William Erskine Atwell

The Pauline theory of the inspiration of Holy Scripture

William Erskine Atwell

The Pauline theory of the inspiration of Holy Scripture

ISBN/EAN: 9783337283865

Printed in Europe, USA, Canada, Australia, Japan

Cover: Foto ©Lupo / pixelio.de

More available books at **www.hansebooks.com**

THE Pauline Theory of the Inspiration of Holy Scripture:

AN INQUIRY INTO THE PRESENT UNSETTLED STATE OF OPINION
CONCERNING THE NATURE OF PERSONAL INSPIRATION;
WITH THE VIEW OF PLACING ON A CONSISTENT
AND SCRIPTURAL BASIS THE INSPIRATION
OF HOLY SCRIPTURE.

BY

WILLIAM ERSKINE ATWELL, D.D.,

EX-SCHOLAR OF TRINITY COLLEGE, DUBLIN; RECTOR OF CLONOE.

Ἡμεῖς δὲ οὐ τὸ πνεῦμα τοῦ κόσμου ἐλάβομεν, ἀλλὰ τὸ πνεῦμα τὸ ἐκ τοῦ Θεοῦ, ἵνα εἰδῶμεν τὰ ὑπὸ τοῦ Θεοῦ χαρισθέντα ἡμῖν.—1 COR. ii. 12.

Καὶ διὰ τῆς πρὸς τὴν ψυχὴν αὐτῶν, ἵνα οὕτως ὀνομάσω, ἀφῆς τοῦ καλουμένου Ἁγίου Πνεύματος, διορατικώτεροι τε τὸν νοῦν ἐγίνοντο, καὶ τὴν ψυχὴν λαμπρότεροι.—*Orig., Cont. Cel.*, Lib. vii., c. iv.

London:
HODDER AND STOUGHTON,
27, PATERNOSTER ROW.
—
MDCCCLXXVIII.

PREFACE.

A SUBJECT which relates to the operations of the Divine Spirit on the spirit of man, is, no doubt, intrinsically abstruse. Nevertheless, it has for many years appeared to me that there must be some influential cause besides at work, largely contributing to the present unsettled state of opinion on inspiration. What in the pure light of Scripture is clear, may become cloudy when compressed within the artificial enclosure of an arbitrary definition. Thus it really happened that the Pauline idea of inspiration has been lost sight of in the surrounding gloom of human improvement. In fact, the impossibility of adjusting the deductions of reason which proceed on uncertain principles, to the explicit statements of Holy Scripture, accounts for much of the present discontent occasioned by the inconsistencies abounding in many modern treatises on the subject.

All the lines of Scripture converge to the person and work of Christ. This work—the great scheme of human redemption—the Saviour promised, to unfold by the Paraclete to His apostles, after His departure; for previously they were not prepared to understand fully, and accept, this mystery of the Gospel. "I have yet many things to say unto you, but ye cannot bear them now. Howbeit, when He the Spirit of Truth is come, He will guide you into all *the* Truth—πᾶσαν τὴν ἀλήθειαν." Now it is to be observed that the guidance here promised is one into the *knowledge* of all the truth. Accordingly, it has been my object in this essay to show that in St. Paul's exhaustive analysis of the subject, this knowledge is the resultant of the two distinct spiritual forces of revelation and inspiration.

In fact, the apostle teaches that, while the lower parts of human nature cannot apprehend the higher truths—the deep things of God—"God hath revealed them unto us by His Spirit." Again, unless the mind and heart be prepared by inspiration to grasp and comprehend the revelation, in any particular case, vouchsafed, it must remain for ever unknown. "Now we have received, not the spirit of the world, but *the Spirit which is of God*, [the exact scriptural idea of inspiration,] that we might know the things that are freely given to us of God," *i.e.*, the revelations graciously presented.

The idea here brought out, and insisted on, in these pages, is that inspiration is a *preparation* of the mind and heart, through the agency of the Holy Spirit, which transforms its character from the natural state (ψυχικὸς) to the spiritual (πνευματικὸς). This transformation is absolutely necessary, since "the natural man receiveth not the things of the Spirit of God, for they are foolishness unto him, neither can he *know* them, because they are spiritually discerned."

Thus the agency of the Spirit in the work of inspiration, is twofold: 1st, to remove prejudice, and thus gain a favourable consideration for the revelation presented; 2ndly, to improve and quicken the intuitional consciousness, and so to fit the mind for the full and clear apprehension and accurate knowledge of the truth which that revelation was intended to convey.

The Donnellan Lectures of the Archdeacon of Dublin were preached before the University in 1852. Two years previously, Mr. Robertson, of Brighton, one of the master spirits of the age, expressed himself strongly on the unsettled state of opinion respecting the nature of inspiration; for in a remarkable discourse he enumerates among the questions into which the subject breaks itself up, this one touching its very essence, 'What is meant by inspiration?'

Dr. Lee, equally sensible of this unsettled state of opinion, notices the fact as existing, and " prevalent even with well-informed persons;" and observes, " So far as relates to the direct arguments which may be deduced from the expressions of the sacred writers in proof of their inspiration, but little remains to be said that has not been forcibly said already. With reference, however, to the *nature* of inspiration itself, and to the possibility of reconciling the unquestionable stamp of humanity impressed upon every page of the Bible, with that undoubting belief in its perfection and infallibility which is the Christian's most precious inheritance,—it may be safely maintained that in English theology almost nothing has been done, and that no effort has hitherto been made to grapple with the difficulties of the subject."

In my mind, the expressions of the sacred writers themselves furnish the only reliable data from which to deduce *also the nature* of inspiration, or the Divine influence, which pervades and quickens the Bible. In my humble, but decided opinion, the co-operation of the Divine Spirit with the spirit of man is explained by St. Paul in terms so clear and cogent, that no additional light has been thrown on the union of the human element with the Divine by any uninspired writer since the days of the apostles. So that if the great question left to our age to solve be this, 'What is the nature of inspiration?' its solution must be sought only in the Bible itself.

No *à priori* assumptions can supply the place of this appeal to the holy volume. The results of such assumptions are perfectly well known. A talented author of great ability and high attainments has tried this plan. Assuming with little variation Perrone's definition of the inspiration of Holy Scripture, and even before he had made a transition to it, from personal inspiration, taking this arbitrary definition, coupled with the infallibility of Scripture, as his point of departure,—although he must have been aware that eminent theologians of our Church were not universally agreed on either position,—Archdeacon Lee has produced a treatise, elaborate and learned, on the Nature of the Inspiration of Holy Scripture. While he proceeds on these principles, (it may be asked,) can any writer have a well-grounded hope that he shall be able to settle the vexed question, 'What is meant by inspiration?' Judging, however, from the complaints of many, so rife since the publication of this work, who objected to the line of reasoning adopted, the definitions and divisions employed, as well as the arguments used, it can be confidently affirmed that the question 'What is the nature of inspiration?' is as unsettled as ever.

We must therefore conclude that, this failure admitted, no one can approach the solution of the problem by *à priori* assumptions.

> Si Pergama dextrâ
> Defendi possunt; etiam hâc defensa fuissent.

I have, moreover, endeavoured to show that the idea of inspiration borrowed from Perrone by Mr. Litton exactly, and with a small addition by Dr. Lee, harmonizes badly with the use of this word in our Prayer Book.

The distinction between revelation and inspiration given by Dr. Lee has been the subject of severe criticism. Undoubtedly, it does not agree with the view of St. Paul. Dr. Henderson is of opinion that the distinction itself must be given up, as unnecessarily clogging the question.

Notwithstanding, on scriptural grounds, I am bold to say, there is a well-marked line of demarcation separating them, though this is not the one held by Dr. Lee, which besides (it has been argued) is not drawn sharply enough, so as to avoid confusion. Neither for this definition of inspiration, nor for the distinction here drawn between revelation and inspiration, can I find any substantial supports in the early Christian Fathers. On the other hand, the Pauline views of both are sustained by many such.

Lastly, I have shown that St. Paul's view of inspiration of Holy Scripture is more entitled to the rank and title of a theory than either the Organic or Dynamic, with this unquestionable advantage, that it is certainly true.

Two of our ablest prelates, the Bishop of Winchester and the Bishop of Gloucester, whose praise is in all the churches, have spoken. The former feels that the present unsettled state of opinion on the subject causes "great anxiety, and not without reason." The latter, advising the rejection of " all the distinctions and definitions which were drawn up for no other purpose than to meet real or supposed difficulties," suggests that the holy volume itself should explain to us the nature of that influence by which it is pervaded and quickened."

I have therefore humbly tried both to show why these distinctions and definitions should be discarded, and, by positive teaching derived from Scripture, to supply the desideratum here indicated.

CONTENTS.

CHAPTER I.

THE PRESENT STATE OF THE QUESTION.

                                                  PAGE

Unsettled state of opinion, in our day, as to the nature of inspiration—The Old Roman Catholic division of inspiration into 'Revelatio' and 'Directio Divina' generally prevailed at the Reformation period—None of the authors cited really held that the directio divina *alone* was inspiration as it is now regarded by modern writers—The true distinction between revelation and inspiration—The Pauline view of inspiration—This is the orthodox view as taught by the Anglican Church—St. Paul's analysis of the facts of the case ought to have led to a more accurate definition of inspiration than that which is now received and borrowed from Perrone . . . . 1—47

CHAPTER II.

INVESTIGATION OF THE NATURE OF INSPIRATION, AND ITS RELATION TO THE AUTHORITY OF HOLY SCRIPTURE.

The correct scriptural idea of inspiration—Its close connexion with revelation sometimes the source of confusion—Wrong methods of theorizing—Bishop Ellicott's advice touching these methods, and hint of the true method—What Dean Alford considers to be the key to the whole question concerning the nature of the inspiration of Holy Scripture—Professor Lightfoot on this point in Gal. i. 15, 16—A strange conjecture of

Augustine bearing on the same point—Relation of inspiration to the Divine authority of the Scriptures—Mr. Swainson's pertinent remark on this matter—Source of error in the ambiguities of language · · · · · · 48—76

CHAPTER III.

DEFINITION OF INSPIRATION.

The sense in which revelation and inspiration are now understood by many theologians altogether abandons the popular employment of the terms—Results arising from this abuse of language—The definition now commonly adopted and derived from Perrone is not properly at all a definition of inspiration—Scriptural definition of inspiration in general—Starting from an *à priori* assumption such as is involved in Perrone's definition, must lead to errors and inconsistencies—St. Paul's idea of the nature of inspiration is presented in the form of a true constructive system—Logical method of arriving at a scriptural definition of inspiration—*Preparation* in man for the exercise of any charism of the Spirit is the proper idea of this influence as to its effects—Hence the inspiration of Holy Scripture consists in the qualification to write, not in the act of writing · · · · · · · · · 77—103

CHAPTER IV.

THE DISTINCTION BETWEEN REVELATION AND INSPIRATION.

Two principles which must guide to a true determination of this distinction—The true subjective character of inspiration set forth in the Communion Service of our Church—Objections to the commonly received definitions of inspiration and revelation—The true nature and extent of revelation was lost sight of at the time of the Reformation both by Lutherans and Roman Catholics; and still continues so—The distinction between revelation and inspiration not deducible from the different characters of isolated passages of Holy Scripture—Cardinal Cajetan and Melchior Cano on Revelation and Divine direction—Remarks of a very able critic on the distinction as drawn by Dr. Lee . . . . 104—131

CHAPTER V.

THE NATURE OF INSPIRATION DEDUCED FROM ITS RELATION TO REVELATION.

None but the *spiritually prepared* can receive and understand the revelations of God—There can be no revelation without inspiration: for without the latter the former would be unintelligible—Thus Perrone's definition, and those derived from it, are untenable—Bretchneider makes inspiration a species of revelation, reversing the view of the old Roman theologians, who regarded inspiration as the genus, and revelation and Divine direction its species—An excellent passage of Dr. Lee which might have suggested to him the true nature of inspiration . . . . 132—159

CHAPTER VI.

THE DIFFERENT KINDS AND MODES OF INSPIRATION.

The inquiry as to the inspiration of the Bible must be postponed to that of the inspiration of the writers—The former is a result terminating in the written word, the last step of many in the series—Revelation, inspiration, knowledge, expression in words—The common definition of inspiration, as a Divine direction, partakes more of the nature of revelation—Inspiration is either (i.) primary and personal, or (ii.) secondary and Biblical—Again, personal inspiration is either (1) intellectual, or (2) moral—General definition which includes every form of personal inspiration—Moral inspiration, as taught in our Church, has the essential characteristic of all inspiration, namely, preparation . . . . 160—191

CHAPTER VII.

THE SAME SUBJECT FURTHER CONSIDERED.

PAGE

Question examined whether poets, philosophers, and men of genius are inspired; at most only a quasi-inspiration can be accorded to the naturally gifted—Mr. Robertson not very consistent on this point—Forms of inspiration, erring in defect or excess: 1st form, a guidance to the external act of uttering in words or of writing Divine truth; 2nd form, a guidance limited further to the written expression; 3rd form, an undue extension to poets, philosophers, and skilled craftsmen—The two first forms are not supported by the early Fathers, who claim to be themselves inspired, yet do not attach unerring accuracy to their own oral or written statements of religious truth   192—222

CHAPTER VIII.

PROGRESS TOWARDS A SOUNDER AND MORE SCRIPTURAL VIEW OF INSPIRATION.

The popular definition, as a special guidance to writing, of recent date; such a limitation was proposed in 1689, and is sanctioned neither by Scripture nor antiquity—A regard to the Pauline synthesis would have led to a more accurate view—With the exception of one remarkable passage in Origen (given in the title-page of this essay) the question of the *nature* of inspiration was really overlooked by the Fathers—Thomas Aquinas sheds some rays of light on the surrounding gloom—He states the conditions on which revelations are intelligible and communicable—Progress to more correct views marked in Hengstenberg, Hävernick, Twesten - · · · · · · · 223—257

CHAPTER IX.

THEORIES OF THE INSPIRATION OF HOLY SCRIPTURE.

The formal idea of inspiration is *preparation*—This has three constituent elements—What is a legitimate theory of inspiration?

What a non-legitimate?—The Organic, Dynamic, and the Latitudinarian theories in the Essays and Reviews do not proceed on right principles as to their construction—Philo's theory of inspiration is rather a classification of the different species of prophecy, and therefore is rather a theory of prophecy than of inspiration—Origen occupies the unique position of being the only ancient Father who gives the true nature of inspiration clearly and fully as a preparation for the reception of Divine revelations . . . . 258—305

CHAPTER X.

GENERAL REMARKS AND CONCLUSION.

Is St. Paul's full and complete proof that the written word is the word of God, to be regarded as a theory of the inspiration of Holy Scripture?—Arguments in support of this view summed up—The usual argument against this position answered—The inconsistencies which have arisen from making a definition like Perrone's the starting-point, are attended with one advantage, furnishing a test by which the doctrine may be tried . 306—326

APPENDIX.

NOTES AND ILLUSTRATIONS . . . . . 327—338

ERRATA.

The footnotes in pages 15 and 16 ought to change places.

Page 18, in note *, the reference should be to page 235.

,, 66, line 6, for *is* read *it*.

,, 96, line 20, for . *The* read *; the*.

THE INSPIRATION OF HOLY SCRIPTURE.

CHAPTER I.

THE PRESENT STATE OF THE QUESTION.

A QUARTER of a century has now passed away, since the distinguished author of 'The Mission of the Comforter' mournfully called attention—in an utterance still as fresh as when he pronounced it—to a desideratum in theology. When he said, "An intelligent theory upon the subject of inspiration is a most pressing want of the day," he only expressed the general feeling of the divines of his own time. But these words were oracular; for during all that period they have never ceased to echo the same note on the ear of the religious world.

In a similar strain, and about the same time, Mr. Robertson of Brighton, one of the great thinkers of the age, notices the same want, and points out many of the obstacles to be met and encountered before the desired goal can be reached :—

"This is the deepest question of our day, the one which lies beneath all others, and in comparison of which, the questions now agitating the popular mind—whether of Papal jurisdiction, or varieties of Church doctrine in our own communion—are but superficial: it is the grand question of Inspiration, which is given to this age to solve."

Of the many difficulties surrounding the problem, this brilliant writer, among others, mentions the following :—

"What the Bible is, and what the Bible is not? What is meant by inspiration? Whether inspiration is the same thing as infallibility? When God inspired the minds, did He dictate the words? Does the inspiration of the men, mean the infallibility of the words? Are the operations of the Holy Spirit, inspiring men, compatible with partial error, as His operations, in sanctifying them, are compatible with partial evil." *

It would be presumption in me to attempt a discussion of the many nice distinctions of the various phases of the subject here presented. I may, however, be permitted briefly to touch upon a few of the more important; feeling unequal to bear the burden of the many weighty principles involved, lest, if too

---

* Without committing oneself to the views of the eminent writers here referred to on all points, it can be safely said that no men were more competent to give an opinion on the present state of the question.

heavily equipped, I might not find it easy to reach the end of my journey.

Within the limits of a short sermon, Mr. Robertson wisely took the shortest method of treating a subject so abstruse and so complicated, in a single, but very remarkable, aspect of the question. "Upon these things (he observes) there are many views, some of them false, some superstitious; but it is not our business now to deal with these: our way is rather to teach positively than negatively. We will try to set up the truth, and error may fall before it."

While approving, and also endeavouring to follow this method, I am obliged to mark out for myself a wider range.

The importance of this question in its present theological bearings, is forcibly brought before us very recently in an able treatise:—

"The indeterminateness of current opinions regarding the nature of inspiration and regarding consequent principles of interpreting Scripture, are to a great extent the vantage-ground from which the Christian faith is assailed in the now notorious 'Essays and Reviews.' How indeed can we settle the meaning of Scripture, or even combat for its claims upon us, until we have realized definite notions of what is involved in its being given of God, and yet coming through man."* If, says Augustine, the authority

---

* Hebert's Neology, page 136.

of the divine Scriptures is shaken, the Christian faith will falter, and with it will Christian practice also falter.*

The present unsettled state of the question has also been strongly felt by the learned Bishop of Winchester, Dr. Harold Browne, whose weighty words deserve the deepest consideration :—

"The historical sketch, thus rapidly given, seems to show that there have been always slight differences of tone and opinion touching this important question, but that these differences have never so markedly come out as in the nineteenth century. The subject *at present* causes great anxiety, and not without reason." †

Let so much suffice to indicate the unrest, and discontent, which at this moment prevail concerning the nature of inspiration, personal and Biblical.

Of the ablest and most erudite treatises lately published on the subject, there is no end to the complaints of hostile criticism. On the contradictions and inconsistencies originating (it is alleged) from the confusion of thought and language in their authors, how much has been said by men of the highest character as theologians, and of known ability and great learning?

---

* "Titubabit fides, si divinarum Scripturarum vacillat auctoritas: porrò fide titubante, charitas et etiam ipsa languescit."—*Aug. de Doct. Chr.*, i. 41.

† 'Aids to Faith,' page 301.

The subject is too sacred to be handled in a controversial spirit. I cannot, therefore, bring myself to think that writers, as remarkable for piety as for scholarship, would, from any lower motive than the love of truth, feel dissatisfied with the current views of inspiration, had they not just, at least very plausible, grounds for these complaints.

Now—to come at once to the root of the matter—if there really be, as is alleged, palpable errors and inconsistencies in treatises which hold the notions popularly entertained, whence do they arise?

In this essay it will be shown—

1. That these authors generally take their answer to the question, 'What is inspiration?' not from the Bible, but from the traditions of Roman theology, and that this does not give the true scriptural idea of inspiration.

2. That there is a real distinction between Revelation and Inspiration; but that this is not the one derived from the view of inspiration transmitted to us from the theology of Rome, resolvable into the elements of 'Revelation' and 'Assistentia et Directio Divina.'

3. That the marvellous manner in which inspiration is interwoven with revelation, sometimes hides from view the very nature of inspiration.

4. That the ambiguity of language has told powerfully upon writers, who profess "to abandon altogether the popular employment of the terms revelation and

inspiration." For nothing more exposes men to the subtle inroads of inconsistency than the arbitrary employment of words. Thus, violence being done to their established use, on which depend the rule and norm of speech, an unfailing *Nemesis* is sure to reassert nature's outraged rights. And so it happens that the abandoned meaning is again restored to its legitimate place, from which it had been forcibly expelled.

I shall then endeavour, in the first place, to present what I am convinced is the true and scriptural idea of the inspiration of Holy Scripture, exhibited in a correct analysis of St. Paul's theory. And next I shall explain how the record of a Divine revelation is truly expressed in "words which the Holy Ghost teacheth."

This analysis, it may be seen, rejects, as unsound, the present popular view of inspiration, borrowed from the dogmatic theology of Rome, and stereotyped in the conventional language of the day.

My conclusions, however, lead me to the highest form of verbal, though not mechanical, inspiration; for they are by no means identical.

In modern times, theories of inspiration date from the era of the Reformation. Now in the strife and heat of party spirit then prevailing, opinions were often hastily taken up, and as hastily renounced. As at that time men had no very definite notions concerning the distinct and proper functions of revelation and inspiration, for communicating Divine knowledge, inspiration generally signified with them the whole compound process* by which something was infused into the mind. The question ventilated at that stirring epoch, with much subtlety and earnestness, was, whether the Holy Spirit inspired only the matter, or both the matter and the words.

Mosheim, in his 'Elementa Theologiæ dogmaticæ,' presents a clear account of the progress of this notable controversy. He states that Luther held the view that the *matter* only was inspired; and generally, that the theologians of the sixteenth century were of the same opinion; but remarks that the adherents of the Church of Rome attacked this view. Reasoning, that if only the matter were inspired, the prophets and apostles might have erred in their enunciation of the truths inspired, they came to the conclusion that both the *matter* and *form* were inspired by the Holy Spirit.

Mosheim winds up his narrative in these terms: "Our theologians deserted the view of Luther; and at the end of the sixteenth century, and the beginning of the seventeenth, adopted the view that the Scripture was inspired by the Holy Spirit, not only as to its matter, but also as to its form. This opinion took its first rise in Saxony, and then spread over almost

---

* Even in our own day Dr. Henderson holds this view: 'Divine Inspiration,' p. 12.

the entire Church. Yet some of our divines are unwilling to give up the view of Luther."

Some time afterwards, the Church of Rome, however, yielded a point in the direction of the Lutheran view; for a controversy having arisen between two parties in the Roman communion—the Jesuits and Jansenists—in 1586, the former at their public lectures in Louvain set forth, among other propositions, (1) "That for anything to be sacred scripture, it is not necessary that its several words be inspired by the Holy Spirit." (2) "It is not necessary that the several truths and their meaning should be immediately inspired by the Holy Spirit to the writer himself," (non est necessarium ut singulæ veritatis et sententiæ sint immediatè a Spiritû S. ipsi Scriptori inspiratæ)," the business was settled in this way. To end this domestic quarrel, an apostolical breve in 1588 from Pope Sixtus V. commanded all parties to desist, until the matter should be determined finally by the Holy See. To this day it remains undecided—*adhuc sub judice lis est.*

It is indeed not strange to find men to be so easily shaken in their opinions, when they entertain such wrong conceptions about the nature of inspiration*— a purely subjective influence as to its effects—transforming it into the objective transmission of thoughts

---

* This great abuse of language, producing much confusion of thought, has come down to more recent times. Thus, treating of the degrees of inspiration, Bishop Wilson says, " By the inspiration of suggestion is

and words, and thus confounding it with revelation. In fact, revelation is altogether ignored in the proposition above referred to.

The Tridentine Council gave no definition of inspiration; but a widespread distinction existed among Roman and Lutheran theologians of the complex conception that went under the name of inspiration. This was its division into 'Revelatio' and 'Assistentia et Directio* Divina,' to which already I have alluded.

Thus Melchior Cano, Bishop of the Canaries, and before him Cardinal Cajetan on the part of Rome,† besides Calixt on the side of the Lutherans, upheld this distinction; but none of them limited inspiration to the contracted bounds of the 'Assistentia et Directio Divina,' which, if not revelation, is rather a result of inspiration than inspiration itself.

Cardinal Cajetan (born 1470), in his Commentary on Luke i., published 1528, writes: "Unde clare apparet Lucam scripsisse ex auditû ab Apostolis, et

---

meant such communications of the Holy Spirit as suggested and detailed minutely every part of the truth delivered."—*The Evidences of Christianity*, by Daniel Wilson, vol. i., p. 508.

In like manner M. Athanase Coquerel defines the word. "Inspiration is a transmission of ideas from God to man."—*Christianity*, p. 202.

* "Another degree of inspiration is the inspiration of direction," (also mentioned by Wilson); and yet inspiration itself, in the popular definition, is direction or guidance. Thus the genus is transformed into a subordinate species.

† Perrone is our authority for the view *now* received, and left undecided by the Church of Rome. He teaches "libros sacros esse conscriptos utpote Spiritû S. afflante, *Saltem* quoad res et sententias."

non revelatione sibi immediatè factâ : divinâ tamen gratiâ dirigente et servante ne in aliquoerraret."

Melchior Cano (born 1523) in very decisive terms gives the view of the Church of Rome: "Ipsi vero fatemur singula quæque, sive magna seu parva, a sacris authoribus Spiritû Sancto dictante, esse edita : id a patribus accepimus, id fidelium animis inditum, et quasi insculptum est. Id itaque et nos ; Ecclesiâ præsertim magistrâ et duce, retinere debemus. Non enim asserimus per immediatam S. Spiritûs revelationem, quæ quidem propriè revelatio dicenda sit, quamlibet Scripturæ partem fuisse editam. Sive ergo Matthæus et Joannes, seu Marcus et Lucas ; quamvis illi visa, hi audita, referunt, non egebant S. Spiritûs novâ revelatione: egebant tamen peculiari S. Spiritûs directione." (See p. 126, 'De Locis Theol.,' lib. ii.)

This view, though unsupported by Scripture, it must be admitted was, in some measure, necessitated by the prologue to the book of Ecclesiasticus, which with Roman Catholic divines is canonical.

The question now arises, Is this *direction* rightly denominated, at the present time, inspiration ?

Cajetan and Cano did not, in their day, think so. And yet both were very familiar with the term inspiration. What then ? Why did they not use it in this sense ? Doubtless because, with them, inspiration, as something infused into the mind, cannot apply to the external act of writing. According to the teaching of their Church, inspiration was this infusion by the Holy Spirit of the matter and form of the revelation. In their view, inspiration of the Holy Scriptures had a generic signification, including under it 'Revelation' and 'Divine assistance and direction.' The idea then adopted by Roman Catholicism, was indeed—though not the scriptural one—very ancient and very general. This may be aptly exemplified by the classic phrase "divinely inspired dreams," where the revelation, as a subordinate species, is included in inspiration. And the whole process, whereby the Divine Spirit imparts the knowledge of things revealed, enabling the prophet or apostle to record the same faithfully and accurately, was called inspiration. Time rolled on, and was changed, and men were changed in it. What the earlier divines left undone, their successors tried to complete.

The old division of Biblical inspiration into revelation and Divine direction, was at length transformed into the new division of revelation and inspiration,—a subordinate species, as I have said, of inspiration taking the place of inspiration itself,—and the long-desired definition of inspiration, after centuries of misgiving, came into the light of day, emerging from its hiding-place in that division. The finishing stroke of this tedious work was made when the dogmatic theology of Rome supplied a definition of this so-called inspiration. In that Church, Peronne's is now accepted as the authorised definition. This, which is the parent of the popularly received definition, is thus expressed, "Inspiration is that peculiar impulse of the Holy Spirit, moving to write, His direction and aiding presence ruling the mind and heart of the writer, so as not to suffer him to err, and so as to cause him to write what is agreeable to the will of God." *

It will be observed how the tendency to narrow the limits of revelation gradually advanced among Roman Catholic divines, who, as I have already remarked, felt themselves obliged to modify their views in accordance with the sentiments expressed in the preface of the book of Ecclesiasticus. These sentiments imparted much force to the division above referred to, and it spread far and wide. No writer has so fully and so clearly stated the view which prevailed in the early stages of the Reformation as Cardinal Bellarmine: "God is the author of all the Divine Scriptures; but He nevertheless assists the prophets in one way; and others, especially the historians, in a different way. For He was wont to reveal the future to the prophets, and at the same time to assist them, lest they should introduce anything false into their writings; and thus the prophets had no other labour than that of writing or dictating. But to other writers

---

* "Inspiratio est singularis ea Spiritûs Sancti moventis ad scribendum, impulsio, directio ac præsentia mentem animumque Scriptoris gubernans quæ non sinit eum errare; efficitque ut scribat quæ velit Deus."—*Prælectiones Theol.*, Perrone.

God did not always reveal what they should write; yet He excited them to write the things which they had seen or heard, and of which they had the recollection: and at the same time He assisted them, lest they should write anything false. This assistance did not exempt them from the labour of thinking and inquiring what, and how, they should write." *

The time, however, had not yet arrived for reducing inspiration to the dimensions of this second term of the division. Still it may be safely affirmed that every modern, and the commonly received definition of inspiration, has in this lucid statement been forestalled by Bellarmine.

And no less safely may it be affirmed that this is not inspiration in the mind of Bellarmine, as it was not in the minds of Cajetan and Cano. So much have recent authors in our day mistaken the true nature of this sacred influence.

It is indeed to be observed, that revelation is not excluded by those theologians, even in the record of matters cognizable by unaided human reason; but only *express* revelation. For in the passage cited in Basil

---

* "Deum quidem esse autorem omnium divinarum Scripturarum, sed aliter tamen adesse solitum prophetis, aliter aliis præsertim historicis. Nam prophetis revelabat futura et simul assistebat ne aliquid falsi admiscerent in scribendo: et ideo prophetæ non alium habuerunt laborem quam scribendi vel dictandi: aliis autem scriptoribus Deus non semper revelabat ea quæ scripturi erant sed excitabat ut scriberent ea quæ viderant vel audierant quorum recordabantur: et simul assistebat ne falsi aliquid scriberent: quæ assistentia non faciebat ne laborarent cogitando et quærendo quid et quomodo scripturi essent."

by Cano, these words occur, " hæc supernaturali lumine et *expressâ* revelatione ut scriberentur non egebant."

Now the direction and assistance of the Holy Spirit mentioned, is, if anything, a veritable undoubted revelation; while, on the other hand, the absence of supernatural light shuts it out from the category of inspiration.

Such is the perplexity involved in the new distinction introduced between revelation and inspiration; and in the new definition of what late writers please to call inspiration. All this would have been avoided, had they, according to the Pauline conception, regarded inspiration as an effect produced by the Spirit of God preparatory to the knowledge of Divine truths, presented by revelation to the mind and heart of the apostle or prophet; and the things recorded as constituent parts of one entire narrative. Then there should be no reason to deny inspiration to be necessary to the full and clear understanding of the whole, though separate portions of it could be comprehended by the light of nature.

Previously, however, to entering on the examination of the scriptural view of the nature of the inspiration of the Bible set forth by the apostle Paul, it may be useful to clear the way by removing two misconceptions lurking in the minds of theorists, who aim at being "wise above that which is written." One of these relates to the extent of revelation, the other to the nature of inspiration.

The reader has no doubt anticipated much of what I am about to say, in the remarks already made on the little support which the current views respecting the nature of inspiration in this nineteenth century derive from the vacillating and shifting opinions of the authors of the post-reformation period, concerning the question, What is inspiration?

So much reason had Mr. Robertson to include among the many difficulties by which the subject is embarrassed, the primary question, "What is meant by inspiration?"

But fresh difficulties have started up, and have disturbed other inquirers, who ask, What is revelation? What is the distinction between revelation and inspiration? How much then is the embarrassment multiplied?

I do not know any treatise where these questions are answered in exact accordance with the statements of Holy Scripture, above all with the Pauline exposition of them in the second chapter of 1 Corinthians.

1. Very great confusion both of thought and language has generally shrouded the whole subject in darkness, in consequence of authors narrowing the field of revelation beyond what Scripture warrants; and excluding from this category all Divine disclosures through ideas supernaturally suggested to the minds of the holy apostles and prophets.*

---

* See Doddridge *in loco.*

Now, that this was one of the many ways (πολυτρόπως) in which God, by His Spirit, revealed Himself, and His will to mankind, can on scriptural grounds be incontestably proved.

In the sixteenth chapter of St. Matthew, our Lord asked His disciples, "Whom say ye that I am?" Simon Peter answered, "Thou art the Christ, the Son of the living God." Jesus answered and said unto him, "Blessed art thou, Simon Barjona, for flesh and blood hath not *revealed* it unto thee, but my Father who is in heaven." As if our Lord had said, Thou hast not learned it by human report, or by the unassisted sagacity of thine own mind, but my Father has disclosed it to thee, and wrought in thy soul this cordial assent in the midst of those various prejudices which present circumstances might suggest.*

God had not revealed this great truth by any special vision to St. Peter, nor in any way different from that in which He had manifested it to the other apostles, who had heard Christ's words, and had seen His miracles. In these respects all were on terms of equality. Special suggestions, therefore of God's Spirit to Peter's mind gave a peculiar colour and meaning to the signs of the Messiah's character and mission, supplied as they were by the sayings and doings of their common Lord and Master. Moreover, as we shall show that the condition of the

---

* See Chapter V.

intelligibility * of a revelation is the inspiration of the mind to which the revelation is presented, this revelation implies that Peter's mind and heart had been opened by the Spirit of God, so as rightly to understand the disclosure of the truth conveyed to his soul, and clearly expressed in his answer.

I must not, however, anticipate what next comes to be considered.

Again, in 1 Cor. xiv. 30, St. Paul instructs the Christian prophets of the Church at Corinth in the proper and edifying use of their gift, and advises, " If anything be revealed to another that sitteth by, let the first hold his peace." Here is a clear case of a revelation imparted to a person sitting in an assembly of Christians, by divinely suggested thoughts.

Again, when Christ instructed His disciples, at what times they should be delivered up to councils, not to premeditate, for it should be given to them in that hour, what they should say; or when He promised that the Comforter should recall to their remembrance what He had said unto them; new instances rise up to view of revelations by suggestion, of the same kind as those referred to.

Once more: Jesus of Nazareth, as very man in whom dwelt all the fulness of the Godhead bodily, while He tabernacled in the flesh, being like His brethren in all things, sin only excepted, was favoured with express revelations,—voices from heaven, angelic

---

* See Eph. i. 18.

visitants. But as He enjoyed an unbroken communion with His heavenly Father, the more frequent revelations which He received, were not express, but ideal and suggestive.*

Picture in imagination the All-merciful approaching the grave of Lazarus, and Mary falling down at His feet. Behold the sympathy of Jesus for the weeping broken-hearted sister! Her sorrows touched His human soul at a tender point, and He wept. What a sight this for the contemplation of men and angels!— a scene in which the truest emotions of man's nature are drawn out in their loveliest form. They come to the tomb. "And Jesus lifted up His eyes, and said, Father, I thank Thee that Thou hast heard me." †

Was not He, who, as the Son of Man, prayed to the Father, in very deed a fit recipient of Divine revelations? He, who was one Christ, by taking the manhood into God; and who, though one with the Father, yet, O ineffable mystery, prayed to the Father, and obtained by direct revelation an assurance that His prayer was heard! Compare Matthew xxvi. 53.

All these, on the unquestionable authority of Scripture, are properly and truly revelations; and to be called such. So far had Melchior Cano, and those who had adopted the view that "express

---

* See Dr. Salmon's Sermons, p. 44, 1861.

† Thomas Aquinas, the great luminary of the scholastic age, enumerates suggestion as a class of revelations : see p. 109.

revelations" are only those which are correctly denominated revelations, deviated from the scriptural standard.*

In matters of so delicate a nature, and having regard to the fact that, even after nineteen centuries have almost passed away, the questions are still asked, "What is revelation?" "What is inspiration?" an appeal must be made, not to human conjecture, but to Divine certainty.

In the second chapter of his epistle to the Galatians, St. Paul says, "Then fourteen years after I went up again to Jerusalem with Barnabas; and took Titus also with me. And I went up by *revelation*." On this passage Professor Lightfoot remarks,—and his remark strongly corroborates the view which I have taken,—"In Luke's narrative (Acts xv. 2) he is said to have been sent by the Church at Antioch. The revelation either prompted or confirmed the decision of the Church. Here there is no contradiction. The historian naturally records the external impulse which led to the mission: the apostle himself states his inward motive. What I did, he says, I did not owing to circumstances, not as yielding to pressure, not in deference to others, but because the Spirit of

---

* The immense range of this class of revelations can be understood from these pertinent remarks of Jerome : "Pharisæi stupent ad doctrinam Domini, et mirantur in Petro et Johanne quomodo legem sciant, qunm literas non didicerint. Quidquid enim aliis exercitatio et quotidiana in lege meditatio tribuere solet, illis Spiritus Sanctus *suggerebat*."—*Ad Paulin.*, Ep. liii., t. i., p. 271.

God told me it was right. The very stress which he lays on this revelation seems to show that other influences were at work." In the preceding chapter St. Paul also refers to *internal* revelation, verse 16: "When it pleased God to reveal His Son in me." Olshausen proceeds a step farther, and shows how, by a superior inspiration and internal suggestive revelation, the Divine Spirit enabled the blessed apostles to unfold the mind of the Spirit, not only in the new disclosures made to themselves, but also in the right understanding of the old. "The apostles, like all other writers of the New Testament, had in the *illumination* of the Holy Spirit the full authority to pass beyond the standpoint of consciousness in the Old Testament writers, and to unveil their innermost truth of the thought according to the sense of Him who promised and foretold. If, therefore, Jewish learning also has made similar applications of Old Testament passages, still the distinction of the apostolic mode of procedure from the Rabbinical always consisted in this, that the learned Jew acted merely according to the arbitrary manner of human beings, by which their acuteness often degenerated into mere conceits; while the apostles, *guided by the Spirit*, ever unveiled infallibly the true sense of the predicting Spirit (2 Peter i. 20, 21)."

Now what is the guidance of the Spirit but a revelation, or an unveiling rather, to their own spirits, of truths which otherwise they could not expound to others, but which, by inspiration or "the illumination of the Holy Spirit" being enabled to understand,* they were fitted to explain? For, as is stated by a very able writer,† if this guidance participate not largely of the nature of revelation, it is nothing, or an unintelligible impulse.‡

Writers have embarrassed the subject immensely by confounding this class of undoubted revelations with inspiration. They however hide the confusion by applying to this mode of revelation the designation of 'direction.' Still it may be asked can anything be more a revelation than the suggestions of the Spirit which such supernatural direction really implies?

Thus Quenstädt, quoted by Dr. Lee (who appears himself to use the word suggestion in the same sense, though it is hard to see the meaning which either attaches to the word), writes: "Each and all such matters were *not only* committed to writing, under the infallible assistance and *direction* of God, *but* are to be ascribed to the special *suggestion, inspiration,* and dictation of the Holy Spirit."

Now it is not easy to understand the double aid referred to in this perplexing sentence, since the reason added seems to be itself merely a repetition of the infallible assistance and direction. The reason

---

* Eph. i. 18. † *Journal Sac. Lit.*, April 1866. p. 170.
‡ Of the large scriptural sense assigned to revelation, see Eph. i. 17; Philip. iii. 15.

is thus given: "For all things which were to be written were in the very act of writing suggested by the Holy Spirit." And this only becomes intelligible on the supposition that with Quenstädt inspiration was something different from 'Divine direction,' as was indeed to be expected in a Lutheran Professor of Theology of that period. Quenstädt was born in 1617.

Again, Dr. Lee remarks, "We have reason to believe that, in general, the Divine communications were not committed to writing for some time after they were received: there are even instances of several years having elapsed before they were placed on record. Now in all such cases, where it was the will of God that a record of a revelation should be preserved as a guide and a rule for future ages, the co-operation of the Holy Spirit was indispensable, in order both to bring the original communications before the mind of the sacred writer in its primitive perfection, and to enable him to record it with infallible accuracy."

Here it is to be considered, in the first place, whether in this vague statement, leaving undefined the steps by which the sacred writer was guided to such infallible utterance, this co-operation of the Holy Spirit can in any proper sense of the word be denominated inspiration, although it may be fairly called 'direction.' In the second place, no notice or account is taken of the fact, that the original communications of our Lord to His apostles were generally misunderstood, or only partially understood by them.

A presentation to their minds at a future time of these communications, with every additional information, which only then they were able to bear, and by inspiration able to receive, and thoroughly to comprehend, gives to them an indisputable title to the name of revelation.

I cannot see any valid reason for calling ideas suggested for the first time to the mind by the Holy Spirit, a revelation; and refusing this designation to a former communication, now perhaps forgotten, when it is amplified and presented in a new light,— when, that is, the apostle, through inspiration able to bear it, can receive the communication, not certainly "in its primitive perfection," but in a much higher state of perfection.

Besides, if this illumination and quickened intuition be inspiration, (as it really and truly is—and this I shall presently show,) I ask, is that which, on Scripture authority, I have called revelation, also inspiration? So much for this mode of revelation, which cannot be confounded with inspiration.

But, to do the old authors—from whom this distinction is borrowed—justice, they instead call it by another name, 'directio.' Thus, when the many ways in which Divine truths have been supernaturally revealed, are classified—such as visions, ecstasy, dreams, audible voices, symbolic acts, Urim and Thummim, angelic appearances, spirits of the departed,—another mode, viz., that of the Divine suggestion of thoughts to the mind, must be added to the number.*

Indeed, short of this more comprehensive enumeration (as I shall show more fully hereafter), a legitimate designation is scarcely given to the Bible, when we call it 'a Divine revelation.' And this sentiment is in unison with the view of Bishop Stillingfleet: "The primary notion of a prophet doth not lie in foretelling future events, but in declaring and interpreting to the world the mind of God, which he receives by immediate revelation from Himself."

II. Inspiratio ($\theta\epsilon o\pi\nu\epsilon\upsilon\sigma\tau\iota a$) signifies the inbreathing of God. The ordinary use of the term, it has been truly remarked, confuses the distinct conceptions of breathing into, and breathing out.

We cannot fail to perceive in St. Paul's view of the matter, that an influence of a peculiar kind, infused by the Holy Spirit into the spirit of the apostle or prophet, is that which is properly called inspiration. But an outflowing energy, enabling him to commit

---

* Since writing the view here given by me, of the comprehensive scriptural meaning of revelation, I have found with much pleasure its strong confirmation in the very learned treatise of Dr. Henderson, even while he confounds revelation with inspiration as many of the reformers had done. "The modes of Divine revelation, or the exertion of inspiring influence, which it pleased the author of all wisdom to select, are the following: *direct internal suggestion*, audible articulate sounds, the Urim and Thummim, dreams, visions, and the reappearance of the departed."

to writing what had been revealed, can, in no legitimate sense of the term, be denominated inspiration.* For the latter is not inspiration, but prophecy, (προφητεία) the external act of utterance, or teaching, as explained above by Stillingfleet. And it is noteworthy that in our Lord's division of the Scriptures into "the law of Moses, the prophets, and the Psalms, prophecy has its larger and more correct signification.

When the Holy Ghost breathed this hallowed influence into the prophets and apostles, they became bearers of the Spirit (πνευματοφόροι), *i.e.*, inspired and fitted for the prophetic office.

In former times, before the necessities of the case had forced theorists—as each new theory was started—to attach a new meaning to the word, inspiration (though generally taken for the whole combined internal result of inspiration and revelation) had been very rarely confounded with the outward act of expression, or προφητεία. The prophet's office was to declare the truths revealed to him. And he was duly qualified for that work by the infused gift of inspiration.

Thus Theophilus ad Autolycum, (ii. § 9,) refers to this as the qualification for the prophetic enunciation

---

* I cannot read Philo in the sense given by Dr. Henderson and Dr. Lee, (see p. 262,) as if "he divided inspiration into two species, 'ερμηνεία and προφητεια." Philo says, "they differ," but does not say that either of these two modes of expressing God's will is inspiration.

of these truths in the following words: "The prophets inspired by God Himself."*

But to proceed. Both in revelation and inspiration there are to be considered, first, the Divine act, and next the effect produced on the mind. These are often not kept distinct ; in the same manner as invention is used ambiguously,—sometimes denoting the act of inventing, sometimes the thing invented.

To enable man, who by his unaided natural faculties cannot grasp the spiritual truths conveyed to his mind by revelation, a power of recipiency is divinely imparted, and a distinct recognition that the things revealed are not the natural offsprings of his own mind.

As intromitted forces, acting on man's intellectual and moral faculties, the radical and essential difference of each (which must exist *in the things themselves*) cannot be in the Divine agents—whether the Father, or the Son, or the Holy Spirit be the operating cause ; nor in any external results produced ; but in the influences wrought upon the mind. Now such are the following :—

In revelation there are presentations to the mind— something objectively given, such as thoughts, supernaturally suggested to the understanding, or objects of some kind to the spiritual faculties.

In inspiration there are no presentations. It is

---

* προφῆται ὑπ' αὐτοῦ τοῦ θεοῦ ἐμπνευσθέντες.

simply and solely a Divine subjective influence, wrought on the mind and heart by the Spirit of God. This is called by Bishop Wordsworth, "a Spiritual Transfiguration," see page 107. To objectify inspiration is entirely to mistake its true nature, function, and office. A subjective influence on the human soul, produced by the operation of the Holy Spirit, is the formal and proper idea of this imparted gift. And this perfectly accords with the analogous influences of the same Divine agent recorded in many passages of Scripture,* as when He imparted courage and strength to Samson, and quickened intelligence in works of art to Bezaleel and Aholiab.

Moreover, this mistaken view has a double aspect: whether the object be something infused into the mind, or some *result* of this sacred internal influence *extraneous* to the mind.

In the former sense, inspiration wrongly moved in the sphere of objectivity when there appeared in the Jansenist controversy (A.D. 1586) the proposition "non est necessarium ut singulæ veritates et sententiæ sint immediatè a Spiritu Sancto ipsi scriptori *inspiratæ*."

In the latter, when Dr. Lee, with equal error, fixes on the objective results of inspiration. This distinguished Biblical scholar asserts in very positive terms, from which I am forced to dissent, "The inspiration of the authors of the Bible was an energy altogether

---

* This is also the idea of our Church. See the prayer for the Church Militant in Communion Service, quoted page 107.

objective, and directed to supply the wants of the Church. The inspiration of the Christian is altogether *subjective*, and directed to the moral improvement of the individual."* Again, "the true idea of inspiration is altogether objective, extending to every portion of every book."†

Now I submit that we cannot define inspiration, either intellectual or moral, in the manner here indicated, from the *terminus ad quem*,—that is, from results. In both cases, inspiration was an accomplished spiritual fact within the soul of the sacred author, on the one hand, and of the Christian believer on the other, antecedently to the results which they were intended to produce. In other words, inspiration was objective in neither; for on the same ground that you call the inspiration of the sacred writer objective, you must call that of the Christian, also, objective, according to the orthodox teaching of our Church: " Grant to us Thy humble servants that by Thy holy *inspiration* we may think those things that be good, and by Thy merciful guiding may perform the same;"‡ and, without doubt, the performance of the things that be good, is as much objective, as the speaking or writing the things that are true. To which we may add, that if the guiding in the one case is not inspiration, so neither is it

---

* See ' Inspiration of Holy Scripture,' 2nd ed., p. 243.
† See page 31, *ibid.*
‡ Collect for Fifth Sunday after Easter.

in the other, as is stated in the popularly received definition of inspiration. Hävernick states in what "the essence and subjective peculiarity" consists. (See chap. viii. of this essay.) The very compound term itself, θεόπνευστος, clearly indicates an intromitted influence of the spirit, and consequently disowns and repudiates any definition of inspiration which refers to an outcoming operation such as that of recording revelations. This latter, in fact, was a subsequent transaction in all cases, so that revelation and inspiration had exercised their full effects in producing knowledge of the truth, before it was expressed orally or in writing.

And yet such a definition, arbitrarily chosen by the Church of Rome, was the one commonly adopted by Protestant divines.

The consequence was, that this view necessitated the introduction of several theories to meet the difficulties involved in such a definition. But unfortunately many, thinking that none of these theories rested on a solid scriptural foundation, have in recent times sown broadcast opinions subversive of the certainty itself of God's holy word.

At any rate, none of these is the view that St. Paul takes of the inspiration of Holy Scripture,—that is, of the process by which, in fact, Scripture had become the word of God.

With the apostle, perfect knowledge of things Divine is the result of the combined forces of personal inspiration and revelation; and this sanctified knowledge emerges into what may be called an inspired verbal record.

Assuredly this was the process that prepared St. Paul, by the spiritual aids graciously vouchsafed, to communicate in writing to the Christians of Ephesus the hidden mystery of the call of the Gentiles. He speaks of his knowledge, intimate and profound, of that mystery (in what he had written to them), and how God had fitted him for the apostolic office. These are the words in which he describes how he had acquired that knowledge. "How that by revelation He made known (ἐγνώρισε) to me the mystery, whereby, when ye read, ye may understand *my knowledge* in the mystery of Christ."*

Having now stated the results of my investigation as to the nature and function of inspiration, and also those of revelation, in qualifying the sacred writers for recording the knowledge communicated to them by those gifts, it remains to explain the steps of the process given by St. Paul in the second chapter of 1st Corinthians, through which the Scriptures had become the word of God.

I reserve my further strictures on the wrong and illogical definitions which are embodied with, or underlie, the ambitious theories of the inspiration of Holy Scripture hitherto propounded, until I have explained the Pauline view fully set forth in the

---

* Eph. iii. 3, 4.

second chapter of the 1st Corinthians. Sufficient attention has not been paid to the luminous statement of the apostle in that wonderful chapter in which he clearly expounds all that can be understood concerning this mysterious subject.

Confining ourselves to this exposition, supported by Scripture reference only, we tread on holy ground; and have reason to hope that we shall escape the hidden perils of an unknown region; walking over fields of sacred literature, in the foot-prints of the apostles and prophets, and of our Lord Himself.

The warning voice, too, still ringing in our ears. " Put off thy shoes from thy feet, for the place where thou standest is holy ground," reminds us of the duty of humbly divesting ourselves of human preconceptions, before we venture to enter on the interpretation of a profoundly difficult passage of Holy Scripture.

In a faithful analysis of the facts of the case, as presented by St. Paul, the following points are obvious to all who bring to the subject minds unwarped by prejudice in favour of some arbitrary definition of inspiration.

The definition should follow, not precede, an inquiry into the nature of the thing defined.*

1. For the revelation of spiritual facts, two things are needed: first, a Divine truth; and next a spirit that can receive it. Accordingly, the apostle proceeds

---

* Vide Whately's Logic, 4th ed., p. 255.

to show (verse 7) how "we speak the wisdom of God," which before was hid in a mystery; that in fact this mystery, which treats of the doctrines of the gospel, relating to human redemption, cannot be conveyed to the mind through the unaided natural inlets of knowledge, whether of sense, or conception, or imagination. "Eye hath not seen, nor ear heard, neither have entered into the heart of man, the things which God hath prepared for them that love Him."

At this point, the very important question suggests itself: 'To what powers of our mental constitution are revelations of the higher truths, in the last resort, addressed?' The apostle answers negatively: not to *natural* sensation,—"Eye hath not seen, nor ear heard;" nor to *natural* conception nor imagination,—"neither have entered into the heart of man," etc.*

Moreover, reason cannot by any scientific analysis discern the truths of God—the mysteries of the kingdom of heaven. For the instrument of science is observation, internal and external; and this calls in the aid of sense, or the exercise of conception and imagination. By none of these powers can you by searching find out to perfection the Almighty, nor any of the deep things He wills to reveal. All these powers convey to our minds only earthly and human things, not spiritual truths which "the natural man cannot know, because they are spiritually discerned."

---

* See Chapter VIII. of this Essay.

There then only remains the Divine power of intuition, which brings us directly *en rapport* with the universal mind, "in whom we live and move and have our being." This takes place whenever He is pleased to reveal to us, duly prepared for their reception, some glimpses of eternal truth—coruscations of "the light which no man can approach unto."

In giving expression, however, to the knowledge attained by revelation and inspiration, the logical reason is brought into conscious activity. For the apostle says that in the utterance of suitable words to represent that knowledge, under the teaching of the Holy Ghost, the apostles interpreted spiritual things by spiritual words (verse 13): see an example in page 42.* This also clearly implies that the words were not directly dictated by the Holy Spirit; but that the Divine Spirit revealed truths to the mind, either *indirectly* by expressive forms presented to the imagination, or *directly* by the ideas which He suggested to the understanding.†

---

* Πνευματικοῖς πνευματικα συγκρίνοντες, *i.e.*, which we also speak or discourse or treat upon (such is the meaning of λαλοῦμεν) in spiritual words,—Alford on 1 Cor. xii. 3. For the meaning of συγκρινειν, see the Septuagint, Gen. xl. 8, 16, and 22, and Numbers xv. 34. I prefer this translation to that which makes πνευματικοις the dative 'to spiritual persons' (p. 38).

† The distinction of revelations into those of the *indirect* representations of images set before the imagination, and of ideas *directly* suggested by the Divine Spirit,—the former being generally the objects of revelation with the order of the prophets, and explicitly stated by them; the latter, the objects of their revelations to which the other writers of the sacred books only refer,—gives an intelligible meaning to the view of

2. In the next place, designating those profound truths "the deep things of God," τὰ βάθη, the apostle goes on to say that the Holy Ghost is the revealer of them (ver. 10): "God hath revealed them unto us by His Spirit: for the Spirit searcheth all things, yea the deep things of God." The gifts of men of genius are concerned with their natural spiritual perceptions, or what St. Paul calls "the spirit of the man," by which "the things of a man" are known; whereas the thoughts of prophets and apostles were employed on "the things of God, which no man knows, save the Spirit of God."

Very appropriate to this subject are the well-considered words of Archbishop Sumner: "What the heart cannot conceive, the counsels which are too profound for man's faculties to reach, God may reveal. No one knows what is passing in the thoughts of his friend, or his companion, till they are disclosed. No man knoweth the things of a man save the spirit of man which is in him. "The Spirit of God is in this respect like to the spirit of man." . . . For just as the secrets of a man's heart, though they cannot be discovered, may be revealed to his friend, so the

---

the German professor Sack alluded to by Hävernick.—Introduction, § 12, and of which view the Translator said he could form no idea.

"The peculiar character of the Hagiographa is that they do not communicate the thing given in the *revelation-act*, but set forth a *thought-image* springing from the subjective, and yet by no means merely human, excitement of the Spirit presenting the revelation with such a reference to the elsewhere given word of God, that a purer and more living understanding of the latter thence proceeds."

Divine Spirit, who only knows "the deep things of God," can reveal them to the human spirit.

3. In the third place, St. Paul (ver. 12) points out, in very precise terms, the nature and function of inspiration. Its function is to qualify and prepare the mind and heart for the reception—intelligent and cordial—of the truths communicated by revelation. "Now we have received, not the spirit of the world, but the Spirit which is of God, that we *might know* the things that are freely given to us of God." And as to its nature, the effect produced is, in fact, a character divinely impressed on the human spirit by the informing Spirit of God. Thus Mr. Swainson aptly describes inspiration as the new "spiritual condition of the writers;" and the learned Bishop Wordsworth, "a spiritual transfiguration."

We have seen (p. 7) that both Luther and his adversaries understood inspiration to mean an inbreathing into the mind, whether of the matter, or of the matter and form. Both confine it to the knowledge imparted *previously* to its being expressed.

There is then no assumption whatever in affirming that without such an influence as this—which as to its nature and origin is properly inspiration—no knowledge of things Divine would accrue from a revelation. For "the natural man receiveth not the things of the Spirit of God; for they are foolishness unto him, neither can he *know* them, because they are spiritually discerned" (ver: 14).

The higher powers, therefore, of man's spirit, by which only adequate conceptions of God, and of the profound truths of Christianity, as a scheme of redemption, can be formed, must be fitted for their reception (compare St. Paul's words, 2 Cor. iv. 6). Only can they come within the sphere of human cognition, when inspiration has imparted to the spiritual faculties of the apostles or prophets a quickened intuition and a keener perspicacity than they are naturally endowed with. Thus gifted, they have a power of recipiency which enables them to grasp these eternal truths, as far as Divine Wisdom sees fit to reveal them. For—to quote the same prelate once more—" As the things of God do not enter into the heart of man, that he can naturally comprehend them, so likewise there must be a *preparation* of the heart to receive them."

Such inspiration is sometimes represented as seeing with the Spirit bestowed by this influence—its effect being described as "the Spirit which is of God." Thus the son of Sirach (Eccles. cxlviii. 24) says of Isaiah, "He saw by an excellent Spirit, what should come to pass at the last," etc.; and still more in keeping with this idea are the following remarkable words in the Wisdom of Solomon:* "And Thy counsel who hath *known* except Thou give wisdom; and send Thy Holy Spirit from above." So also in Psalm

---

* Chap. ix. 17. βουλήν δε σου τίς έγνω εἰ μὴ σὺ ἐδωκας σοφίαν καὶ ἐπεμψας τὸ ἅγιον σὸν πνεῦμα ἀπο ὑψίστων.

cxliii. 10, to the teaching of God's good Spirit is ascribed the source of righteous conduct.* "Having ears to hear," is another form of expressing the gift of inspiration.

Here, then, the combined result of revelation and inspiration culminates in *knowledge*, which the man who solely depends on the natural unaided powers of his mind, does not and cannot receive,—a knowledge called by our apostle (2 Cor. iv. 6) "the light of the knowledge of the glory of God in the face of Jesus Christ," as relating to the scheme of man's redemption. "Thou gavest also Thy good Spirit to instruct them" (Neh. ix. 20), points to the same conclusion. For these words describe how the gifts of the Spirit were bestowed on certain chosen elders, by which they were enabled to assist Moses in teaching the refractory children of Israel in the wilderness.

Even now the doctrine taught by Paul, is the wisdom of God in a mystery. The light of the Holy Spirit must be imparted to the mind and heart before any one rightly knows Jesus Christ, and Him crucified, as the Lord of Glory. This is the precious gift of which St. John speaks, "ye have *an unction* from the Holy One, and ye *know* all things."

---

* This is the orthodox view of inspiration expressed in the Collect for Whit Sunday, and accepted by our Church : " God, who at this time didst *teach* the hearts of Thy faithful people, by sending to them *the light* of Thy Holy Spirit, grant us by the same Spirit to have *a right judgment* in all things, and evermore to rejoice in His holy comfort," etc.

4. Lastly, the *knowledge* of such truths being firmly grasped by the inspired subject of those Divine communications, and being clearly presented to his mental vision, in full and exact proportions, finds, according to the laws which govern human thought and language, a natural and spontaneous expression, in words not the product of human wisdom, yet having a human element. For these words spoken by man ("which *we* also speak," or discourse of, λαλοῦμεν, ver. 13,) exhibit the manifest traces of the channel through which they flow. Nevertheless are they, all the while, words which the inspired do form and utter, under the moulding hand of the Spirit, and the immediate result of His teaching—ἀλλ' ἐν διδακτοῖς πνεύματος ἁγίου; * *i.e.*, we discourse or set forth (such is the force of λαλεῖν) in suitable spiritual words the knowledge imparted to us. This observation confirms the interpretation I have given to πνευματικοῖς in page 33.

---

* Clemens Alexandrinus indicates the manner in which the Holy Spirit teaches the words—namely, by impressing His mind on them. He teaches the meanings (τὰς δόξας) which He has of the things, stamping, as it were, His mind on the forms of expression employed. The Spirit teaches the meanings, "ἃς τὸ ἅγιον πνεῦμα περὶ τῶν ἔχον πραγμάτων, εἰς τὰς λέξεις, ὡς εἰπεῖν, τὴν αὐτοῦ διάνοιαν ἐκτυπωσάμενον, διδάσκει. κ. τ. λ. Thus is it, through the knowledge divinely imparted to the inspired prophet or apostle, that the words expressing it are invested with their meanings, in the mind of the Spirit. Thus also (in his 'Admonitio ad Gentes,' p. 51,) Clemens says, "Jeremiah the prophet, or *rather* the Holy Spirit in Jeremiah," etc., indicating how the Spirit is the author of the words. By correcting himself he implies that only in a certain sense the words are those of the Holy Spirit.

Possessing then a knowledge so perfect and so exact of a matter thoroughly understood, and his mind deeply imbued with the Spirit's teaching, and this moreover powerfully influencing those faculties which are subservient to the use of language, the prophet or apostle cannot fail to deliver spontaneously the burden of the Lord, in suitable terms—

"Verbaque provisam rem non invita sequentur."

According to the commonly received view of inspiration, some have thought that the writers were left to themselves, and got no assistance from the Spirit in the utterance of the truths imparted to them. Such an objection disappears on the principles laid down. Chalmers, using inspiration in an objective sense, puts the case in its strongest form : " Strange that with the inspiration of thought, the revelation should make pure ingress into the minds of the apostles, but, wanting the inspiration of words, should not make pure egress to that world in whose behalf alone this movement originated in heaven, and terminated on earth." The revelation was not "abandoned to itself," as is supposed, in the minds of the apostles, since they had been fitted by the teaching of the Divine Spirit to express it accurately; and may have been further assisted (though this is not stated by St. Paul) in those silent and rapid processes of thought which subserve the use of language.

In no part of the wide field of this investigation are we so apt to lose our way, and to choose devious paths, as that on which we have now entered. Here we stand on debateable ground, and it behoves us to secure a firm footing. Only shall this be possible if, disengaging ourselves for a moment from the tangled web into which speculation has woven this mysterious subject, we turn to the Holy Scriptures for guidance and instruction.

A careful exegesis of this very remarkable passage will show that the words are not themselves infused, as it were, by silent dictation; but that they are the outcome of the Spirit's teaching, by which the knowledge had been produced.

For the first clause of the 13th verse,—"which things also we speak, not in the words which man's wisdom teacheth,"—fixes the meaning of the construction ἐν διδακτοῖς, followed by the genitive of the agent, Πνεύματος ἁγίου. It shows that the words are the natural issue of the knowledge imparted. That the first clause fixes the meaning of the second, "in words which the Holy Ghost teacheth," follows necessarily from the parallelism here instituted between the two kinds of teaching.

For what is to be understood by "which things also we speak, not in the words which man's wisdom teacheth"? How does human wisdom teach men to express the knowledge they have acquired of scientific, or religious, or moral, or political subjects, the things about which the wisdom of this world is exercised?

By experienced masters, their pupils are indoctrinated in the principles of these several departments of human knowledge. Next, the truths involved are brought out, and explained. Lastly, when the pupils are by such training well instructed and thoroughly conversant with the subject, and acquire an accurate knowledge of the leading questions of each branch of study, they are themselves in a position to express the knowledge so acquired in appropriate terms— the natural outcome of such knowledge. Those utterances which now flow spontaneously and unbidden are "the words which man's wisdom teacheth." How? By the modes and processes of instruction which had prepared their minds for taking in the knowledge of the truths, afterwards to be enunciated by themselves, for the benefit of others.

In like manner, the Divine Spirit was the instructor of the prophets and apostles. By inspiration and revelation He imparted to them a full and accurate knowledge of the mysteries of the kingdom of heaven; thus fitting them to express that knowledge "in words which the Holy Ghost teacheth" through the appliances aforesaid.* By these, in His wisdom, He had prepared and equipped them to announce

---

* I find that Cyril of Alexandria has given the same interpretation, clearly stating that "the prophets were taught by the Holy Spirit, not by a mere verbal message, but by the Spirit flashing on their minds the knowledge of each thing." οὐ διὰ μόνης ἀπαγγελίας οἱ προφῆται κατὰ

accurately and faithfully the Divine truths disclosed, and thus to discharge the duty of Christian prophets or teachers. I say to announce (λαλειν) as distinguished from λεγειν, to say, [see Alford, in 1 Cor. xii. 3, on λαλῶν λέγει,] what He had revealed.

Moreover, the matter of some Divine truth being presented by revelation to the mind of the apostle or prophet, which by inspiration had been prepared to comprehend it, in what form of words does he proceed to express it?

He does not employ "the words which man's wisdom teacheth," such as those used by philosophers and orators, who treat a religious question as a human speculation; but regarding it as a revelation from heaven, he puts the knowledge communicated into a form of expression derived from the past and present instruction of the Divine Spirit, "comparing (or interpreting) spiritual things with spiritual,"—expressing, that is, these spiritual things by spiritual words.

For example: when by revelation it became known to St. Paul that the Gentiles were to be admitted equally with the Jews into the Gospel covenant, he did not reason in such words as these, "The Gentiles are of one blood with the Jews, and God is no respecter of persons;" but, taking up the language of the inspired prophets, through whom the Holy

---

καιροὺς ἐδιδασκοντο, τοῦ 'Αγιου Πνεύματος αὐτοις ἐναστράπτοντος τὴν ἑκάστου γνῶσιν· κ. τ. λ. To this matter I shall again refer in Chap. X.

Spirit had spoken, he says, "Praise the Lord, all ye Gentiles, and laud Him, all ye people;" and again, "there shall be a root of Jesse, and He that shall rise to reign over the Gentiles, in Him shall the Gentiles trust:" using these quotations, and by them interpreting the revelation vouchsafed to Himself. "We have," says Theodoret, "the testimony of the Old Testament, and by it we confirm the New,"* a dictum fully as true when applied to the original recipients of the New Testament revelations, as to future readers of them.

Alford's remarks on 2 Tim. iii. 15 are most important, while they show how almost impossible it is now to keep quite distinct the respective meanings of inspiration and revelation. Θεόπνευστος, which is common to Jews, Greeks, and Romans; as applied to the prophets, only differs in this, "that we ever regard one speaking prophecy as more immediately and thoroughly the mouthpiece of the Holy Spirit, seeing that the future is wholly hidden from men, and God does not in this case use or *inspire* human testimony to facts, but suggests the whole substance of what is said, direct from Himself."

The mode however (above considered) of the prophet's finding, under the Spirit's teaching, a fitting expression for the knowledge imparted to him, is something very unlike dictation.

---

* Ἔχομεν γὰρ τῆς παλαιᾶς διαθήκης μαρτυρίαν καὶ δι᾿ ἐκείνης τὴν καινὴν βεβαιοῦμεν.

But a more direct suggestion of *the words themselves*, which the latest writers insinuate, if any meaning attach to the generalities employed, would be sheer dictation—a theory now entirely exploded, and, as incompatible with the facts of the case, quite untenable. Words nevertheless uttered by men whose minds and hearts were filled with the Holy Spirit of God must be regarded as the words of the Spirit. "If" (says the gifted Chalmers) "God fits men to speak, He speaks by them." So Clemens Romanus, ad 1 Cor., s. 45,* calls the Scripture the true words of the Holy Ghost.

In the same train of thought, Clemens Alexandrinus, quoting 1 Cor. iii. 2, remarks, "The Holy Spirit who was in the apostle, using the voice of the Lord,† says mystically, "I have fed you with milk," etc.

To sum up, under their proper heads, the foregoing analysis of the Pauline view of inspiration of Holy Scripture, may be useful.

1. Revelations are presented to the minds of the sacred writers in any of the various forms which seem best to the Spirit of wisdom.

2. Their minds and hearts are enlightened and

---

* τὰς ἀληθεῖς ῥήσεις Πνεύματος τοῦ ἁγίου.

† τὸ ἐν Ἀποστόλῳ Ἅγιον Πνεῦμα τῇ τοῦ κυρίου ἀποχρώμενον Φωνῇ. Pædagog., lib. i., c. 6, p. 106. Again, in his Fragments, we read that the Holy Spirit impressed His mind on the words of Scripture teaching the meaning of the things τὴν αὐτοῦ διανοίαν ἐκτυπωσαμενον. See note to page 38 of this essay.

opened, by the inspiration of the Holy Spirit, to comprehend fully the import of those revelations, and disposed to accept the truths involved in them, with a distinct consciousness that they are not the natural products of their own thoughts.

3. By this twofold operation of the Divine Spirit, there arises a complete knowledge (as far as the Spirit sees fit to reveal) of the truths conveyed, and an earnest desire to communicate that knowledge to others.

4. According to the laws which govern human thought and language, their conceptions of such truths—clearly and distinctly presented to their spiritual vision—are clothed in appropriate words. Moreover, these words, resulting in the manner described from the teaching of the Holy Ghost, by whose presence they were filled and actuated, and which, no doubt, would have a powerful effect, by excluding extraneous thoughts, and by concentrating their ideas on the matter before them, in those rapid and silent processes of thinking that unconsciously accompany the utterance of verbal signs, are truly said to be "words which the Holy Ghost teacheth."* Now the aggregate of these utterances constitute the holy volume, which is therefore God-inspired.

In St. Paul's view, then, we have a just theory of

---

* In verse 13, the verb in ἃ καὶ λαλοῦμεν is "we discourse or reason about," as distinguished from λέγων, which is simply to say. See John viii. 25.

plenary inspiration; for if the Spirit led the sacred writers into all the truth, giving them precise and clear notions on each matter, so as effectually to exclude error, and by concentrating their thoughts so as to prevent extraneous matter from disturbing their ideas, direct the current of these thoughts in their proper channel, He would, in the fullest sense, have virtually superintended the writing—only short of prompting the very words themselves. Superintendence, however, in this point of view is indirectly making ample and sufficient provision against error.

Here, if anywhere, it is unsafe to dogmatize. The Holy Scriptures tell us of a guidance, promised by the Saviour to His apostles. But this is a guidance into the knowledge of the truth. The Comforter was to guide the apostles into all the truth, and to show them things to come (John xvi. 13).

Now, instead of this, in the popular definition of inspiration, is substituted a guidance into the form of words used by the writers for expressing the knowledge conveyed to them by inspiration and revelation—an assumption of the same stamp as that of the infallibility of the Church of Rome.

But manifest it is that the Holy Spirit, by inspiration and revelation, had guided into those truths the apostles of Christ, some time—it may be many years —previously to their writing a standing record of them; and also previously, in reference to the influences exercised on their minds and hearts at the times in which they committed them to writing.

Thus inspiration has had its effect on their minds and hearts, before they, orally or in writing, had expressed the knowledge of the truths divinely communicated to them.

CHAPTER II.

THE TRUE NATURE OF INSPIRATION: ITS RELATION TO THE AUTHORITY OF THE BIBLE.

SUCH is the present state of the question of inspiration—a question not easily disentangled from the errors which have involved it in much obscurity. A wrong idea of its nature, perpetuated by an equally wrong distinction between revelation and inspiration, had rendered any attempt to remedy the evil hopeless: so long as traditional dogma, instead of appeal to Holy Scripture, had been made the starting-point.

Mr. Morell was, I believe, the first who had the courage to cast off, in his 'Philosophy of Religion,' the commonly received notion of inspiration, as a direction to the external act of speaking or writing. But he has not sufficiently discriminated inspiration from revelation.

At this point I am arrived at the third cause assigned for the many inconsistencies and errors complained of in treatises on inspiration, namely, "the marvellous manner in which inspiration is interwoven with revelation, sometimes hides from view the very nature of inspiration."

So intimate indeed is the connection, that inspiration often gives revelation; and with Mr. Morell this became a general principle.*

The saying of our Lord, "Blessed are the pure in heart, for they shall see God," he pushes to an extreme, and considers such purity the measure of the degree in each, of his intuition of Divine things. On this head it has been well remarked that if one man be of a purer heart than another, he must enjoy a higher form of inspiration; and if he have a higher religious character in this respect than an apostle, he would have a higher intuition of Divine truths, and know them more infallibly. Be this as it may, it is nevertheless certain that inspiration sometimes induces and gives revelation, clearing away, as it were, obscuring clouds which hide from view the realities of the spiritual world. Such is a true revelation, or unveiling, of things previously hidden from man. David notes this spiritual insight, as the result of inspiration: "Open Thou mine eyes, that I may behold wondrous things out of Thy law." A similar effect is described in Luke xxiv. 45. And in the case of Lydia (Acts xvi. 14) we have the moral effects of inspiration.

* Mr. Morell seems to be deeply imbued with the views of Schleiermacher.

As on a clear night, countless stars of different magnitudes are visible to the naked eye, in the blue vault of heaven, while many more remain unseen by that organ: yet if the power of vision were increased a hundredfold, how many shining orbs of light would be discovered for the first time? So it may be with inspiration. The enlargement and purification of the human faculties, imparting quickened intuition and a perspicacity otherwise unattainable, give a power of recipiency to the mind, and may also bring into light many new truths hitherto unperceived.

As therefore inspiration is so nearly allied to revelation, they are often used—where they ought not—interchangeably, as if synonymous. And truths revealed by suggestion, or recalled to memory by the Divine Spirit, which, committed to writing, form a large portion of the holy volume, are ascribed to inspiration, and even sometimes called inspirations.* With greater propriety, however, ought such truths be called revelations, in the same sense and manner as the whole Bible is called a revelation.

Now as to theories of inspiration of Holy Scripture, the great aim of any writer should be to give a rational and scriptural account of the connection between personal inspiration and revelation

---

* A luminous writer, the late Archbishop Whately, seems to use these words indiscriminately; and in one place to employ inspiration, where St. Paul has revelation.

of the sacred writer, and the truth of the written record.

The usual method of proceeding, however, is very different. This is to determine beforehand the most plausible ground (as it appears to each theorist) on which to base the certain and undoubted truth of the words uttered by the sacred writers. It is nevertheless to be observed that *à priori* notions, if not checked and confirmed by clear Scripture proofs, are unsafe to depend on, involving more or less of doubtful assumptions. Moreover, such tests are useful and even necessary to apply in the case of any theory, however satisfactory, at first sight, it may seem. And thus too by the way of exclusion, we can approach nearer and nearer to a true view of the question under consideration ; or arriving at the conclusion (which I believe will be the actual result) that no theory hitherto devised, if subjected to the scriptural test, can be entertained, we shall instinctively turn to the Scriptures of truth, having discarded all theoretical considerations whatsoever.

So keenly have the disappointing results of modern speculation on the subject been felt by the learned and thoughtful Bishop of Gloucester, Dr. Ellicott, that, on a careful review of the present state of the question, he advised the rejection of theories, and, instead, recommended a thorough examination of the several notices of inspiration, in the Bible itself.

" We heartily concur with the majority of our

opponents in rejecting all theories of inspiration, and in sweeping away all those distinctions and definitions which only, in too many cases, have been merely called forth by emergencies, and drawn up for no other purpose than to meet real or supposed difficulties. . . . The holy volume itself shall explain to us the nature of that influence, by which it is pervaded and quickened. Nothing can be less tenable than the assertion that there is no foundation in the gospels and epistles for any of the higher or supernatural views of inspiration. . . . We assume that what Scripture says is trustworthy, and so conceive that it may be fittingly appealed to as a witness concerning its own characteristics." *

With much diffidence in my own ability to cope with the intricacies in which this subject is involved, I have tried to work out the investigation recommended by this excellent prelate. For there can be no doubt that many commencing an inquiry into the nature of inspiration, have taken for their starting-point, not the word of God, but the traditional definitions and divisions of the Roman theology, to which their ingenuity is tasked to make the former agree.†
Now it being impossible effectually to accomplish this, they have so darkened the simple scriptural

---

* 'Aids to Faith,' p. 404.

† This is an undeniable fact. It is not, however, insinuated here that the eminent authors who accepted those definitions and divisions had any leanings to the Roman theology.

account of inspiration, that the faith of many in the Divine authority of the written word has been shaken in no small degree. For theories not based on sufficient data, erring sometimes in defect, sometimes in excess, have naturally weakened men's reverence for God's word, and not seldom have produced and promoted infidelity.

To investigate the nature of inspiration in the notices of this influence presented in the pages of Scripture is as legitimate as it is safe. It is not reasoning in a circle to assume the truth of the Bible, and from it to deduce the nature of the inspiration of Holy Scripture. For on independent grounds, not accessible to the attacks of unbelievers, and on evidence the most unquestionable, it has been proved that the Bible has come from God.

Writers on the evidences of the Christian religion have proved its Divine origin, and therefore its truth, in so convincing a manner, that their arguments have never been answered. They are unanswerable. "Scripture" (says Hooker) "teacheth us that saving truth which God hath discovered unto the world by revelation ; and it presumeth us taught otherwise, that itself is divine and sacred."—*Eccl. Polity*, book iii., chap. 8.

The Divine authority of the New Testament has been established in a way so strikingly effective by our great writers on Christian Evidences, that nothing is now wanted to prove that it has really come from God. Besides the evidence peculiar to the old canonical Scriptures, the New Testament stamps on the Old the Divine superscription. Our Lord and His apostles repeatedly cite and freely appeal to the books of the Old Testament. The phrase, too, so often employed by Christ for the purpose of impressing and definitively determining and settling His own dictum "It is written," fixes the Divine imprimatur on all the books of the old canon received by the Jews.

Although I have treated in the first place 'the present state of the question of inspiration,' I admit that a methodical discussion of its nature should be postponed to the inquiry into the Divine authority of the Holy Scriptures, which latter inquiry is independent of the former, however intimately related the things themselves may be to each other.

Here I must do myself the pleasure of introducing the pertinent remarks of Mr. Swainson, who has contributed much to the dispersion of the cloudiness of this confessedly abstruse subject.

"The question, then, as to the authority of the New Testament is of one kind; the question as to the manner and nature of its inspiration is of another. They differ as to the place which they take in theological inquiry; they differ as to the objections by which they are affected. The authority of the volume, and of the several books which it contains, depends on the position and character of the respective writers, on their competency to speak to the things which they attest, and on their truthfulness in giving their testimony. And these must be judged of by the ordinary criteria: Are they, or are they not, worthy of credit? And this distinction has been lost sight of quite as much by opponents of the faith of our Church as by its upholders. If some of the latter have rendered themselves liable to the charge that the arguments are illogical, and their reasonings circular, equally short-sighted have their opponents been, who, in the overthrow of a humanly conceived theory of inspiration, have exulted as if they had thrown discredit upon the facts from which the theory was inferred. But we of the present day must take warning from the history of the controversy: we must not assume the inspiration of Scripture to prove its truth, and then assume its truth to prove its inspiration. We must inquire carefully and painfully on what grounds we accept it as true; and then we may inquire humbly and earnestly whether we are able to form any adequate conception of the spiritual condition of its writers." *

The fact is, neither the theories nor the definitions of inspiration, nor the divisions employed, in the most elaborate treatises on the subject, are strictly in accordance with God's word. The writings of the Old Testament and the New have been unanswerably proved to be God's word. The *fact* of the inspiration

---

* 'Authority of the New Testament,' by C. A. Swainson, M.A.

of the Divine word passing to us through a human channel, coming however from the pure source of Divine truth, may be accepted as proved; and this inspiration, extending to every word, although not mechanical, to be really and truly verbal. For it is a wrong representation of the matter to suppose a verbal inspiration to be necessarily mechanical.

But when we proceed to the further question, 'What is the nature of that inspiration?' we have not, it has been alleged, sufficient data—data of that kind which some, who accept only such facts as are addressed to and attested by their own experience, deem sufficient to build a complete theory on.

We have, however, a perfect right, notwithstanding what Roman Catholic controversialists say to the contrary, to appeal to the Scriptures—antecedently proved to have come from God—for the elucidation, as far as it has pleased its Divine Author to have given it, of the nature of that sacred influence on the mind and heart, which is properly denominated inspiration. And the facts, attested by the sacred writers, furnish data of another kind, which must also command our assent, and be therefore accepted as a sufficient groundwork of a legitimate theory; just as much as, in the world of matter, physical theories are based on facts received on the evidence of our senses.

Now it will be seen that the above-mentioned elucidation in the hands of St. Paul, only stating the facts of the case as known to himself, without entering into the mysterious laws of the workings of the human spirit, and those of the Divine Spirit on the spirit of man, has a pre-eminent claim to the rank and title of a theory of the inspiration of Holy Scripture.

Even in physical theories, where we group together facts according to general laws, however well the facts seem to be ascertainable by the use and exercise of our natural faculties, we know almost nothing of the nature of the mysterious agencies themselves of which we would give the theories. The facts of universal gravitation, electricity, and magnetism are well known, and yet what in themselves are gravitation, electricity, and magnetism? Even in theories of these, there are ultimate facts beyond which we cannot go, and of which the only account we can render is that they are.*

In the present case, the facts are: the Spirit of God, the spirit of man, the revelation presented to the latter; the personal inspiration, which prepares the human Spirit for that revelation. Knowledge produced by this twofold operation, the expression of that knowledge in words, the outcome of this Divine teaching of the Holy Ghost. These facts, so grouped in logical sequence, is the theory of St. Paul, by which he proves that the written word is the word of God.

---

* See Chapter X. for a fuller discussion of this point.

In the analysis here given, Dean Alford's acute and very valuable suggestions have been attended to. "Two things," says this learned commentator, "I would earnestly impress on my readers: first, that we must take our views of inspiration, not, as is too often done, from *à priori* considerations, but entirely from the evidence furnished by the Scriptures themselves; secondly, that *the men* were inspired, and *the books are the results* of that inspiration. This latter consideration, if all that it implies be duly weighed, will furnish a key to the whole question."

Now it is to be observed, that the tendency of writers on the subject in our day has been rather to postpone the consideration of the inspiration of the *men*, to that of the books composed by them. This tendency, moreover, has been encouraged into a growing habit by the prevalent belief that 'revelation,' in Scripture terminology, refers to the utterances of the inspired writers, and not to the Divine communications made to them. Thus modern authors begin their inquiry in, and rest satisfied with, that which is more properly the record or book of a revelation than a revelation itself. And yet it is only by studying the latter that you can understand the true nature and character of the former.*

On the contrary, the true language of Scripture is, "The Lord God revealeth His secrets to His servants

---

* Mr. Litton, referred to in Chapter III., is one who does not adopt the sage advice of Alford.

the prophets" (Amos iii. 7). In the same sense, St. Paul uses the word when he says, "I will come to visions and revelations of the Lord;" and speaks of "the abundance" of those revelations vouchsafed to himself; and so in other places, of which Gal. i. 15, 16, and Eph. iii. 3—5, may be taken as samples. For Gal. i. 15, 16 is not an exception. In this passage St. Paul says, "But when it pleased God, who hath separated me from my mother's womb, and called me by His grace to *reveal* His Son *in me*, that I might preach Him among the Gentiles."

Here Professor Lightfoot, following Grotius, very strangely interprets *in* me (ἐν ἐμοὶ), contrary to the weight of evidence and of the best authorities, as the equivalent of *through me* (διὰ με); meaning thereby that God revealed His Son through the preaching of Paul.

Now this interpretation is untenable. For the phrase, so understood, renders the following clause (ἵνα, "in order that I might preach Him," etc.) a mere tautology. The words ἐν ἐμοὶ can only mean, in reference to Paul, God's revelation made *in* or *to* him. In the latter sense, it is understood by Irenæus as referring to Paul's miraculous conversion, "revelare Filium Suum in me ut evangelizarem eum in Gentibus . . . . revelatione ei de cœlo factâ et colloquente cum eo Domino."—*Irenæus, Ad Her.*, lib. v., c. 12, p. 417.

A revelation within his soul is the view of Beza,

Olshausen, Semler, Cocceius, Winer.* So much for the tendency to which I have called attention.

The question of the authority of Scripture established on prior and independent grounds,—resting, in fact, on the proof that it has a Divine origin,—can be and has been treated apart from its inspiration. And yet there is an intimate and inseparable connexion between them, which ought not, as sometimes it has been, overlooked.

Those who place the authority of Scripture in its inspiration, can be reconciled with others who attach

---

* Beza: "ἐν ἐμοὶ" *i.e.*, Mihi: sed tamen videtur quiddam etiam amplius significare."

Semler: "Rectius omnino faciunt interpretes qui post Chrysostomum, ἐν ἐμοι. Sic explicant, ut excludat externum omnem magistrum, sicut. 1 Cor. ii. 10; Eph. iii. 3."

Cocceius: "Multis ostendit Deus Filium Suum, sed non revelat; quia *in* multis non est, non habitat."

Winer: "1 John iv. 9, ἐφανερώθη ἡ ἀγάπη τοῦ Θεοῦ ἐν ἡμῖν; to have the love of God revealed *in* us is something more than to have it revealed to us."

Professor Lightfoot marks three separate stages in the apostle's consecration to his ministry, of which the third is the entering upon his office. I should rather lay down these stages as the following:

1. His predestination to this office (ὁ ἀφορίσας με. κ.τ.λ.)
2. His call to the apostleship, which took place on his way to Damascus (καλέσας).
3. The revelation of His Son to him or in him afterwards.

For all three were preparatory to his preaching the Gospel to the Gentiles (ἵνα, etc.)

Even Lightfoot notes this, subsequently, in reference to Paul's journey into Arabia: "In the midst of such scenes, his spirit was attuned to harmony with his Divine mission, and *fitted* to receive fresh visions and revelations of the Lord." And again, "St. Paul says, 'I conferred not with flesh and blood, but departed into Arabia.'" See 2 Cor. iv. 6.

this mark of honour to the apostolic office and commission.

The point of union exists in the fact that the inspiration of Scripture—which is its essential characteristic—is the result of the personal inspiration and revelation imparted by the Holy Spirit to the writers who were invested with this official authority. This is the extrinsic, that the intrinsic, source of the authority of Holy Scripture. In this the formal, in that the essential authority consists. Its authority is the only safeguard of religion and virtue.*

Many, overlooking this distinction, important and all-pervading, between form and spirit—of which the application is as easy as it is general in every department of theology—have run into extreme views on this and kindred subjects.

A Divine fire burns through the Bible, and thus a sort of divinity is by many, and among others by Coleridge, assigned to that blessed book. Now while in this sense, as God's word, it is the sword of the Spirit, and as such a powerful mean by which God acts upon the human mind, in another and higher sense the Bible is a revelation of the mind of God.

In the former, every good and pious book, as Baxter's 'Saint's Everlasting Rest,' or Bunyan's 'Pil-

---

* This essential authority in its important results is thus stated by Augustine: "Titubabit fides si divinarum Scripturarum vacillat auctoritas: porro fide titubante charitas et etiam ipsa languescit."—*De Doctr. Christ.*, i. 41.

grim's Progress,' might claim to rank with the Bible. But the Bible is more than a storehouse of influences adapted to move and stir up in its unnermost depths the spirit of man—which above all other books it is fitted to do : it is the record of the revelation of God to man ; and in this sense it is unique, and claims an authority peculiarly its own.

The simple truth may be briefly stated thus. The authority of Scripture depends on its being the word of God ; and because it is the word of God, and the result of the Spirit's teaching, it has this intrinsic property of being inspired,—that is, of coming to us through men, fitted by the inbreathed energy of the Holy Spirit to take cognizance of and fully comprehend the truths revealed to them.

This Θεοπνευστια, whose function it is to purify, prepare, and duly qualify for the reception of those truths, the human channel through which, by Divine appointment, they were designed to flow to mankind, is followed by προφητεια,* their oral or written announcement. On this point see Hengstenberg, quoted further on in this chapter.

Such, in brief, on examination, will be found the plain statement of the manner in which authority, both formal and essential, attaches to the utterances

---

* Thus Augustine defines a prophet, " Nihil aliud est propheta Dei, nisi enunciator verborum Dei hominibus." See also ' Aids to Faith,' p. 84, for the true meaning of ' prophet,' ‫נב‬. Echo ad instar, nihil profert, nisi quod prius accepit. Profert, i.e., λάλει, as in p. 42.

of the inspired servants of God, and invests their united record with the rank and title of 'the word of God.'

Perhaps the greater number of the difficulties which embarrass this question are to be attributed to the imperfection and abuse of language; and this is the fourth cause assigned by me for the inconsistencies of writers on the subject of inspiration.

Scarcely any two authors agree in the meanings they affix to the principal terms employed. How different the answers they give to the questions—What is inspiration? What is revelation? What is the nature and extent of each? If the Redeemer promised a guidance into all the truth to His apostles, what is the nature of that guidance, and how far does it extend? If the whole Bible be the revelation of God to man, is it so that parts of it are not revelations? When the Holy Spirit, by the suggestions of ideas to the minds of the inspired, guides and directs, are these suggestions to be accounted with some inspirations, or, as I think, more correctly to be reckoned among revelations?

This is only a small catalogue of the ambiguous terms and phrases which, unfortunately, will be found, not only in different authors, but also in the same, to be used variously, thereby giving rise to damaging inconsistency.

What consequences are to be expected from such abuse of language? Hear a competent judge in matters of this kind—Mr. Locke,—

"I am apt to imagine that, were the imperfections of language, as an instrument of knowledge, more thoroughly weighed, a great many of the controversies that make such a noise in the world would of themselves cease; and the way to knowledge, and perhaps peace too, lie a great deal opener than it does."

Speaking of revealed truths, he remarks: "These, which are conveyed to us by books and languages, are liable to the common and natural obscurities and difficulties incident to words: methinks it would become us to be more careful and diligent in observing the former, and less positive and imperious in imposing our own sense and interpretation of the latter."

Again: "Men take the words they find in use amongst their neighbours, and that they may not seem ignorant what they stand for, use them confidently, without much troubling their heads about a certain fixed meaning, whereby, besides the case of it, they obtain this advantage, that as in such discourses they seldom are in the right, so they are as seldom to be convinced that they are in the wrong; it being all one to go about to draw these men out of their mistakes who have no settled notions, as to dispossess a vagrant of his habitation who has no settled abode."

I introduce these severe, but well-considered, remarks of our world-renowned philosopher, than whom none better understood the danger of the unsteady use of words. This inevitably happens when terms, not generally well and clearly defined, are employed in an unusual sense.

I have no doubt that the distinguished authors with whom I differ had carefully and honestly weighed and measured their words. Yet when the ablest men venture to employ the principal terms here concerned—Inspiration and Revelation—in a sense "which altogether abandons their popular use;"* if "the good Homer sometimes nods," they cannot expect to be always on their guard against the insidious abuse of words; for in the course of their discussions, the proper and true etymological meanings may intrude stealthily and unperceived; and at a moment when they are not aware, warp their judgments and disconcert their reasonings, and thus unconsciously involve them in contradictions and inconsistencies.

Now finding themselves unfortunately riveted to errors, they usually take another step, and seek to find, if possible, in the Fathers of the early Christian Church, passages in support of such views. For this is often an easy task, since these generally eminent and pious men wrote so much, and spread over so deep and stormy a sea of bold and often not strictly reasonable conjecture, that it is not hard to fish out of it a sentence here and there, which may seem

---

* Lee's 'Inspiration of Holy Scripture,' note [2], page 29.

to favour the most plausible guesses at recondite truth.

Come from what quarter they may—*fas et ab hoste doceri*—the following are admirable words :—

"More than any other subject of human knowledge, Biblical criticism has hung to the past; it has been hitherto found truer to the traditions of the Church than to the words of Christ. It has, however, made two great steps onward—at the time of the Reformation, and in our own day. The diffusion of a critical spirit in history and literature is affecting the criticism of the Bible, in our own day, in a manner not unlike the burst of intellectual life in the fifteenth or sixteenth century. Educated persons are beginning to ask, not what Scripture may be made to mean, but what it does."

Now in reference to the bearing of these observations on the inquiry into the nature of inspiration, I may be permitted to remark that nothing can be plainer—if we seek our information from Holy Scripture—than St. Paul's statement of the manner in which the knowledge of Divine truth had been produced in the mind of prophet or apostle.

This knowledge was supernaturally imparted by the Divine Spirit through the conjoint operation of revelation and inspiration, being in fact the resultant of these spiritual forces.

Yet, if it be said, as it has been, that revelation alone conveys this knowledge; and if inspiration be shifted from the inwardness of its proper function and province, as the act which prepares and enlightens the mind for taking in and comprehending the revelation, to the position of an act operating outwardly as a guidance to a verbal expression, what follows?

On this, *supposition regarding the nature of inspiration*, it follows that the patriarchs receiving revelations were not inspired because they did not record them. That, moreover, whatever revelations have been given to the servants of God, if they were treasured in the silent depths of their hearts, imparting consolations of the purest kind, there had been no inspiration. Simeon, to whom "it was revealed that he should not see death before he had seen the Lord's Christ," had not been inspired, though he *understood* the revelation, and under this influence had "come *by the Spirit* into the temple" to witness the realization of his long-cherished hope!

Nor had St. John been inspired when he received Divine revelations which, until some time afterwards, he had not committed to writing, although he expressly states that he was under that sacred influence *when* the revelations were vouchsafed to him: "I was *in the Spirit* on the Lord's day, and heard," etc.

Again, try the question of the nature of inspiration on the disputed point, "Why from a multitude of writings extant among the ancient Jews and Christians,* a selection of certain books was made to the exclusion of others?"

Here disjoin inspiration from the combined acts of the Spirit,—namely, inspiration, properly so called, which fits the mind for the intelligent reception of the revelation vouchsafed,—and limit it to the record of the knowledge communicated by revelation alone —supposing this to be possible,—and what follows next?

The next step is to assume, in order to meet the difficulty, that a prophet too may have revelations without inspiration, if the revelation be unrecorded; and, what is stranger still, may not be under this Divine afflatus when he commits to writing the thoughts in his mind for the benefit of others.

So when a difficulty arises in 2 Chron. xxvi. 22, that an undoubted prophet, of the highest order, wrote a Book which has not been inserted, by the Jewish Church, in the Old Testament canon, an hypothesis is started, that this prophet was not inspired. "Now the rest of the acts of Uzziah, first and last, did Isaiah the prophet, the son of Amoz, write."

In support of this extraordinary position, Augustine is quoted. Still, this eminent Father, with all his love for speculation, who could invent an argument for the Assumption of the blessed Virgin, "ex convenientiâ rei," *i.e.*, an *à priori* reason of what ought

---

* Chrysostom, on 1 Cor. ii. 9, remarks, πολλὰ διεφθάρη βιβλία καὶ ὀλίγα διεσώθη.

to have been,—thus supplying what the Scriptures had omitted,—falters here. For he hesitates, and doubtingly gives his opinion. ("Cujus rei fateor causa me latet nisi quod existimo," etc.) "Of which thing I confess the cause is to me unknown, if it be not that even those to whom the Holy Spirit was wont to reveal what ought to be of authority in religion, could write some things as men by historic diligence; other things, as prophets by Divine inspiration: and these were thus distinguished—the former were to be attributed to themselves, but the latter to God speaking through them."

This gratuitous hypothesis is completely overturned by the unanswerable and decisive remark of Dr. Moses Stuart: "The manner of appeal to the works in question, which are now lost, both in Kings and Chronicles, shows, beyond all reasonable doubt, that they were regarded as anthoritative and sacred."

Indeed it is on this very ground that the New Testament lends its authority to the Old. The writers of the New Testament, who were unquestionably inspired, quoting with approval, incorporate in their writings the passages cited, and thus make them their own. In like manner the author of Kings and Chronicles, supposed to be Ezra, being inspired, adopts and appropriates, and throws the halo of his own inspiration around any books to which he refers the reader. For this reference really implies that it would be needless and supererogatory on his part to repeat what has been already placed on record; which it would not be, if it were not of equal authority with his own writings. These, it is highly probable, were extracted from the public records of the nation; as we read of the acts of Solomon, and frequently of the books of the Kings of Israel, and of the Kings of Judah; and of the book of Jehu, in which was written the acts of Jehoshaphat. And Isaiah wrote the acts of Uzziah; out of which, and such like books, Ezra composed a brief history.

In the same manner the inspired authors of the New Testament quote the old prophets; and giving the words of the Septuagint version, often differ from the Hebrew original. This adoption of the Greek translation stamps with Divine authority the passages so transferred to their own writings.

But the inconsistency does not end here: those who accept Augustine's view, must, with it, hold the opinion that inspiration does not apply to works composed by historic diligence; for he divides the writings of the prophets into two classes—what they write as men by historic diligence, and what as prophets by Divine inspiration.

Now if, as some think, several portions of Holy Scripture be not the record of revelations, but of the fruits of historic research; and if, according to this Father, these be written without inspiration, where is the agreement with Augustine of those writers who maintain, with Melchior Cano, that inspiration as 'a direction' was necessary to the faithful record of information derivable from man's unaided powers of investigation?

For it would be a most gratuitous assumption to assert that the prophet Isaiah was not inspired in precisely the same circumstances as those in which other writers were; or that an original writer, such as Isaiah, was not inspired, while a compiler like Ezra was.

Besides, the προφητικον πνεῦμα, and absence of inspiration, in a prophet composing a book, cited with approbation by an inspired writer, in the volume itself of inspiration, tally together badly. For these reasons, it need surprise no one, that Augustine, who defines a prophet, "nothing else than the utterer of the words of God to man," should have faltered in hazarding such an opinion.*

I cannot, however, feel that omission of some divinely inspired books from the canon mars the collection, as if it produced a hiatus in its continuity. For the canon may, and doubtless is, still complete. We have not in the gospels all the words and acts of

---

* When the trammels of the traditional dogmas of his Church hamper him, it is not easy for one of its bishops, however pious and clear-headed, to keep clear of the danger of being truer to the traditions of his party than to the words of Christ and His apostles. Thus Augustine could find an argument for the worship of the sacramental bread, from the text "worship at His footstool"—adorate scabellum pedum ejus; and in the entire absence of Scriptural references find a reason for upholding the assumption of the mother of our Lord, "ex convenientiâ rei."

the Lord Jesus; and yet for the blessedness of faith, what we have are sufficient and ample. "These are written that ye might believe that Jesus is the Christ, the Son of God; and that believing ye might have life through His name."

It is scarcely fair to assert that any book not received into the canon was rejected "as being human and fallible." Thus it cannot be affirmed that the book of Ecclesiasticus is such on *that* ground; but because, as Hävernick remarks,* the canon had been closed when the grandfather of the translator had composed the book in Hebrew or Arämaic. The *only* answer then why the book was not admitted into the canon, according to Hävernick, was 'that the already firmly established authority of the canon prevented it."

Even were the Hebrew edition extant at the time the canon had been closed, its omission would be no proof that it was rejected as uninspired, but only that the canon was deemed to be complete without it, as it was without the book which Isaiah composed.

The scriptural investigation of the nature of inspiration cannot be safely conducted on any preconceived assumptions whatsoever. Herein lies the danger. Sure that the Holy Scriptures are the words of the Spirit, spoken through human agents, we rightly pronounce

---

* 'Introduction to the Old Testament,' chapter i., § 7, p. 29.

those words to be sacred and divine. Nevertheless, if we make this character of the verbal signs our starting-point, and from it proceed to analyze the nature of inspiration, we are driven to devise the most plausible hypothesis in our view, to secure the absolute infallibility of Scripture. Perhaps our hypothesis is not the only one that can be conceived for that end; and, if so, it may turn out that we have not hit on the right one. Hence the supposition that the Divine Spirit guided the apostles and prophets into unerring words, cannot be laid down with safety as the point of departure in this inquiry. And a theory of inspiration built on this principle, unless such be expressly stated in Holy Scripture, cannot be entertained. The principle is unphilosophic, and a theory based on it cannot repel infidel objections. Now there is, as has been already said, a guidance spoken of there, but it is a guidance into all the truth—into the certain *knowledge* of the mysteries of the kingdom of heaven, into the knowledge of the deep things of God. If, therefore, we wish to understand *the nature of inspiration*, it is indispensable not to begin with hypothetic conjectures, but to follow the apostolic precedent. This is the course adopted by St. Paul. He shows how from two factors—revelation and inspiration—there results the *knowledge* of Divine truth; and how the apostle or prophet, *thus* taught by the Holy Spirit, expresses such truths, *suo more*, but yet with a mind and heart penetrated by His sacred presence, thereby uttering words which bear the Divine impress.*

It is only by thus entering into the inner chamber of consciousness that the nature of Divine inspiration can be understood;—the very idea is lost when we seek its nature in the outward acts of speaking and writing. Before one word is written or spoken, inspiration had exercised its influence, and attuned the mental and spiritual powers to apprehend and receive the truth.

Then in virtue of their commission, and impelled by a sense of duty, these men of God officially communicated to others that knowledge of Divine truth which had been imparted to themselves. And the inspiration which they had received in order "that they might know the things freely given to them of God," enabled them to teach others the truths conveyed to their own souls by the Spirit of God, according to the dictum of the Redeemer Himself: "We speak that we do know."

The idea of inspiration, as ancillary to the acquisition of Divine knowledge, made a deep impression on the mind of Irenæus: "After our Lord's ascension, His apostles were endued from on high with the power of the Holy Spirit; and were filled with and had a perfect *knowledge* of all things. They departed

---

* How the words flow from this divinely acquired knowledge is thus expressed by Solomon: "The heart of the wise teacheth his mouth, and addeth learning to his lips" (Prov. xvi. 23).

into the most distant lands, and preached one and all these saving truths of the Gospel."

How strongly the idea of the guidance of the Spirit of God to knowledge had also impressed itself on the minds of the sacred writers, is strikingly exhibited in the book of Job, where this inward guidance is expressly called inspiration: "There is in man a spirit; and the inspiration of the Almighty giveth them understanding."*

The Spirit of God calls out an answering spirit in man, and bestows upon it His gifts in the exact measure and proportion which are necessary to the clear and accurate knowledge of the truths to be imparted. And this knowledge relates either to truths now for the first time disclosed by revelation, or those recorded which have been already revealed, in both of which the preparatory enlightenment and quickened intuition of inspiration are absolutely required.

This extensive range of the knowledge of things Divine gives a peculiar force to the words of St. Paul (1 Cor. xiii. 2): "And though I have the gift of prophecy, and understand all mysteries, and *all knowledge*," etc. ($\pi\hat{a}\sigma a\nu$ $\tau\dot{\eta}\nu$ $\gamma\nu\hat{\omega}\sigma\iota\nu$),—a knowledge promotive of the gift of teaching, which is $\chi\acute{a}\rho\iota\sigma\mu a$ $\delta\iota\delta a\sigma\kappa a\lambda\acute{\iota}a\varsigma$ (Rom. xv. 14).

---

* Job xxxii. 8, רוּחַ הִיא בֶאֱנוֹשׁ וְנִשְׁמַת שַׁדַּי תְּבִינֵם. This is rendered in the Septuagint version, Πνεῦμα ἐστιν ἐν βροτοῖς· πνοὴ δὲ παντοκράτορος ἐστιν ἡ διδάσκουσα.

As bearing on this subject, the note of Professor Burton on 1 Cor. xii. 8 is judicious and pertinent: "If the order observed in this verse corresponds with that in ver. 28, σοφία applied to the apostles, and meant a full and perfect knowledge of all the doctrines of the Gospel; γνῶσις applied to the prophets, *i.e.*, the expounders of Scripture, and meant an understanding of the Old Testament."

So also Hengstenberg, on 1 Cor. xiv. 6, remarks, what, viewed in respect to the manner of receiving it, is revelation; the same when viewed as to its manner of delivery is prophecy. "We have here a double pair of corresponding parts: revelation and prophecy constitute the one, knowledge and doctrine the other." (See page 62.)

While Dr. Lee makes the important observation that, in consequence of the harmonious union and mutual balance of the several charisms in the minds and hearts of the apostles and prophets, provision was made for securing them from error of every kind, he falls into the strange mistake of substituting that which is properly inspiration for knowledge, "unclouded insight and clear perception (γνῶσις)."— Appendix M, page 556.*

---

* See Neander's Church History, vol. I, § 1, page 259, for the function denoted by the λόγος γνώσεως.

CHAPTER III.

DEFINITION OF INSPIRATION.

HAVING investigated the true nature of inspiration in the Scriptures themselves, I next proceed to give its definition conformably to that nature.

Now the scriptural view of its nature as operating on the minds and hearts of the servants of God, who were the chosen instruments of transmitting to us the truths revealed to them by the Father of Lights, has been fully set forth by me in the precise terms of St. Paul. And it is to be hoped that a view which uses the term in its true etymological sense, shall not land us in any of the inconsistencies about which in recent treatises on the subject complaints have been so rife.

It is indeed to be much regretted that Dr. Lee, whose indefatigable industry in collecting an immense mass of materials—patristic, mediæval, and modern—bearing on the several questions into which he breaks up the problem, is beyond praise, should have employed the term inspiration in a sense opposed to its established radical signification.

The result, as was to be expected, must exhibit itself, in many of the great authors cited by him,* holding views of inspiration at variance with his own. His definition of inspiration is thus expressed: "The actuating energy of the Holy Spirit in whatever degree or manner it may have been exercised, guided by which the human agents chosen by God have officially proclaimed His will by word of mouth, or have committed to writing the several portions of the Bible."

On this definition I venture to make a few remarks.

1. It is too vague and general, and does not, therefore, convey any precise information.

2. The real essential difference does not appear, veiled by the cloudy phrase—"in whatever degree or manner it may have been exercised."

3. What is here described is not inspiration, but the result of inspiration. A guidance to an external act, contrary to the very nature of the thing defined, which is an inbreathed energy, gives not a correct idea of its nature. There is, as I have shown, an inward guidance to knowledge, both promised by Christ and expressly specified by St. Paul.

4. Even if admissible, this definition is defective,

---

* This is a matter of the greater surprise, since Dr. Lee's reading had discovered to him the fact that the Fathers in regard to the condition of the sacred writers under the influence of inspiration "strongly insisted upon the notions of quickened intuition and enlightenment the faculties of the prophet."—Appendix, page 501, 2nd edition.

since it omits an essential element embraced in the scope of St. Paul. This is the impartation of *knowledge*.

"We have received (says the apostle) the Spirit which is of God, that we might *know* the things that are freely given to us of God." Therefore to confine the influence to the expression of the truths revealed, fails to present a just idea of this operation of the Divine Spirit on the soul of man. Its real work was an accomplished fact within the soul, before the utterance followed, and its function was to aid in imparting the knowledge of the truth, for Divine truth must be known before it can be expressed. Inspiration, in its primary signification,* is an influence of the Spirit of God on the hearts and minds of individuals, infusing into them those principles and motives of action which fit them for the performance of any of the works pertaining to the divers gifts of the Spirit. For thus "all these worketh that one and the selfsame Spirit, dividing to every man severally as He will."†

It is indeed a manifest abuse of language—ignoring the very etymology of the term—to refer inspiration solely, or at all, to the outcome of the sacred influence of the Holy Ghost on the mind and heart of the prophet or apostle, and passing

---

* The inspiration of a book can be understood only in a secondary or derivative sense.
† 1 Cor. xii. 11.

over the inward process by which he comes to "know the things freely given to him of God," to fix attention merely on their outward expression. The definition, therefore, which omits the essential and distinctive characteristic of this influence, is erroneous and illogical. Moreover, by excluding a part which the Scripture includes, it has bred vast confusion—perhaps more than is to be found in any other department of theology.

In fact, the definition above referred to, nearly formed on the Roman model, as enunciated by Perrone, is rather a statement of the resulting accuracy of expression, oral or written, of that knowledge which inspiration fitted and prepared the servants of God for accurately proclaiming, than a definition of inspiration itself.

Truly this inspiration it was which gave him a disposition to receive, and a quickened intuition to grasp and clearly perceive, the revelations which the Spirit had presented to his enlightened faculties; accompanied with a distinct consciousness of their Divine origin, and so not to be mistaken for the natural conceptions of his intellect, or creations of his imagination.

It has been justly remarked, that "so long as the mechanical theory of inspiration was generally maintained, there was no want of distinctness or consistency in the views put forward." But after this theory lost ground, and could no longer hold its position, vagueness, confusion, and inconsistency took the place of what had been precise, distinct, and accurately defined.

Then the intricacies of the subject sprouted up in abundant variety; and notwithstanding all that has been written up to this day, on no one question in theology has so much dissatisfaction been expressed as on the doctrine of Biblical Inspiration.

It may be interesting to trace to their sources the perplexing difficulties by which the subject at present is embarrassed. The new theories, and the definitions on which they have been constructed, involve so much of assumption and conjecture, that there is not likely soon to be an end of the difficulties engendered.

Much perplexity has arisen from the use of equivocal language. When writers use words in an avowedly new sense, it is next to impossible to avoid the danger and to escape the charge of inconsistency. For example, 'revelation' now refers to a Divine presentation to the mind of prophet or apostle, now it is taken for the prophetic utterance expressed in the word of God. One time 'inspiration' denotes an influence of the Holy Spirit on the mind, giving it a recipiency to enable it to grasp and understand Divine revelations; at another time it represents a power imparted for guiding a writer to the true and accurate expression of the truths revealed.

The effect too of the written word on the soul of

a Christian reader, called spiritual illumination, is by some taken for a revelation, by others for an inspiration, the same in kind as the apostolic. Once more: the act of the Holy Spirit on the believing heart of the Christian, imparting sanctifying grace, has been also called inspiration: so many and so serious in their effects are such ambiguities; and how extremely hard to disengage and draw them out of their hiding-places into the light of day.

Nothing, however, has so much tended to obscure the subject as a culpable neglect of following the luminous synthesis of St. Paul. Instead of investigating the nature of Biblical inspiration, as this great teacher had led the way, modern authors take a different course. He, adopting a true constructive plan, commences with its origin in the mind of the apostle or prophet, and proceeds thence to the united result of the action of personal inspiration and revelation, in producing the certain knowledge of Divine truth within the mind of the inspired; and, lastly, to the expression, oral or written, of that knowledge.

They make assumptions at the starting-point; and with them the starting-point is the written form in which the writers expressed the revelations with which they had been favoured. Moreover, while they call this record a revelation, and all parts of Scripture, viewed objectively, inspirations,—these authors, reversing the method of St. Paul, do not, by a correct analysis, retrace the steps of the Pauline synthesis. On the contrary, confessing—it is not easy to say why—man's ignorance of the steps of the process* described by St. Paul, they are content to substitute for it an assumed guidance to the words, which is not the guidance promised to the apostles by the Lord Jesus. For whether St. Paul, entering more minutely into details in the second chapter of 1st Corinthians, indicates the two spiritual forces—revelation and inspiration—which united give knowledge; or in other places, more briefly refers only to revelation, one of the factors: knowledge of Divine truth ($\gamma\nu\hat{\omega}\sigma\iota\varsigma$) is the focus where the rays of both concentrate. The rays reflected from this point of union, and falling on the pages of Holy Scripture, image forth the written word of God.

Hear now the apostle stating, "How that by revelation He (Christ) *made known* unto me the mystery, as I wrote before in few words: whereby, when ye read, ye may understand *my knowledge* in the mystery of Christ: which in other ages was not *made known* unto the sons of man, as it is now revealed unto His holy apostles and prophets by the Spirit."†

---

* The process is indeed beyond human comprehension; but the steps of this process are expressly and fully indicated by St. Paul. See this point examined more fully in pages 55—58.

† Ephes. iii. 3—5.

That the knowledge of the writer was not the result solely of revelation, while inspiration merely directed the utterance, is evident besides from indisputable facts in the history of the apostles.

Neither St. Peter nor St. Paul fully understood the truths involved in their respective visions, however profoundly they might think on them, until the illumining power of inspiration had afterwards supervened, as well to dislodge their deep-rooted prejudices, as to teach them clearly the real import of the revelations wrapt up in the visions.

The utterance too was the natural outflow of the knowledge imparted by the spiritual energy exerted on their minds through inspiration and revelation. This is strikingly evidenced by the difficulty the sacred writers sometimes felt, when the thoughts crowded upon them, of giving a distinct expression to their sentiments.

Attention has been called to the fact, that conceptions may crowd in the mind of a sacred writer, whilst the mode of giving utterance to them may not be supplied. This has been remarked in the case of St. Paul, and the passage (Rom. viii. 26, 27) clearly shows how impossible it is to dogmatize on the subject: "The Spirit helpeth our infirmities: for we know not what we should pray for, as we ought: but the Spirit itself maketh intercession for us with groanings that cannot be uttered. And He that searcheth the hearts knoweth what is in the mind of the Spirit, because He maketh intercession for the saints, according to the will of God."

I have said that the ordinary definition of inspiration, as limited to speaking or writing, is too contracted, and therefore does not present a correct view of the thing to be defined in the light of Holy Scripture.

The logical method of proceeding in such cases is to give a definition of inspiration in general; and to arrange under it, as one of its species,—marked by its essential difference,—the inspiration of Holy Scripture.

What then is Divine inspiration in general? I submit the following: The supernatural actuating energy of the Spirit of God on the mind and heart of an individual, preparing him for the reception and for the manifestation of any of the gifts which he vouchsafes to bestow.

Conformably to this, supported by 1 Cor. xii. 11, I define the inspiration of Holy Scripture, the supernatural energy of the Holy Spirit on the minds and hearts of certain chosen servants of God, preparing them for the reception and clear knowledge of Divine truths presented to them by revelation—accompanied with a distinct consciousness of its Divine origin—whereby they may be qualified and moved to express accurately the knowledge so imparted.

Both these definitions exactly correspond with the Pauline idea, and are strongly confirmed by Solomon's profound saying in Prov. xvi. 1, "The preparations of the heart in man, and the answer of the tongue, are from the Lord."

As to the common restricted use of inspiration, it is to be observed that the apostolic fathers refer to inspiration as a fact merely. Speaking of it in general, and though quoting passages in the Old Testament in which such phrases as λεγει τό πνεῦμα τὸ ἅγιον occur, they do not give any more definite account regarding the manner of this influence.

Thus Ignatius (ad Magnes., c. 8) says, "The most Divine prophets have lived according to Jesus Christ. For this reason they have been persecuted, *inspired* (ἐμπνεύμενοι) by His grace, that unbelievers should be firmly persuaded that there is one God who has manifested Himself through Jesus Christ His Son, who is His eternal Word." Again, in his Epistle to the Philadelphians, c. 5, he writes: "I also love the prophets, as having announced Christ; who were partakers of the same Spirit as the apostles. . . . But there is one Paraclete who has worked in Moses, the prophets, and apostles."

As to the restricted use among the moderns of inspiration to the composition of the Bible, Hagenbach remarks: "The doctrine of inspiration, as set forth in the New Testament, stood in close connexion with the doctrine of the Holy Spirit and His work. But the fathers did not think so much of the exertions of the apostles as writers, as of the power which was communicated to them of teaching, and of performing miracles. (See Chapter VII. for a misapplied quotation of Tertullian.)

Preparation indeed in man for the enjoyment and exercise of any of God's gifts is everywhere ascribed to a Divine origin. Thus Barnabas, in his Catholic epistle, echoing the words of St. Paul in the sixth chapter of Ephesians, writes: "Do not in bitterness lord it over your male and female servants, who trust in the Lord; lest you may not fear the same God, who is over you both: since He came to call, not from respect of person, but those whom the Spirit has prepared ($\dot{\eta}\tau o \iota \mu a \sigma \epsilon$)."

Our definition of inspiration in general, embraces that species of it which among the gifts of the Spirit is the grace of sanctification. And both the Lord Jesus, to whom the believer is united, and the Holy Spirit, the cleanser of the heart, are called in Scripture the gifts of God.

Jesus said to the woman at Jacob's well, "If thou knewest the gift of God, and who it is that saith to thee, Give me to drink, thou wouldest have asked of Him, and He would give thee living water."

St. Peter, in like manner, addressed Simon the Magician, who thinking that the gift could be turned to worldly profit, offered him money. "Thy money perish with thee, because thou hast thought that the gift of God may be purchased with money."

In the true scriptural idea of inspiration, viewed in

general as a powerful act of the Divine Spirit on the spirit of man, for the purpose of imparting some charism, the strength as well as the mysterious nature of the influence is set forth. Here, as indicative of guidance, a remarkable phrase occurs in the Pauline epistles, " led of the Spirit."

Melville, in one of his thoughtful sermons, explains the nature of this guidance. " We mean that the Spirit literally leads him by dwelling in him, residing in him, as a quickening and actuating principle. Thus it is that man is led. The Spirit of the Most High has taken possession of him, and strengthened him by the renewing process, which leaves out no desire, no affection, no faculty. By becoming a new creature, he craves new objects, new scenes, and new associations; so that, through simply being made willing in the day of Christ's power, he is led away from a life of sin . . . and in this respect it may be affirmed that the Christian is led by the Spirit of God."

There are many points of coincidence in the different forms in which inspiration—as a mighty energy of the Holy Ghost—may exhibit itself. Thus our Lord describes the new birth by the impulsive and invisible force of the wind: " The wind bloweth where it listeth, and thou hearest the sound thereof, but canst not tell whence it cometh or whither it goeth; so is every one that is born of the Spirit."[*]

---

[*] John iii. 8.

The same actuating energy is displayed in the inspiration of the sacred writers. The hand of the Lord—the emblem of His power—is upon the prophets. They are impelled by a Divine energy or afflatus: they are moved or borne along by the Holy Ghost, ὑπὸ πνεύματος ἁγίου φερόμενοι.* So similar in their effects are the influences of the Divine Spirit in imparting the manifold gifts which He vouchsafes to bestow on the children of men. The Agent the same, and so many points of resemblance existing in His diversified operations, naturally one formula ought to embrace in one definition the gift which one and the selfsame Spirit bestows, " dividing to every man severally as He will."

Moreover, a suitable modification being introduced for expressing the knowledge communicated to the inspired, we shall arrive at a more correct definition of the inspiration of Holy Scripture than the now popular one, derived from Roman theology and the Latin Vulgate. For Perrone's definition has, if not borrowed from, been sustained by, the Vulgate translation of certain passages in the Bible. These are Gen. ii. 7, "and breathed into (*inspiravit*) his nostrils the breath of life." Also 2 Tim. iii. 16: "Omnis Scriptura divinitus inspirata," is the rendering of the compound word θεόπνευστος, God-inspired, as if something (words) were infused into the minds of the inspired. This

---

* 2 Peter i. 21.

interpretation, however, is not necessary, any more than that the idea suggested by our version, "*given by inspiration,*" denotes something really given or presented to the mind of the inspired. The wrong view of inspiration, commonly entertained, keeps up and fosters the confusion generated by such improprieties of language. Inspiration of Holy Scripture is the supernatural energy of the Divine Spirit, exercised on the minds and hearts of certain chosen servants of God, to prepare and qualify them for accurately expressing the knowledge of the truths communicated to them. Inspiration, in fact, is a mean to a divinely instituted end beyond.

It only creates confusion to extend the definition to the outcoming result of committing to writing the truths revealed: in the same manner as it would be unjustifiable to extend the definition of inspiration as a gift of the Holy Spirit, which "cleanses the thoughts of our hearts," to the perfect love of God, and the promotion of His glory, which is a consequence for which we pray, springing from that inspiration," (Collect for Communion Service;) or to blend into one heterogeneous compound the "holy inspiration by which we think the things that be good," with "the merciful guiding by which we perform the same." (Collect for Fifth Sunday after Easter.)

Equally, and in the same way, the definition of the inspiration of Holy Scripture is unwarrantably spread out into a guidance to the external acts of speaking and writing.

In a word, inspiration of Holy Scripture, *ex vi terminorum*, and regarded as an effect, is in the qualification for writing, not in the act of writing itself. Omitting the former, and making it the latter, is taking the very heart out of it.

The accuracy of the definitions of inspiration, general and special, which, with fear and trembling, I have ventured to give,—for the feeling is a painful one when one finds himself, even for the truth's sake, coerced to run counter to the views of men distinguished alike for learning and ability,—can be judged by their exact adaptation to the several different cases, recounted in Scripture, of the Holy Spirit's energizing power. The analogy of these cases proves incontestably that the true definition of the inspiration of Holy Scripture cannot include its prophetical announcement in words spoken or written. In all, it was some supernatural new character, or property, infused into, and impressed upon, the soul for some particular "manifestation to profit withal;" for which manifestation, such operation of the Spirit was the due preparation. (See p. 36.)

Examples of this kind were the instances in which the Holy Spirit moved and actuated men that were raised up for defending the cause of God's people by superhuman deeds of valour.

Thus "the Spirit of the Lord began to move

Samson in the camp of Dan."* Here, and again when he rent a lion in pieces, and when it is said that "the Spirit of the Lord came mightily on him;"† and it is worthy of notice that the same phrase is used in the case of Balaam: the powerful energy of the Spirit, imparting to him supernatural strength, was a special gift—a foretaste of the Divine aid by which he should be enabled to conquer the enemies of his country. "And the Spirit of the Lord came mightily upon him, and the cords that were upon his arms became as flax that was burnt with fire, and his bands loosed from off his hands." ‡

The inspiration of Samson, or this gift of the Spirit, is that which qualified him for the feats which he achieved against the Philistines, and urged him on to their performance. So the gift of inspiration is that which qualified and prompted the sacred writers to express the revelations which God's Spirit had presented to them. In like manner, were Bezaleel and Aholiab *prepared* by the Spirit, through knowledge imparted, to execute cunning works for the tabernacle.§ Similarly, "the Spirit of God came on Saul, and he prophesied." Here again is clearly indicated, first the inspiration—the gift which on a particular occasion the Spirit conferred on the first king of Israel; and, secondly, its expression, "he prophesied."

---

* Judges xiii. 25.   ‡ Judges xv. 4.
† Judges xiii. 25.   § Exod. xxxvi. 1.

DEFINITION OF INSPIRATION. 93

All these examples of analogous cases corroborate in a striking manner my former statement, that the ordinary notion of inspiration confounds this gift of the Spirit, with that of προφητεία, which is the expression of the knowledge imparted by inspiration and revelation.

On these principles will appear the unfairness of Mr. Litton's criticism on Dean Alford's decisive judgment concerning this moot-point : " The men were inspired ; the books are the result of that inspiration." Mr. Litton remarks, " If by this statement is meant that the apostles, though as witnesses of Christ, and founders of the Church, they were inspired, were not inspired to write the books of Scripture, it is liable to the objections above advanced (that the Bible *is* not, but *contains* the word of God, etc.) If, on the other hand, it also implies the latter, it is not easy to see what additional light the learned author has by this distinction thrown upon the subject."* (See p. 58 of this essay.)

In order to understand these observations, it is to be noted that Mr. Litton's instructive volume was published several years after Dr. Lee's treatise on the Inspiration of Holy Scripture. And doubtless as he gave a different definition of inspiration, he felt a new difficulty to have sprung up, not sufficiently

---

* 'Guide to the Study of Scripture,' p. 122. See Exod. xxxvi. 1. "God gave them a quickness of apprehension and sagacity beyond which was natural to them "—*Bishop Patrick.*

provided against in the former; and tried to improve on it, by omitting the clause added by Dr. Lee to Perrone's definition. Mr. Litton accordingly defines inspiration of Holy Scripture—"a special influence of the Holy Spirit, whereby the writers of Scripture were, *in act of writing*, supernaturally preserved from error, and enabled to transmit, in its integrity, the original revelation as they received it."

The hypothesis that the gift of inspiration can be properly applied to books, and the further hypothesis that there is another special guidance (without producing any scriptural proof) needed, over and above that to the clear and precise knowledge of the truths revealed,—hypotheses invented to meet the necessities of the case,—are objections common to every form of the Roman definition of inspiration. But a new objection started up to Mr. Litton's view: "Prophecies uttered under the impulse of the Spirit, were not perhaps committed to writing for some time afterwards;—what guarantee would there be that they were correctly recorded, had not the prophets or other persons been inspired for that very purpose, viz., to record correctly what had been uttered?" He therefore limited this inspiration to writing: and quaintly adds in a note, "Jeremiah prophesying was in one sense inspired: Jeremiah, commissioned to record his prophecies for the benefit of future ages long after they were delivered, needed a further gift of the Spirit to preserve him from error; and this is the gift to which the term inspiration is *here* confined." Such are a few of the perplexities by which arbitrary assumptions have entangled the all-important subject of inspiration, each author being forced to abandon the position occupied by his predecessors.

Now all this confusion might have been avoided by a proper and legitimate use of words. For this end, inspiration must be applied only to the subjective effects of the Spirit's influence. To extend its use to any external product of the mind, is improper and misleading.

Undoubtedly the true view of the inspiration of Holy Scripture is educible from Alford's statement, when rightly explained, that the books are "the results" of the personal inspiration of the writers. But why was the idea that "inspiration should be applied, not to the men, but to the books," at all introduced? For the purpose, it seems, of guarding against error, that might arise from failure of memory, or the admixture of the human element with the Divine. A superintendency of a peculiar kind for this end was deemed necessary, in addition to the original afflatus. In reference to this assumption, it may be observed, that this superintendency may be really involved in the spiritual appliances already employed for conveying the clear and accurate knowledge of Divine truth to the mind of the writer. For it was a part of the promised gift of the Spirit, implied in suggestive revelations, to supply the defects of memory, and to fix the thoughts upon the proper matters to the exclusion of things irrelevant.

It is a mere play upon words to apply inspiration to books in the same sense as to their composers.* In the former it is applicable only in a figurative and secondary sense, denoting its derivative influence and power, as the sword of the Spirit upon the soul of man.

In this sense, indeed, the Bible is inspired, and the Scriptures living oracles. The Spirit of God animates them. They are saturated and bathed with the Divine light. They are light. "Thy word (says the Psalmist) is a lamp unto my feet and a light unto my path;"† and if at any time that is ascribed to the composition which can be strictly applied only to the composer, as when it is said that the Scripture is endued with foreknowledge—"The Scripture, foreseeing that God would justify the heathen, through faith, preached before the gospel unto Abraham, saying, "In thee shall all nations be blessed,"‡ The metaphor in the words *foreseeing* and *preached* is patent to all.

The long reign of the Organic theory, which extinguished the human element in the word of God, had been, I have no doubt, the occasion of perpetuating

---

* Mr. Gaussen goes so far as to say that inspiration is not in the men, but in the books.
† Bishop Wordsworth.
‡ Gal. iii. 8.

the idea, without attaching any definite meaning to *it*, that the Bible, as a person, was literally inspired. But it is manifest, on the least reflection, that inspiration in its primary and direct signification belongs only to persons. And this is the clear purport of Dean Alford's dictum, "the men were inspired; the books the results of that inspiration." For he is not speaking of these men as the organizers of a Church system, nor as witnesses of Christ; but as the authors of the books which bear their names. Moreover, if a lucid exposition of the formula 'the men were inspired, the books are the results of that inspiration,' exhibit, on the unassailable ground of Scripture, how their compositions were the true and genuine fruits of that inspiration, what necessarily follows? That Alford, treading in the footsteps of St. Paul, has thrown a flood of light on this mysterious subject, when he fixes attention on the perfect certainty (for such is the true inference) of their compositions. For he points out how the writers were taught by the Divine Spirit, through inspiration qualifying and preparing their minds, accurately and faithfully to express in words the revelations imparted to them.

Thus, with much reason, Dean Alford* considers that this, if all that it implies be duly weighed, furnishes the key to the whole question. For, in fact, this is equivalent to the apostle's statement, resting

---

* Alford's Greek Testament, Prologomena, chap. i., p. 21. Fifth edition.

on no assumption, only indicating the steps by which the sacred writers were taught the knowledge of Divine truth, and qualified to express it.

Before the light of this clear statement vanishes the hazy assertion, "Jeremiah delivering a prophecy by word of mouth, is not secured in the same way as Jeremiah recording it in writing."

In both cases, what was it which enabled the prophet to transmit securely to future ages the revelations with which he had been favoured? The answer is: The complete and perfectly clear knowledge which revelation, aided by inspiration, had imparted to him.

In both cases,—the oral and written expression of the knowledge communicated to him, and to which he was moved by the Spirit of God,—the great secret of its accuracy turns upon the perfect command and mastery he now had of the matter revealed, which a clear, distinct, and full knowledge supplied. For just in proportion as one masters a subject, can he speak or write correctly on it.

In reference to the sacred writers, the knowledge imparted by revelation and inspiration finds its natural and spontaneous expression "in words which the Holy Ghost teacheth," since this Divine agent is Himself the Revealer and Inspirer.

The naturalness of the expression is evinced by the fact that the words are marked with the individual peculiarities of the several speakers or writers. Thus the Divine and human mutually interpenetrate in giving a character to every word of Holy Writ. The human characteristic, observed by all, implies that the words employed are the immediate fruit of their knowledge. The Divine characteristic is stamped on the word, since they are taught by the Holy Spirit, through the sanctified appliances of inspiration and revelation.

Are we now to assume in addition a *new* superintendency, besides the one provided by the Spirit, for fitting the writer to express the knowledge divinely communicated by the instrumentality of inspiration and revelation? Are we to assume such, while we have a real superintendency supported by Scripture, and not resting on any *à priori* conjecture whatever, and this in a matter so far beyond the sphere of natural reason that assumption is not allowable? What, then, have been firmly established on this debateable point on the sure ground of Holy Scripture?

1. The sacred writers exhibit a human element in the peculiarities of style belonging to the different authors, and in their manner of inculcating the same doctrines. This is the more noteworthy, as many have remarked, when it is considered that they were all devoted to the same cause, and were all supernaturally qualified for the same work by the same Spirit. Yet it may be questioned whether any profane authors, who agree in general principles, exhibit a greater diversity of natural character than

those do, in their cast of sentiment and manner of thinking.

2. In the next place, it must be admitted as proved, apart from all hypothetic reasoning, that the conjoint effect of revelation and inspiration was to convey to the minds of the sacred writers the *knowledge* of truths neither attainable nor cognizable by the unassisted powers of man.

3. Thirdly, a supernatural unknown guidance to writing is the essential difference* in the popularly received definition of inspiration, whereas the essential difference of scriptural inspiration as given by St. Paul is the preparation of the mind by the Spirit for the intelligent reception of the truth presented by revelation, " that we might *know* the things freely given to us of God."†

In fact, the essential difference of this operation on the mind and heart must exhibit the steps of the *modus operandi* of the Divine Spirit for producing the knowledge of Divine truth. Now in the two passages of the Bible where the word occurs, no mention is made of any such guidance, enabling men to write accurately. "Every scripture is God-inspired" (2 Tim. iii. 16) leaves the *modus operandi*, which is properly the act of inspiration, undetermined; while the Pauline view in 1 Cor. ii. shows that it at least includes much more than is contained in the

---
* Inspiration being regarded as an energy or gift of the Spirit.
† ἵνα εἰδῶμεν τὰ ὑπὸ τοῦ Θεοῦ χαρισθέντα ἡμῖν.

definition which makes inspiration simply guidance to recording revelations, and therefore that this is not inspiration at all. Besides, to the passage in Job, "There is a spirit in man, and the inspiration of the Almighty giveth them understanding,"* this definition is entirely inapplicable. On the other hand, its agreement with St. Paul's idea is very—I may say singularly—striking: "Now we have received, not the spirit of the world, but the Spirit which is of God, that we might *know* the things that are freely given to us of God."†

"We might know," and "the inspiration of the Almighty giveth them understanding," are points of contact in the statements of Job and Paul which undeniably prove that the common definition, judged by Scripture, is at fault, since it omits the principal element which enters into the conception of inspiration.

So great, indeed, has been the confusion engendered by the inconstant and indeterminate ideas as to the nature of inspiration, which for centuries have prevailed in the Christian world, that I felt it expedient to impress by every kind of argument, and with what might otherwise be deemed unnecessary repetition, the true scriptural character of that holy influence.

Coupled with revelation, their united influence had been generally denominated inspiration; and in this sense I have observed many author susing the phrase,

---
* Job xxxii. 8.   † 1 Cor. ii. 12.

"a revelation communicated by inspiration." While with them inspiration moved in the sphere of objectivity, confusion was unavoidable; the term being as well applied to the thing communicated as to the men to whom the communication was made.

Now the latter is essential to the former, which is a complex conception comprising both revelation and inspiration. In fact, the religious truth is conveyed by the Spirit through the joint instrumentality of revelation and personal inspiration. Hence in a proper discussion of the question of the inspiration of Holy Scripture, the nature of personal inspiration is of primary consideration and importance.

Two things, for the sake of clearness, are to be kept quite distinct: 1. The knowledge communicated by personal inspiration and revelation. 2. The expression of that knowledge, which constitutes the Holy Scriptures. Now the latter is the point at which theories are called in, and from which they all diverge.

I have also taken pains to impress as forcibly as possible, that in its true scriptural idea inspiration is simply a state of the mind superinduced by the Holy Spirit; in fact, a transformation* of its character of ψυχικὸς into the πνευματικὸς, and this is confirmed by the analogous idea of moral inspiration. Thus when a man felt himself wanting in energy, and not equal to some great enterprise, the Spirit some-

---

* See page 27.

times had breathed into his soul the needed courage and determination. Moreover, in its suggestive form I have tried to keep revelation distinct from inspiration, in order to avoid confusion. Olshausen, in describing the hindrance mentioned in Acts xvi. 6—10, well remarks, "The manner in which Luke describes this hindrance is calculated to bring to view the operation of the higher $\Pi\nu\epsilon\hat{\upsilon}\mu\alpha$ in the souls of the apostles. The $\psi\upsilon\chi\acute{\eta}$ of the individual who had received the Holy Ghost was in no way identified with the Spirit as to take away a full consciousness of the distinction which existed: he could, on the contrary, very clearly distinguish the impulses of his own soul ("They assayed to go," etc.,) from the suggestion of the Spirit. The former often prompted to what was erroneous or unsuitable; the latter, in such cases, checked the soul and guided it to what was right. ("The Spirit suffered them not.")

CHAPTER IV.

REVELATION AS DISTINGUISHED FROM INSPIRATION.

In accurate definitions of revelation and inspiration,—and it is fundamental to our present inquiry, where abuse of language has been productive of so much disorder, to define these terms accurately,—there must enter the intrinsic and distinctive characteristics of each; for otherwise their proper meanings cannot be determined and fixed. But correct definitions, thus framed, will indicate the true points of difference by which they are really discriminated.

This is all the more necessary, since the distinction between them is by some overlooked, by some denied, and by others deemed needless; and not unfrequently by many laid in something which cannot in any respect be regarded, in the light of Scripture or of reason, as their true essential characteristics. As to the determination of the true distinction, the following has been the course of my thoughts.

1. I have been deeply impressed with the strange view, now popular, and shared by many authors, con-

cerning the nature of inspiration, which has led to its confusion with revelation.

2. In the second place, as I have already observed, inspiration and revelation are so interlaced, that it is not easy to consider them separately. In fact, the gift of inspiration, which enlarges, exalts, and purifies the human faculties, imparting a quickened intuition, and a perspicacity naturally unattainable, gives a new power to the spiritual organs, which may bring into light many new truths hitherto unperceived.*

Now this is a true revelation or unveiling of things previously hidden from man; and I have given in page 49 three remarkable instances of revelation produced by inspiration. From this undoubted fact I inferred that as inspiration is so nearly allied to revelation, they are often used—where they ought not—interchangeably, as if synonymous. And truths revealed by suggestion, or recalled by memory through the aid of the Spirit, which, committed to writing, form a large portion of the holy volume, are said to be inspirations. With greater propriety ought these truths to be called revelations, in the same manner as the whole Bible is called a Revelation.

3. Besides, it has occurred to me that the distinction between revelation and inspiration is often laid in some things which in no respect can be regarded in light the of Scripture or of reason, as their true

---

* Bishop Patrick, on Exodus xxxvi. 2, gives the true idea of inspiration.

essential differences.* There are two principles to guide us in the inquiry: 1. Their essential differences cannot be sought in anything extraneous to the spiritual moments themselves of inspiration and revelation *as effects on* the spirit of man. 2. That which belongs to the one cannot be predicated of the other. Both these principles militate against the distinctions set forth in their commonly received definitions; from which it may be presumed that one or both of the latter are logically unsound.

If indeed the essential characteristics of these influences of the Spirit of God on the spirit of man are to be found in their effects on man's spirit, you cannot look for them either in their operating agents or in any subsequent act of the man who was the subject of those influences. In fact, inspiration had been a transaction already accomplished, within his mind and heart, before he uttered or wrote a word. In the same manner, the revelation, aided by inspiration, had presented to his mind's eye the knowledge of the truth conveyed, before the prophet or apostle "spake what he did know," or placed it on record as an integral portion of the Bible-revelation. The true essential characteristic mark cannot, therefore, be found in the common definition of inspiration; and hence it must be rejected as illogical.

---

* The peculiar properties of revelation and inspiration, by which they are severally discriminated from other gifts of the Spirit, are their essential differences.

It remains, then, that we should state the precise essential differences of inspiration and revelation, and give their correct logical definitions.

Of inspiration, the essential difference is *preparation* of the mind for the intelligent reception of Divine truth. Of revelation, the essential difference is the *presentation* of objects to the mind, so prepared by inspiration as to comprehend their import.

Definition of inspiration: The actuating energy of the Holy Spirit, exerted in preparing the spiritual and intellectual faculties of certain chosen servants of God, so as to enable them fully and truly to comprehend and receive the revelations presented to their minds, and thus to qualify the inspired accurately to express the knowledge imparted.

Definition of revelation: The supernatural presentation to the mind, through sense, or conception, or imagination, of objects, for the purpose of disclosing Divine truths, to faculties prepared for their reception by inspiration, with a distinct consciousness that the objects presented to the mind are not the natural suggestions of the mind itself.

The real distinction consists in this: that in revelation there are presentations to the spiritual vision; in inspiration, none. The subjective character of the latter in the Communion Service of our Church is clearly set forth—"beseeching Thee *to inspire* continually the universal Church *with the spirit* of truth, unity, and concord." (See page 26.) The combined result of inspiration and revelation, I repeat, is *knowledge*, as is very clearly set forth by St. Paul; and the utterance of that knowledge is prophecy, or teaching; while its written expression is the word of God. Thus our Lord, who brought down from heaven the mysteries of Divine knowledge, says, in His memorable interview with Nicodemus, "We *speak* that we do *know*, and testify that we have seen."*

The utterance in words of that knowledge is moreover said to be taught by the Holy Ghost, since the knowledge † of which it is the expression comes from His teaching, or from a heart abundantly supplied with the gifts of the Spirit. Animated by faith in the truths revealed, " we," says the apostle, " also believe, and therefore speak." ‡

Thus these men of God were taught and prompted, nay, constrained by a Divine impulse, to deliver to mankind the heavenly knowledge conveyed to their minds, with the sanctity and definite colouring of truth, which the vague definition of Scribe, inspiration, bequeathed to us by the Church of Rome, does not possess. Any further and more direct aid of the Spirit, as if putting the words into the mouths of the inspired, would be dictation pure and simple— a view now generally exploded, and contrary to the analogy of God's dealings with the free subjects of His kingdom.

---

* John iii. 11.
† As in the phrase " it seemed good to the Holy Ghost and to us."
‡ 2 Cor. iv. 13.

That revelation is distinct from inspiration, and that the true idea of the function of the latter in reference to the former is to impart a capacity and qualification for comprehending it, is evident from the fact that in Holy Scripture men such as Pharaoh and Nebuchadnezzar had revelations which they could very exactly describe, and yet could not understand.* Even the inspired did not always comprehend the *full* meaning of the revelations vouchsafed to them, the Spirit having enlightened them only so far as it seemed best to Him.†

Whatever may be alleged in support of the assertion that revelation and inspiration are also discriminated by the sources from which they proceed,—revelation being the peculiar function of the Son, and inspiration the result of the agency of the Holy Spirit,—such view is opposed to both the principles laid down.

These are not radical and essential distinguishing marks of those respective influences, such as exist in their own nature and effects; nor is it so that what, in this respect, belongs to the one cannot be predicated of the other: for if the agent be the discriminating mark, and it be said that revelation is the peculiar function of the Son; and yet if revelation be also the work of the Father and the Holy Spirit, (as the Scriptures teach explicitly), such is not a sufficient discrimination to constitute the essential difference we are in quest of, however truly it may

---

* Gen. xli. 1, and Dan. iv. 4. † Dan. xii. 8.

be said that the Son is the Revealer of the Father's will.

I cannot concur in the view of M. Gaussen, of Geneva, whom in this matter Dr. Lee follows, that "the real question which our inquiry is concerned with, is the result of this influence, as presented in the pages of Scripture, not the manner according to which it has pleased God that this result should be attained." This view, in my humble opinion, is a very unphilosophic and a very unsafe principle to start from. For limiting, in this way, the consideration of the Spirit's agency to that of its results, as presented (in your judgment) in Scripture, you miss the proof of the authority that attaches to these results. Assumption, in fact, had thus taken the place of an analysis of the causes which produced them. St. Paul, I submit, should in a point of such extreme delicacy be our guide. He analyzes the causes of the unerring certainty of the verbal expression of the knowledge produced by the joint operation of the spiritual moments of revelation and inspiration.

In my mind, it is an insecure principle to begin with the results. For thus you make certain assumptions concerning the written word, which may not exactly agree with what others—equally competent judges—will accept. How can you answer objections of Mr. Coleridge or his disciples, while they too, beginning with results, form a very different judgment about the nature and characteristic properties of Holy Writ ?*

Once more. The result here, as I have remarked, is the transient external act of speaking or writing; and, in propriety of language, inspiration cannot be predicated of any outgoing action. If inspiration be a guidance, it is a guidance, when aided by revelation, inwardly to the knowledge of the truth, and not a guidance outwardly to its expression.

In fact, this is the guidance which the Redeemer Himself promised to His apostles: "Howbeit when He, the Spirit of Truth, is come, He will guide you *into* all the truth" (John xvi. 13). And it is to be observed that this is said of the mysteries of the kingdom which should be hereafter revealed to the apostles: "I have yet many things to say unto you, but ye cannot bear them now" (John xvi. 12).

Lastly, I have more than one objection to the definition of revelation expressed in this form: "A direct communication from God to man, either of such knowledge as man could not of himself attain to, because its subject-matter transcends human saga-

---

* "When objections are urged against the doctrine of inspiration, on the ground of unreasonableness, and of its opposition to clear features of the sacred writings, the light which the Scriptures really supply, as to the manner in which they were communicated, must clearly be a most important help in removing misconceptions, and in establishing a full harmony between the doctrine and the facts which it professes to explain."—*Rev. T. R. Birks, Modern Rationalism*, etc., page 103.

city or human reason—such, for example, were the prophetic announcements of the future, and the peculiar doctrines of Christianity; or of information which, although it might have been attained in the ordinary way, was not, in point of fact, from whatever cause, known to the person who received the revelation."

In the first place, the Pauline theory,—which, in the present unsettled state of opinion as to the nature of inspiration, I have tried to enforce at great length, pointing out the several steps of the apostle's profound synthesis,—gives a very different idea of the subject from that presented in this definition.

Here revelation, directly and *per se*, gives knowledge; whereas, according to St. Paul, knowledge of this kind is the resultant of the conjoint spiritual forces of inspiration and revelation. Both are necessary to the attainment of the knowledge of "the deep things of God." Without inspiration, revelations could not be intelligently apprehended; and without revelation, our own subjective conceptions of religious truth would usurp the place of the realities of the spiritual world.

In the second place, whatever may be said in support of this contracted view of revelation, regarded as a disclosure to the mind of the inspired, this does not apply to its written record; for revelation, in this point of view, is confined within too narrow limits, when it is alleged that "certain matters stated in the Bible are, strictly speaking, revelations,—that is, are such as, from their supernatural character, or the circumstances of the writer who records them, could not have been known to him without a special communication from heaven."

Now I am free to admit that there are matters which might have been known to the apostles from their own observations, or from other sources at their command. But considering the length of time that may have elapsed since the disciples of Christ had heard the many deep and pregnant sayings of their Divine Master,—perhaps half a century, in the case of John, who of the evangelists records the greatest number,—how needful was it to stir up their slumbering thoughts concerning the great truths which, when Christ uttered them, were only dimly or partially understood? John, fifty years afterwards, through the Spirit's influences, having recalled to his mind the ideas of truths, at first fugitive and faint, but now—his memory being supernaturally refreshed—grasped in their fulness, naturally under the intense feeling of these spiritual influences breaks forth into the lofty language of inspiration: "That which was from the beginning, which we have heard, which we have seen with our eyes, which we have looked upon, and our hands have handled, of the word of life; (for the life was manifested, and we have seen it, and bear witness, and show unto you that eternal life which was with the Father, and was manifested unto us;)

that which we have seen and heard, declare we unto you."*

These thoughts, brought up by the Spirit before his mind in a present living reality, the beloved apostle was as much a subject of revelation as when, in the isle of Patmos, being in the Spirit, there were presented to his mental vision the wonderful revelations which he describes.

Considering, too, the many disturbing causes in the eventful and chequered lives of the apostles, that may have weakened their memories, concerning these and other matters of interest, who can doubt the vast and priceless importance of their Lord's promise to call all things, whatsoever He had said, to their remembrance?

If then, in the language of Holy Scripture, ideas divinely suggested are revelations, the suggestions of the Spirit of God, recalling lost or half-forgotten truths to the minds of the apostles, were beyond controversy undoubted revelations.

It may be admitted that special aid by supernatural revelation was only given when required. If not needed on any occasion, such would be superfluous; and therefore at such times the apostles, left to the use of their own powers, would set forth the truth with equal conformity to the Divine will, as when entrusted by the special aid of a new reve-

---

* 1 John i. 1—3.

lation. For our Lord taught that "every scribe who is instructed unto the kingdom of heaven, is like unto a man that is an householder, which bringeth forth out of his treasure things new and old."*

Still, evident it is that no unerring certainty could be attained by the apostles themselves—and less could the characteristic of infallibility be predicated of their writings—unless the Holy Spirit should have recalled to their recollection the sayings of Christ, and bring again before their minds the truths not fully comprehended, or those partially forgotten, or, lastly, such as were purposely omitted by the Redeemer Himself, but which after His ascension they were to receive.

A view that merges revelation in inspiration, confounding a subjective influence, such as inspiration with revelation, which latter only presents objects to the contemplation of the inspired, must inevitably lead to an erroneous theory of inspiration. This unquestionably proves that the true nature and extent of revelation had been lost sight of or misunderstood at the Reformation period. Such was the mechanical theory of inspiration revived by Carpzov as the upshot of the reaction from the inspiration of things only, to that of both things and words.

"God, by an immediate and mysterious concourse with amanuenses, excited them to the office of writing,

* Matt. xiii. 52.

by which He impelled their will to write promptly, and illuminated their mind, and filled it with the *suggestion of things and words* to be marked down in order that they should write intelligently, and directed their hands that they should write infallibly; not, however, that they should contribute more to the Scripture than the pen of a ready writer."

What, then, are the possible constituent elements of a revelation fully comprehended by the mind of the inspired, and committed by him to writing?

They are threefold :

1. Matters supernaturally revealed which transcend man's natural powers of discovery.

2. Matters now lost or faded in memory, but recalled by suggestive revelation.

3. Matters bearing on the subject, such as men can and will discover by the natural use of their faculties.

Thus a supernatural revelation presented to the mind of the inspired, and aided by suggestive revelations of the Holy Spirit, together with the thoughts arising from the natural use of the powers of observation and reflection, concur in one common object, namely, to adjust and fit into their proper places, and in exact proportions, one complex narrative, so that the whole may be a faithful transcript of the Divine will.

The truth is, a narrative consisting of many divers matters, clustering in the manner described round one central revelation, dovetailed into it, and conjointly with it forming its constituent parts, constitutes one revelation of the Spirit of God, and should be so considered.

In passing, a remark already made incidentally rises up. The suggestion of the Divine Spirit to the writer for this end, and relating to an outward act, is not inspiration, or that sacred influence of the Spirit without which revelations would be impossible. Hence it follows that, in a recorded revelation, it is not a fair representation to isolate a passage from the context, and say, This is not a revelation. For, by itself, though this be not a revelation, yet is it a part and parcel of *the* revelation recorded by the apostle or prophet. And this is the sense in which the objectors use revelation. For example, in the last book of the New Testament we have the Revelation of Jesus Christ, who sent and signified it by His angel to His servant John," and John committed to writing this revelation; for it is added, "who bare record of the word of God, and of the testimony of Jesus Christ, and of all things that he saw." Now the ninth verse of the first chapter,—"I John, who also am your brother and companion in tribulation, and in the kingdom and patience of Jesus Christ, was in the isle that is called Patmos, for the word of God and for the testimony of Jesus Christ,"—is not a revelation, or a part of a revelation, presented to the entranced apostle; still it is a part of *the* Revelation as put on record. And the whole book is rightly denominated, "The Revelation of John the Theologian."

In like manner, the same distinction* is observable in St. Luke's record of the revelations that took place in reference to the conversion of Saul. Ananias, a citizen of Damascus, was favoured with a revelation by vision from the Lord, who spoke to him, and instructed him what he should do regarding Saul, who was struck blind, and was now fasting for three days. This is one of the supernatural parts of the revelation as recorded by St. Luke.

Next, immediately after, and in answer to the instruction imparted by the Lord, Ananias in the conscious exercise of his natural faculties, says, "Lord, I have heard by many of this man, how much evil he hath done to thy saints at Jerusalem, and here he hath authority from the chief priests to bind all that call on Thy name." Lastly, the Divine Voice directs Ananias further that he should obey His commands, inasmuch as Saul was destined to be a chosen vessel to bear His name before the Gentiles, etc.

Here then we have another example of the union of what is strictly a supernatural revelation, with the information which a pious disciple had acquired by the use of his natural powers of observation, so intimately blended that the record makes but one complete narrative of a revelation. In fact, it would

---

* The distinction between a revelation divinely communicated, and a revelation recorded.

be a maimed and imperfect record of a supernatural revelation, should the part, naturally known to Ananias, be removed from the central place which it occupies between the two supernatural extremes. In one word—such passages of Scripture are not *direct* revelations, but as *Scripture records* are indispensable portions of undoubted revelations.

Thus the word of God presented to us in the pages of Holy Scripture is a record of the revelation of the will of God consisting of many parts. These parts, fitting harmoniously together, come directly from the Spirit of truth, or are such as He sanctions, and in their totality constitute the Holy Volume, stamped therefore with the noblest character of truth, which is consistency. The knowledge of that truth, which His apostles were commissioned to deliver to all men, was thus supplied to them.

Their promised instructor, the Paraclete, brought to their remembrance the sayings of Christ, which they might have forgotten. He corrected their knowledge of things which they had only partially comprehended. He imparted to them the knowledge of things to come, and generally a knowledge of such things as they could not acquire by natural means. Lastly, when supernatural aid was not needed, their Divine Teacher sanctioned what they drew from the treasures of their natural resources. The expression in a written record by the sacred authors of the knowlege so supplied, under the teaching and sanction of the Holy Spirit, makes up, in the collective unity of its several parts, the Bible as the revelation of the will of God to man. Revelation understood in this sense: every part of the written word is either a revelation or a part of a revelation. And this refers as well to those portions of the Bible the contents of which had been previously known to the writers, as to those relating to matters unknown to them, or undiscoverable by their unassisted natural faculties.

Truths of the former class are not only sanctioned by the Spirit of God as integral portions of a revelation when it is put on record (and it is in this sense the term is here understood), but also in some cases the Divine Spirit reveals truths already known to man, in order to stamp on them the impress of Divine authority.

Thus conscience approved and accepted the commandments of the moral law, before they had been revealed by word. Conscience, however, being an unsafe guide to finite erring mortals, to make these commandments authoritative, God revealed them from heaven.

Again: whenever the Spirit of Christ had recalled a forgotten fact or truth to the remembrance of an apostle, here was as undoubted a revelation as if a voice from heaven had guided him into the knowledge of that truth or fact. In a word, revelation is to be taken (in the light of Scripture) in a large sense, not only as introducing things entirely new, but as also reintroducing, and shedding fresh light upon, the old, which reason might discover, but did not; or which it had discovered, but could not hold.

We cannot pick out a small sentence, as if it were not a part of a revelation, on the ground that, in and of itself, it is not a revelation, regarding it as merely human, and not coming from God. As little are we disposed to regard a single verse in the Bible as the manufacture of man, because of its unimportance, as to believe that the lowly weed is the offspring of some inferior power, because it wants the loveliness or grandeur of the higher objects in nature.

Such is one of the results of the ambiguity of language in the use of the word 'revelation,'—one time signifying a direct communication to the mind of the inspired, again denoting the record of the knowledge produced by revelation and inspiration.*

The distinction, therefore, which is sometimes drawn between certain matters stated in the Bible that are strictly speaking revelations,—*i.e.*, such as could not have been known to the writer without a special communication from heaven, and other matters which must have been known to him from natural sources of information,—is not the true ground on which to base the distinction between the ideas of inspiration and revelation. For if a reference be made to *what* is inspired (allowing such a use of the word) and *what* is

---

* See Chapter VIII., where this important matter is further discussed.

revealed, there is no distinction between inspiration and revelation. But if inspiration be taken (as it ought to be) for an act of the Holy Ghost, or a state of mind produced by that act, enabling the mind to grasp and receive the revelation vouchsafed, there is a real distinction.

Now if the Holy Spirit recall old ideas to the mind, and suggest new, touching " the deep things of God " which are only spiritually discerned, it is not easy to determine what portions of the sacred writings are not revelations, even including the things which are within the province of natural reason.

The distinction between the matters contained in the word of God here alluded to, I have already observed, had been expressed, in the dogmatic theology of Rome, by 'revelatio' and 'assistentia et directio Divina,' and ages had passed before the latter was metamorphosed into inspiration. The distinction had been first set forth by Cardinal Cajetan, and after him also fully by Melchior Cano; but with both, inspiration was something very different from the 'directio Divina,' being in fact the infusion of the matter and form of the Divine truths recorded in Holy Scripture into the minds of the sacred writers. In other words, inspiration, as the operation of the Holy Spirit, included both revelation and direction. This wider signification of inspiration remained for many generations the standing doctrine of divines; until that Church whose *semper eadem* glory admits no change in matters of faith, changed her doctrine of inspiration into the narrower limits of the 'directio Divina.' Such is the present view of the Church of Rome, presented in the definition of inspiration given by Perrone. And this definition has been generally adopted by Protestant divines in this country. But in Scripture terminology, most assuredly, "a Divine guidance to writing" falls far short of its true idea in the mind of St. Paul. There is indeed a Divine guidance even to writing, but this is not inspiration.

It is something following inspiration, and over-leaping its boundary. As, however, the popular definition, now generally accepted, of inspiration, stands or falls with the Roman division of "Revelatio, et assistentia et directio Divina," it may be not amiss to examine, more minutely than I have hitherto done, this view as prominently set forth by Melchior Cano, who flourished shortly after the Reformation, and whose ideas were cast in the Roman mould.

"We do not assert that every portion of sacred Scripture had been published by an immediate revelation of the Holy Spirit, which is that properly called revelation. But Luke himself committed to writing the things which he had received from the apostles, as he testifies in his preface. And we say that Mark, being requested by the disciples, has written what he had learned from Peter. Whether, therefore, we refer on the one hand to Matthew and John, or on the other hand to Mark and Luke,—although the former relate what they saw, the latter what they heard,—*they did not need a new revelation* of the Spirit, yet they did need a peculiar direction of the Holy Spirit."*

Perhaps the clearest and most convincing evidence of the impotency of this view is to bring it into direct comparison with the Pauline.

According to our apostle, the knowledge of Divine truth is not given by revelation, but is the conjoint result of the spiritual forces of revelation and inspiration. This was the guidance promised by the Saviour—a guidance into the knowledge of the truth. This is the true direction of the Holy Spirit, and not that aiming at the verbal forms of thought.

The facts of the case incontestably prove that the words flowed spontaneously and naturally from the full, clear, and precise knowledge taught by the Holy Spirit, through His gifts of inspiration and revelation, so naturally indeed and fittingly under these influences, as exactly to express the truths in terms at once Divine and human. Thus in a manner analogous to that in which human instruction enables a man to express his knowledge in words which man's wisdom teacheth, Divine instruction, supernaturally imparted, had produced in the apostle or prophet a knowledge of things Divine, that enabled him to express it "in words which the Holy Ghost teacheth." But for the further elucidation of the

---

* 'De Locis Theol.,' lib. ii., p. 126.

division of inspiration into revelation and Divine direction, the passage from Basil by which Cano endeavours to support his view is to be carefully scrutinized. Here is Cano's reference to Basil :—

"What the sacred authors wrote, differ from each other in two respects. First, certain things which they knew only by supernatural revelation, Basil states to be from the Holy Spirit. Next, other things they embraced by natural knowledge,—such things, namely, as they had seen with their eyes, and handled with their hands. Indeed, to be written, these things did not need supernatural light and express revelation; but they did need the presence and peculiar aid of the Holy Spirit, that although they were human and known by natural reason, they should be divinely written free from all error. These are the things, according to Basil, which Paul and the prophets were wont to speak of themselves."

1. In this passage, the common mistake of writers, who hold knowledge to be given by revelation alone, crops up.

2. In reference to the second class of writings which, he says, did not need supernatural light, and express revelation, it is to be observed, that a more correct view would regard supernatural light to be something german to inspiration; and also would hold the revelation of the Holy Spirit through suggestion to be powerfully influential in matters even within the sphere of things naturally cognizable.

3. If it be said that inspiration is not supernatural light, but some vague nondescript direction, enabling to write correctly, what is it? If it be neither supernatural illumination nor suggestive revelation, what is it? Thus, in the last resort, are we driven back to the question which initiated this investigation—What is the nature of inspiration?

A very able writer in the 'Journal of Sacred Literature,' finds himself terribly bewildered on this very point; for, while justly criticising the distinction drawn by Dr. Lee between inspiration and revelation, he imports into the idea of inspiration so much of what really belongs to revelation, as to embarrass a view which, if he had kept their respective ideas distinct, would have been the clearest hitherto advanced.

Taking the wider scope of revelation assigned by me in this essay, the trenchant remarks of this energetic writer are thus summed up:—

"Revelation has a wider scope than simply the communication from heaven of truth absolutely unknown to the recipient of it. It may be very true that inspiration is given to man without, at the time, or, it may be, at any time, making to them a revelation of what was wholly unknown to them. But unless we define inspiration to be a *mere wild unintelligible impulse* to we know not what, we must suppose that it always exerts some influence in the direction of and partaking truly of the character of revelation, as correcting and revising memory, correcting and guiding judgment, correcting and imparting a proper apprehension of the subject in hand.

"All this is of the nature of revelation, or the making known; and if we strip the inspiration which we attribute to a man of everything of this kind, we reduce it to we do not well know what. It is then either *nothing*—absolutely nothing *but a name*, or else a wild, headlong impulse, unintelligible, unreasonable, and ridiculous."*

This powerful and incisive reasoning brought the writer very near to the truth. Rightly he extends the sphere of revelation; but, strangely enough, by adding to the idea of inspiration, what that of revelation, in the common acceptation of the term, lacked. What is this, however, but to confound revelation with inspiration? Had he left the idea of revelation so improved, and as a consequence rather simplified the idea of inspiration by reducing it to its true subjective character and dimensions, which divinely prepared and fitted the mind for the intelligent reception of these comprehensive revelations, he would have avoided the common confusion, and exactly hit on the view of St. Paul. For confusion is only to be avoided by us when we imitate the

---

* This writer says: "The only distinction we can see is that revelation may be described as the matter communicated; and inspiration, as the manner in which it is communicated." This statement, however as regards inspiration is from its vagueness not easily understood.

apostle, and sharpen the line of demarcation which divides inspiration and revelation.

In humble confidence, I apprehend that the time has come in which we must be prepared to return from these nullities to the divinely reasoned and solidly established judgment of St. Paul. His statement cannot be misunderstood or evaded.*

What Christ had delivered to His apostles were facts and truths which came under their cognizance; but at the time they did not fully comprehend them. After their conversion, the Holy Spirit revealed, for the first time, to their minds, enlightened by inspiration, these truths in their spiritual significance. By this inspiration they understood all that was thus and otherwise revealed. Being, moreover, illuminated,—and fully made masters of the knowledge communicated,—they were by this teaching of the Holy Ghost enabled "to speak what they did know," and to commit the same to writing. (See 2 Cor. iv. 6.) The relation of the words to, and their connexion with, the thoughts which they represent, is usually considered the most mysterious part of the whole process. I have carefully examined St. Paul's reasonings on the subject for a solution of the difficulty.

---

* In the hands of Philo, inspiration in an extraordinary degree is reduced to "the wild, unintelligible impulse" described above, which is nothing but a name—precisely because, as most modern writers, he begins with the result—the written prophecy. See Chapter IX.

The apostle shows how the Holy Spirit taught the chosen servants of God to express accurately the Divine truths communicated to them. This is the manner. He presented to their spiritual vision revelations; and as, without suitable preparation, the mind in its natural state could not receive and know these revelations; by a Divine operation He transforms this natural into a spiritual state. This transforming act on the one hand, and the mental effect on the other, is inspiration. So Alford rightly interprets 1 Cor. ii. 14. They could not receive, and they could not know, the depths of this spiritual wisdom, "because they were not fitted for it (being carnal), and because they are to be spiritually judged of by the πνεῦμα of a man exalted by the Spirit of God into its proper paramount office of judging and ruling; and inspired and enabled for that office."

By this gift they were made competent to understand the revelations presented. The words, therefore, flow from a knowledge imparted by this teaching; and the inspired speak out the things made known to them "in words which the Holy Ghost teacheth." In fact, the matter, so brought before the mind, is shaped into a proper form by the Spirit's operations of inspiration and revelation; and this form, in a sense already completed, is projected in representative symbols into the outer world. Such is the written word. The connexion between the matter and the form appeared in a strong light to our Lord as He said, "When they shall deliver you up, take no thought how or what ye shall speak : for it shall be given you in that same hour what ye shall speak. For it is not ye that speak, but the Spirit of your Father which speaketh in you" (Matt. x. 19, 20). Here let it be remarked that reference is made both to the ideas and to the words. For in the phrase πῶς ἢ τί, how or what, πῶς refers to the form or words, and τί to the thoughts or matter. The Saviour, however, seeming to feel the engrossing importance of the matter, as bringing with it the words, omits the πῶς in the second clause.

In the same spirit, St. Paul, exalting his knowledge of the truths revealed to him, speaks rather disparagingly of the manner in which he expressed them : "For I suppose I was not a whit behind the very chiefest apostles. But though I be rude in *speech*, yet not in *knowledge*" (2 Cor. xi. 5, 6).

The distinction of matter and form is similarly alluded to in the words of our Lord related by St. Luke : "I will give you a mouth and a wisdom which all your adversaries shall not be able to gainsay nor resist."

Marvellous indeed is the use of words as connected with the thoughts which they represent ! How instantaneously they spring up unbidden—winged, as it were, with lightning. Our thoughts may, even more than we are aware of, be conceived in words, and, at their birth, come forth in wordy forms. This is one of the mysteries of our spirits, which in the present state we can never fully understand. But confining ourselves always to scriptural certainty, we can say that, in whatever conjectures we indulge concerning those winged messengers of thoughts, the latter are viewed in God's word as having a special and distinct importance—a something ($τί$) distinguished from the form of expression—a wisdom ($σοφία$) underlying the utterance ($στόμα$). And this abundantly proves that an exclusively verbal theory does not come up to the scriptural standard.

CHAPTER V.

THE NATURE OF INSPIRATION INVESTIGATED FROM ITS RELATION TO REVELATION.

THE relation of inspiration to revelation will be very forcibly exhibited—and so present in the clearest light the true nature and character of the former as contrasted with the erroneous idea now prevailing—if we consider the connexion of the supernatural revelation of the higher truths with inspiration.

It has been stated that for a revelation of such Divine truths, two things are required. First, the presentation by the Holy Spirit, in some objective form, of thoughts to the mind and heart, external to and therefore not originating from the natural powers of man's mental constitution. These thoughts may be presented either directly, by suggestion of the Holy Spirit; or indirectly, through other forms capable of transmitting them to the mind.

Secondly, there is needed a mind which can receive these higher truths. For St. Paul, speaking of the special revelations vouchsafed to the apostles of Christ, distinctly avers, "Eye hath not seen, nor ear heard, neither have entered into the heart of man, the things which God has prepared for them that love Him. But God hath revealed them unto us by His Spirit." Some inconsiderately apply the words "the things prepared" to the future blessedness of heaven. This, however, was not the idea of the apostle. He speaks not of a future world, but of a present revelation: God *hath* revealed them.

There is *now*, St. Paul affirms, something to be revealed; though not to the eye, nor ear, nor heart, the source and seat of human conception, imagination, and love. It is only to the spirit, and the spirit duly prepared, that it is visible, audible, conceivable, imaginable.

The discussion of this subject by the late Mr. Robertson is admirable, and in a truly philosophic spirit. To the eye there is presented the beautiful in nature and in art; but the beauty is finite, perishable, unsatisfying. The loveliness of the All-beautiful, who is infinite and eternal, is not seen here in a scene so limited and transitory, or, at best, only dimly seen. Observation, too, which proceeds on the testimony of the senses, cannot give a revelation: you cannot by searching find out the Almighty to perfection; nor any of the eternal truths which He has revealed from heaven.

For example, " men have supposed they discovered the law of duty written in the anatomical phenomena of disease. They have exhibited the brain inflamed by intoxication, and the structure obliterated by excess. They have shown in the disordered frame the inevitable penalty of trangression. But if a man, startled by all this, give up his sin, has he, from this selfish prudence, learned the law of duty? The penalties of wrong-doing, doubtless; but not the sanction of right and wrong, written in the conscience, of which penalties are only enforcements. He has indisputable evidence that it is expedient not to commit excess : but you cannot manufacture a conscience out of expediency. The voice of conscience says, not, 'It is better not to do so;' but, 'Thou shalt not.' Conscience in morality is the imperative."

Again, the transcendental truths of God cannot gain access to the soul through the natural ear. For such revelation is made through words; and words are but counters—the coins of intellectual exchange. There is as little resemblance between the silver coin and the bread it purchases, as between the word and the thing it stands for. Looking at the coin, the form of the loaf does not suggest itself. Listening to the word, you do not perceive the idea for which it stands, unless already in possession of it. So that apostles themselves and prophets, speaking to the ear, cannot reveal truth to the soul,—no, not if God Himself were to touch their lips with fire. A verbal revelation is only a revelation to the ear. The same may be said of the heart. To this source is referred the power of conceiving and imagining, and the power of loving.

Imagination is creative. Men of genius are creators. But their creations relating to sublunary things and to material subjects still move in the lower region of the merely human. They do not, and cannot, reach the spiritual and eternal truths which God reveals to the humble. The heart, too, is the seat of affection. The union of heart with heart is the purest state of feeling even to the natural man; but the intensest love of the creature only faintly shadows the depth of the devoted feeling which sways the soul of the spiritually minded, who love their God and Saviour in sincerity and in truth.

Now from what has been said, it is manifest that none but the *spiritually prepared* can receive the revelations of God. By none else can they be understood, or even recognized. To the natural man these truths are foolishness; neither can he know them, because they are spiritually discerned. For every kind of truth, and therefore still more for Divine truth, a special capacity or preparation is absolutely indispensable. Hence the pertinent remark of the late Archbishop Sumner: "As the things of God do not enter into the heart of man, that he can *naturally* comprehend them, so likewise there must be a preparation of the heart that it may receive them." As one whose organ of sight is defective cannot form an idea of colours, yet the moment the film which obscured his vision is removed he sees clearly and distinctly, so when the Spirit, transforming the natural man into the spiritual, by preparing his mind and heart for the reception of Divine truth, "takes of the things of Christ, and shows them to the soul," that man, so prepared, gladly receives them, and is fully competent to know them, precisely because they are spiritually discernible.

This great fact of Christian experience can be illustrated by a pertinent example. The death of Christ—especially the death of the cross—presents to the contemplation of the natural man nothing but ignominy, imbecility, and failure of purpose. The spiritual man discovers and discerns in it the enormity and extent of sin which required so vast a sacrifice. He also discerns in it the infinite love of God to fallen man, in providing so costly a sacrifice for sin. And this unmerited mercy of his heavenly Father disposes him to reciprocate God's love, "We love Him, because He first loved us."

Without concurring in all his views of Christian doctrine, I cannot conclude this chapter without expressing my obligations to the singularly remarkable and ably written sermons of Robertson of Brighton. On Inspiration, which this very thoughtful divine considered the deepest question of our day, his views are clear and convincingly persuasive. The scriptural idea of the nature of inspiration, deduced by me from St. Paul's First Epistle to the Corinthians, as a preparation for the intelligent reception of Divine revelations, is powerfully corroborated by an irresistible logic of this eminent man.

I must, however, dissent from him in extending this view of inspiration to believing Christians in general, at least without very considerable modification.* I hold St. Paul's theory to apply specially to apostolic inspiration; for the apostle in the sixth and seventh verses of this second chapter, which is a preface to the view advanced, beginning at the ninth verse, limits the revelations referred to in the tenth to himself and brother apostles: "Howbeit *we* speak wisdom among them that are perfect." (See also Eph. iii. 5.) In speaking of himself, in the second verse, he says, "If ye have heard of the dispensation of the grace of God, which is given me to you-ward;" and adds, "which in other ages was not made known unto the sons of men, as it is now revealed unto His holy apostles and prophets by the Spirit."

If, then, inspiration be a preparation of the mind and heart, effected by the Holy Spirit for the intelligent reception of revelations; and if such revelations, the deep mysteries of the kingdom of heaven, τὰ βάθη, be disclosures made by the Most High to the apostles and prophets, the inspiration of the latter must be extraordinary and peculiar—peculiar, at least, as to a higher degree of light imparted to them.† Besides,

---

* For the sense in which inspiration may be applied to the believer, see p. 37.

† According to Ewald, the difference consists in its object and form, not in its essence.

it is to be borne in mind that the promise of Christ was specially addressed by Him to His apostles in the valedictory interview He had with them before He suffered (John xiv. 26, and xvi. 13).

Again: if, according to St. Paul, inspiration be the necessary preparation, effected by the Spirit of God, for the reception of a revelation, where the latter has been vouchsafed, there must needs be the former inseparably connected with it.

Here, then, we have a test laid down by which to try the accuracy of any proposed definition of inspiration. In every case where an individual has been the appointed medium of transmitting God's revelation to mankind, he must be inspired. If the definition be so framed as not absolutely to require this condition to be fulfilled, it is erroneous, as not giving the true nature and characteristic property of inspiration. Thus Perrone's definition, and those popularly received and constructed on his plan, admit the separation of revelation from inspiration; and are therefore, in the light of Scripture, untenable.

The patriarchs Abraham, Isaac, and Jacob, had "revelations, but were not inspired to record them," as if this were something peculiar to inspiration. St. Luke was inspired, "but we are not told that he ever enjoyed a revelation."

Somehow, these revelations of the patriarchs were handed down to the time of Moses,—whether recorded or not,—if not in writing, orally. Inspiration, as a gift of the Holy Ghost, was given, and antecedently had produced its effect, as a preparation for oral teaching, just as much needed as for a written record, and such is even included in Dr. Lee's definition of inspiration. As to St. Luke, he really enjoyed many revelations, if the word be taken in its scriptural sense, including under it many of the aids of the Divine Spirit usually classed among those of 'assistentia et directio Divina,' which belong not to inspiration, but more properly to revelation. Here is brought out the view which I have taken of the nature of inspiration as contrasted with that so ably enforced by Archdeacon Lee. "It forms" (says this author, p. 324,) "a prominent feature of the doctrine of inspiration, maintained in these discources, that each writer of Scripture made use, on all occasions, of such materials as were in his power, whether supplied by his own experience, or by the information of others. This principle, as we have seen, forms the foundation of the distinction between revelation and inspiration. The particulars recorded in the pages of Scripture were not all matters of revelation; the sacred writers have touched upon many topics which were not originally communicated to them from heaven; but this circumstance in no respect invalidates the assertion that the narrative of each and every fact of which the Bible takes notice has been handed down to future ages under the influence of inspiration. In other words, the Holy Spirit provided that each portion of the Bible should convey such information as best subserved the Divine purpose, irrespectively of any consideration as to the character of that information, whether it consisted of plain historical facts, or of immediate disclosures of supernatural truths."

Now admitting, in its fullest extent, the truth of this statement, that "the sacred writers have touched upon many topics which were not originally communicated to them from heaven," we must nevertheless insist that, even in such topics, the Spirit's agency as a *revealing* power can be distinctly traced. For suppose (what was really the case) that many of these matters, whether derived from their own experience or from the information of others—above all, what they had heard from the Redeemer Himself—were now in whole or in part forgotten, beyond doubt the Spirit's agency was needed, and graciously exerted, either to suggest or to recall truths which otherwise would be irretrievably lost. Moreover, other inward suggestions of the Spirit might vastly enlarge and improve these very truths. Thus each writer's own experience, and the information he had derived from others, may be greatly modified, if not partly constituted, by undoubted revelations. For such are those secret and silent promptings of the Divine Spirit referred to in Job xxxiii. 14: "God speaketh once, yea twice, yet man perceiveth it not."

In this point of view, there can be no question that

"the perfect understanding" of the sayings and doings of Christ, which St. Luke claims, had been powerfully aided and advanced by revelations.* With the sacred writers, inspiration, rightly understood, had also mightily contributed to the progress of their knowledge however acquired. So gradual, indeed, may the acquisition of this knowledge be, that at last it becomes appropriated; and all *direct* traces of its Divine origin may disappear from the consciousness of the individuals. Moreover, this position is strengthened, if there be taken into account those natural revelations by which God in His good providence makes known His will to mankind. In fact, this view, I repeat, is the only one which consistently assigns to the Bible its true and proper designation—" The Revelation of God."

The facts of history, and information derived from others, are seldom alone the premisses from which the conclusions of the inspired are drawn. For besides the Spirit's aid in recalling the past, other undoubted suggestions of this Divine Agent are usually coupled with the former. So the truths propounded—the inferences of inspired reasonings, in which some of those writers freely indulged, owe their parentage, in an eminent degree, to the revelations of God.

Since, then, revelation runs into, and inextricably blends with, that which is now called inspiration,

---

* See in page 126 a forcible development of this argument by a very clever writer.

both in reference to these respective operations of the Holy Spirit, and also in reference to a supposed difference of character in the composition of different parts of the Bible; and since this difference cannot be maintained, the real distinction between revelation and inspiration cannot rest on such a foundation. The consequence is that the idea of inspiration, derived from such a difference, must be erroneous. The result, moreover, is precisely what might be expected, viz., that revelation entering largely into the idea of inspiration, (as received by Perrone, Dr. Lee, and others,) is confounded with it. The true radical distinction is to be found in the fact that in revelation there is an objective presentation to the mind, in inspiration none, this being a subjective state, and modification wrought in the mind and upon its faculties by the Spirit of God.

Thus, extending revelation to the full limits of its proper sphere, and regarding inspiration as a distinct influence of the Holy Spirit, whereby the servant of God is fitted—by receiving τὸ πνεῦμα τὸ ἐκ τοῦ Θεοῦ —to know the truths graciously revealed, we have a clue to escape from the labyrinth, in whose mazes we were lost.

So much indeed did the acute mind of Dr. Henderson feel embarrassed by the common view of the distinction between revelation and inspiration, that he considers, with many eminent authorities, "the distinction must be given up." Nevertheless there is a real scriptural distinction between revelation and inspiration which I have already pointed out; and this distinction can only vanish in some such view of inspiration as the preceding, which embraces and causes to merge into itself the most general and certain class of revelations—namely, those presented to the mind by the inward suggestions of the Holy Spirit. These, however, as truly and as often are denominated revelations in God's word, as the external, and by a great German author are called 'internal revelations.' A suggestion of this kind is unquestionably a distinct presentation to the mind, and not simply an influence which enlarges and quickens its faculties.

It is in consequence of taking this wrong view of the nature of inspiration that Bretschneider is inevitably led to confound the ideas of inspiration and revelation. For considering revelation by internal suggestion of the Holy Spirit to be inspiration, (he has at least the merit of saying that inspiration is *something*,) he defines inspiration to be "that species of revelation in which God acts without the intervention of external causes."

Dr. Lee rightly remarks that "fresh light is cast upon the nature of the Spirit's agency in the case of the apostles by the statements of St. Paul in his Epistle to the Galatians." For in it he avers, in the strongest terms, that his own knowledge of Christian doctrine had not been derived from the other apostles. "I certify you, brethren, that the gospel which was preached of me is not after man: for I neither received it of man, neither was I taught it, but by the revelation of Jesus Christ" (Gal. i. 11, 12).

The only question is, How did St. Paul obtain this knowledge of the gospel? Dr. Lee's answer is the following: "Did the inspiration of the apostles *merely* consist in the fact of the Divine Spirit kindling a new life in their souls, by which a greater degree of clearness was diffused over their former ideas, how can we account for St. Paul's disclaimer of all the human means which alone could have enabled him to acquire any accurate knowledge of our Lord's teaching?" Hence he infers that it was by a direct revelation the apostle obtained this knowledge, which imparted to him new truths, and gave him "a comprehensive insight into the doctrines of Christianity."

Here more is assigned to revelation than is warranted from St. Paul's express statements, in the second chapter of 1st Corinthians. "The influence of the Spirit" and "the inspiration of the apostles" are identified, as might be expected from the author's definition of inspiration, which is a spiritual energy guiding the sacred writers to proclaim orally or in writing God's will, whether it relates to matters naturally cognizable or supernaturally revealed.

Now if my view be correct, Paul's knowledge of Christian doctrine was the joint result of inspiration and revelation; and the *insight* into these truths, conveyed by revelation, was the office and work of inspiration, which diffused light over both his former ideas, and the revelation itself. For according to St. Paul the measure of the intelligibility of a revelation is the degree of the inspiration which accompanies it.

The extension of the term inspiration from this influence of the Holy Spirit on the mind and heart to the special act by which He imparts revelations to the chosen servants of God—as if inspiration was the infusion of a revelation—has been the fertile source of confusion and perplexity. Thus Quenstedt, who also makes inspiration generically to include revelation, yet admits that, in some respects, inspiration may be rightly taken for and properly called revelation; and further says that he is compelled to the conclusion that the distinction between revelation and inspiration cannot be maintained. Thus too (as I have already observed) it is not surprising that so able a scholar as Dr. Henderson,* entertaining the same view of the nature of inspiration, should find himself embarrassed, and not able to see the way before him. "We use (says this learned author) inspiration in a generic sense, and comprehend under it, not merely the particular species of Divine influence

---

* Dr. Henderson says that no traces of the strict theological distinction between revelation and inspiration are to be found in the Fathers; nor was it at all used by the Reformers. It appears to have been first introduced in the seventeenth century by Calovius, in his 'System. Theol.,' tom. i., p. 555.

which was enjoyed by the sacred writers, but the entire subject of revelation, or the various modes in which Jehovah employed supernatural agency for the purpose of disclosing His will." Holding this view, he also is forced to the conclusion that this theological distinction, though improved by Quenstëdt, and afterwards more scientifically treated by Baumgarten, Seiler, and other divines, ought to be, and has been, abandoned as unnecessarily clogging the subject.

The distinction, however, between inspiration and revelation, which I have drawn out and explained at full length, is a real one, and the line of demarcation is so broad and legible, that by a strict adherence to it no confusion is likely to arise.

The objections, moreover, repeatedly urged, with great force and point, against the former view of inspiration, and which have not been answered, fall perfectly harmless on the latter. Here the subject is simplified, and all distraction of thought avoided, while we cease to objectify inspiration, and learn to confine it within limits proper its of pure spiritual influence. We avoid, as incongruous to the true nature of inspiration, the *contrasted* application of revelation to some passages of Scripture, and of inspiration to all. Thus we shall understand that what some call modes of inspiration, are really modes of revelation: such, in particular, are those internal suggestions of the Divine Spirit which often silently and unconsciously disclose the deep things of God to the soul of man. For St. Paul himself designates as revelations these secret promptings of the Spirit, and it is not easy to see why they should be classed under the head of inspiration. (1 Cor. xiv. 30.)

Nevertheless, hear Quenstedt on the other side, as the representative of those who take the former position, and understand how to them confusion of thought and expression is absolutely inevitable. "Make (says Quenstedt) a distinction between Divine revelation and inspiration. Formally, and by the force of the term, revelation is the manifestation of things unknown and hidden; and it can take place in many and different ways—namely, either by external address or by dreams and visions. Inspiration is the action of the Holy Spirit by which the actual knowledge of things is supernaturally infused into a created intellect, or it is the internal suggestion or infusion of conceptions whether the things conceived were previously known to or hidden from the writer. That (revelation) could precede the writing, this was always conjoined with the writing, and flowed into it. Meantime, I do not deny that Divine inspiration itself can be called a revelation in one respect,—namely, as far as it is a manifestation of certain circumstances, in like manner of the order and mode in which the things were to be marked out and written: sometimes, too, even revelation concurs and coincides with inspiration,—to wit, when Divine mysteries are revealed by being inspired, and are inspired by being revealed in the very act of writing."—*Theol. Didact. Polem.*, p. 68.

It is, on scriptural grounds, impossible to reduce to the one head of inspiration the promised assistance of the Holy Ghost, by which the apostles were guided into all the truth. Their minds and hearts were fitted by inspiration to receive the truths of religion; and these truths were presented to their enlightened understandings in the same manner as the distant invisible stars become visible when the human sight is improved. And yet no improvement of the visual organ could bring within its sphere such objects, unless they were actually in its field of vision. Now what is inspiration but the supernatural improvement, and amplification, of the spiritual vision? Rightly understood, it is therefore in every case subjective, terminating, as the very force of the word implies, in some modification produced in the subject. And this is equally so, whether such inspiration merely subserves an end extraneous to the mind, or aims at moral or intellectual improvement,—whether, in fact, it seeks only to promote the mental condition of the individual, or the interests of the Church; since the former is connected with the latter as cause with effect; and whatever benefit it confers on the Church, is not inspiration, but the fruit of inspiration.

I cannot agree with Archdeacon Lee when he says, "The inspiration of the authors of the Bible was an energy altogether objective, and directed to supply the wants of the Church. The inspiration of the Christian is altogether subjective, directed to the moral improvement of the individual."

Again, both come from God, and are given by God; and therefore I must once more dissent from Dr. Lee when he quotes the passage, "Take no thought beforehand what ye shall speak, neither do ye premeditate; but whatsoever *shall be given you* in that hour, that speak ye; for it is not ye that speak, but the Holy Ghost." Here Dr. Lee remarks, "The objective nature of the Divine influence is denoted by the words 'it shall be *given* you,' which are continually employed by the New Testament writers to express this fact. Thus St. Peter subsequently speaks of 'the wisdom given to our beloved brother Paul;' and St. Paul himself writes, 'When James, Cephas, and John perceived the *grace* that was given unto me.'" Now the very form of expression here used might have cleared up the mistaken view taken of the subject.

Both inspiration and revelation were given to the apostles;—neither was the spontaneous growth of their own minds. But it is not for this reason that an objective character is to be assigned to one or the other. It is because, in the one case, a distinct object or concept is before the mental vision; in the other not so. God gives strength and perspicacity to the powers of the mind; and here God presents no object to the mind. But when by suggestion or otherwise He presents to the enlightened soul truths which He wishes to reveal, the objective nature of these presentations is quite patent. God's gifts are not, however, all objective. It is the nature of the gift that determines which are objective and which are subjective. Such are some of the perplexities arising from objectifying, and thereby mistaking, the true nature of inspiration. But no less originate from the undue limitation, on the one hand, of revelation, and, on the other, from the corresponding undue extension of inspiration to what are really revelations,—that class, namely, so general and diversified, which may be called revelations by internal suggestion.

The revelations of the Divine Spirit vouchsafed to the apostles of Christ were in fact of two kinds : 1. The things brought to their remembrance—"whatsoever He had spoken unto them." 2. The new truths imparted, many of which hitherto they were not able to bear. In these Dr. Lee finds the distinction between revelation and inspiration. Here he says our Lord "separates that exercise of supernatural power which is truly creative, and derived from the eternal word through the Spirit, and which consists in disclosing new truths, from that distinct agency of the Spirit Himself, whereby 'all things are brought to remembrance.'"

I fail to see, in these words of the Redeemer, any reference to a separate agency : more especially as inspiration extends to everything which the sacred writers record—as well to the supernaturally as to the naturally cognizable. In fact, the true distinction does not at all appear in those two forms, which really represent only different modes of revelation. For example, when it was stated in the hearing of the apostles, more or less obscurely, that the Gospel (Matt. xxiv. 14) was to be opened to all, this great mystery was not comprehended at the time; but was subsequently recalled to Peter's remembrance by revelation. And this would be so, whether the matter were disclosed by word, by vision, or by suggestion.* For to recall a truth by suggestion, which truth might otherwise be lost or buried in oblivion, is, in the strictest sense of the term, a revelation. "God hath showed me" (Acts x. 21) is a formula which indicates a revelation, whatever be the way in which God discloses it.

Truths such as this, misunderstood at first, were the very truths that might be most easily forgotten. Herein is the double function of the Spirit displayed most strikingly. This Divine Agent reveals or presents to the mind certain truths; and to fit the mind to grasp and take them in, imparts spiritual discernment and quickened intuition. And it is to be observed that at the very time when the Holy Spirit was given in an extraordinary manner, the truths which, owing to the want of maturing time

---

* Dr. Lee beautifully and correctly marks the progress of St. Peter's knowledge from suggestion to vision. See p. 276.

or a higher degree of illumination to dispel existing prejudices, had vanished, are afterwards revived afresh in living colours, and the inspiration then bestowed becomes the source of their clear and accurate perception.

In the admirable statement given by Archdeacon Lee of the revelations by which St. Peter gradually came to the full knowledge of the truth respecting the call of the Gentiles, the only matter of surprise is why the true nature of inspiration did not flash upon his mind (see p. 276-7). These are his words: "Should it be regarded as a matter of doubt whether his development of the Christian scheme on that occasion (Day of Pentecost) were really a direct result from *the inward suggestions* of the Holy Ghost, such doubt must disappear when the subsequent narrative is considered." The apostle gives expression to these inward disclosures of the Spirit—and every disclosure or unveiling of the Spirit is a revelation—in those words, "The promise is unto you and to your children, and to all that are afar off."

Dr. Lee proceeds: "The account of his ecstatic vision in the tanner's house at Joppa, proves that St. Peter quite misapprehended the bearing of these words. No one can maintain that the knowledge which he derived from that vision was the result of his previous Christian experience. He expressly states that it was a completely new disclosure, which he could not have elicited of himself, but which God unfolded to his view in opposition to his former prejudices;—a fact which clearly indicates that when need required the *Holy Ghost poured new light* upon certain of the apostles' own statements, which had not been previously illuminated for themselves;" and so concludes: "Thus we see how very gradually the whole truth burst upon the apostles. Not even St. Peter's vision displayed it on all its sides; and hence, even of ourselves we can discern how truly Christ could say of the *revelations* to be subsequently given, 'Ye cannot bear them now.'"

Now this very accurate view of the progress of the acquisition of St. Peter's knowledge in every respect confirms what I hold to be the true nature of inspiration as connected with revelation.

The disclosures of the truths which, before they were illuminated, the apostles were not able to bear, Archdeacon Lee very properly calls "*revelations*." These disclosures, made to St. Peter, were first the "inward suggestions of the Holy Ghost." These, however, being not sufficiently "*illuminated*,"—the apostle was not able to apprehend fully their bearing. And this is always the case when a revelation is not accompanied by an inspiration of suitable intensity. So in the present instance when the "Holy Ghost poured new light,"—*i.e.*, vouchsafed to grant a higher degree of inspiration,—the suggestive revelations, imperfectly comprehended before, conveyed an accurate knowledge of this truth to his mind. Then at length St. Peter, thoroughly enlightened by receiving "the Spirit which is of God, in order that he might know" God's gracious communications (χαρισθέντα), was enabled to preach, without doubt or misgiving, the mystery of the call of the Gentiles to a full participation of the Gospel privileges.

If inspiration, as presented in Perrone's and kindred definitions, conveys no information as to its nature,—if, without being blended with revelations, it is we know not what, or, as it has been described, "a wild unintelligible impulse,"—what is it but a name? If it must be blended with revelations in order to make it intelligible, then there may be something real in the complex conception; still something only real when they are mixed together in intolerable confusion.

On the other hand, take inspiration to be the hallowed influence of the Divine Spirit, by which He fits and prepares the mind and heart for the intelligent reception of the revelations presented, and all confusion vanishes. Inspiration becomes perfectly intelligible, and as scriptural as intelligible.

This view takes, as it ought, revelation to have a wider scope and sphere than what the common definition assigns to it. The inward suggestions of the Holy Spirit extends as well to truths partially or imperfectly known, as to those absolutely unknown, like the case considered in the revelations which were vouchsafed to Peter.

All partake of the nature of revelation which discovers or makes known, through the Divine Spirit, what had been previously unknown. And in proof of the scriptural extension of the term, I have already adduced two passages (one in Matt. xvi. 17, the other in 1 Cor. xiv. 30,) which are expressly called revelations. Two others I shall now add where the fact of such communications is clearly set forth. In Nehemiah ii. 4, 8, and 12, Artaxerxes, who sees his cupbearer sad, affectionately asks, "For what dost thou make request?" "So," says Nehemiah, "I prayed to the God of heaven." God, the hearer of prayer, who had already *put it in* Nehemiah's *heart* to build the waste places of Jerusalem, had also put it in the heart of the king to assist this patriot in his good work. In Stephen's apology (Acts vii. 23), a similar form is used concerning Moses: "It came into his heart to visit his brethren the children of Israel." These are all revelations, however silently and imperceptibly they may enter the mind. "For God speaketh once, yea twice, yet man perceiveth it not. In a dream, in a vision of the night, when sleep falleth upon men, in slumberings upon the bed; then He openeth the ears of men, and sealeth their instruction" (Job xxxiii. 14—16). If the dream and vision be the revelation, what is opening the ear and vividly impressing the thing revealed, but inspiration? The great difficulty in our manner of conceiving the nature of Biblical inspiration is the transition from the thoughts communicated by revelation, as illumined by inspiration, to the words by which they may be accurately expressed. Some say that this is effected by Divine suggestion, others by Divine superintendence. Now the suggestion of words, apart from the thoughts of which they are the exponents, is quite inconceivable; and as to the suggestion of thoughts, this I have shown is one of the modes of revelation, and in this sense is so used in Scripture. Again, superintendence as a direction ancillary to the natural employment of language, if not mechanical, must be exerted in the inner sphere of thought. This would take place whenever the Holy Spirit either infused greater energy and perspicacity into the mental powers, or presented the conceptions in a clearer or more definite form.

But all this is really included in the provisions of inspiration and revelation whereby Divine knowledge had been already communicated; and thus most truly may it be said that "the Holy Ghost teacheth them what they ought to say" (Luke xii. 12). Their utterances "were the commandments of the Lord" (1 Cor. xiv. 37). And he who despised them, despised not man, but God, who had given to them His Holy Spirit" (1 Thess. iv. 8).

Inspiration is then, on these grounds, unquestionably verbal. For the character of the thoughts must be impressed on the words, both because to a great extent we think in words, and because the words are the representative signs of those thoughts. If, in fact, the thoughts really come from God through the operation of the Holy Spirit who suggests ideas, and by inspiration qualifies the mind to comprehend them, imparting thereby a clear knowledge of Divine truths, the verbal forms in which that knowledge is expressed must partake of that clearness. If, moreover,—as is usual in speaking of the inspiration of Holy Scripture, and this is countenanced by our Lord Himself,*—the whole process of the Spirit be denominated inspiration, this really extends to the words, or is verbal. Clear words are the offsprings of clear thoughts, and therefore, so far as men think in words, this may be regarded as a truism.

Agreeably to this view, Professor Ebrard remarks, "The position that God Himself dictated the very words, is, to say the least, very mechanical: yet so far it contains a truth, since it is as mechanical to say, with the Rationalists, only the thoughts are from God, not the words, as if there were such a thing as a clear thought which did not bring the words with it."

David says, "The Spirit of the Lord spake by me, and His word was in my tongue" (2 Sam. xxiii. 1, 2). When God fits men to speak, He speaks by them. In the words of the learned author just quoted, "Each writer was an instrument pervaded throughout by

---

* See Matt. xxii. 43; Mark xii. 36.

God, but not a dead organ. The result, therefore, to which we arrive is this, that the Holy Scriptures are thoroughly and really God's word; and thoroughly and really also man's word; and that they share with redemption itself the character of a true God—manhood."

The great perplexity arises from the mysterious connexion that exists between thoughts and their representative words. In any case, if the words are God's words, if they are pure words, if they be spoken by the Holy Ghost, perfect and infallible certainty must be attributed to them. What, however, is the nature and character of that certainty cannot be posited by any *à priori* formula. The point of difficulty is in the transition from knowledge to its accurate expression, and this the philosophic Chalmers saw very distinctly : " There is not one theory, short by ever so little of a thorough and perfect inspiration, but is chargeable with the consequence that the subject-matter of revelation suffers and is deteriorated in the closing steps of its progress, and just before it settles into that ultimate position where it stands forth to guide and illuminate the world. It existed purely in heaven. It was deposited purely by the great agent of revelation in the mind of the apostles. But then we are told, when but a little way from its final landing-place, that instead of being carried forward purely to the situation where alone the great purpose of the whole movement was to be fulfilled, then was it abandoned to itself, and then were human infirmities permitted to mingle with it, and to mar its lustre. Strange that, just when entering on the function of an authoritative guide and leader to mankind, the soil and feebleness of humanity should be suffered to gather around it. Strange that, with the inspiration of thought, it should make pure ingress into the minds of the apostles, but wanting the inspiration of words should not make pure egress to that world in whose behalf alone this great movement originated in heaven, and terminated on earth."

In this powerful statement of plenary inspiration there would, I submit, be greater clearness had the illustrious author distinguished the use and application of personal inspiration and revelation from that to which they tend as their final term, the inspiration of Holy Scripture.

For, 1. Inspiration of thoughts is properly their revelation by suggestion. 2. Inspiration of words sounds like a theory of verbal dictation; for their simple egress would not be inspiration. 3. Words cannot be disjoined from the thoughts so as not to receive a character and colouring from them. I submit that applying inspiration to either thoughts or words, and thus giving an objective signification to inspiration, is both unscriptural and misleading. Though the term 'God-inspired' is an epithet applied to Scripture, still the question is an open one, "In what sense is this epithet applied to the word of God?"

CHAPTER VI.

THE DIFFERENT KINDS AND MODES OF INSPIRATION.

IN the preceding chapters I have endeavoured to point out the positive teaching of Holy Scripture on the all-important question of the inspiration of the Bible, as the record of God's revelation to mankind.

I have shown that a correct notion of that characteristic of the written word, none can expect to reach by any *à priori* assumption, without having previously, and in the foreground of the picture, exhibited the nature of the personal inspiration of the chosen servants of God whom He favoured with revelations.

In brief, it has appeared from this discussion that the inspiration of Holy Scripture is not a simple guidance to a certain result; but the combination of several spiritual influences on the mind and heart, leading to the knowledge of the truth. For thus taught by the Holy Spirit, the inspired is enabled divinely to express that knowledge in appropriate words.

This result is the last step in a process consisting of several parts ; and the guidance to it is no more inspiration than the guidance to works acceptable to God is to be accounted moral inspiration in the Collect for the Fifth Sunday after Easter : " O Lord, from whom all good things do come, grant to us Thy humble servants that by Thy holy *inspiration* we may think those things that be good, and by *Thy merciful guiding* may perform the same, through our Lord Jesus Christ."

The truth is, it is impossible to conceive any reasonable meaning in the commonly received idea of inspiration, as a Divine direction to the utterance of words ; or, if any, what does not rather apply to revelation than inspiration.

For it has been shown that a *Divine direction*, which may correct or refresh memory, which may correct the judgment, which may impart a truer idea of the matter considered than one's own information supplies, is truly, in the scriptural sense of the term, an undoubted revelation. Hence—it has been truly remarked—guidance in the selection of matter for record, preservation from error in the matters recorded, and similar things, partake as much of the character of revelation as information on a subject of which the party had no acquaintance, whether it be a matter of history or of prophecy.

Accordingly, not satisfied with the platitude of an *unknown and inexplicable guidance* to an external act which, wide of the mark, is not, and cannot be, inspiration, I have tried to gain a correct definition more in accordance with the views of St. Paul.

Now, before I enter on the examination of the several humanly-devised theories of Biblical inspiration, which all less or more deviate from the Pauline, it will be my object to give a succinct account of the varieties of opinion which have been entertained, at different times, concerning the nature and extent of inspiration.

This examination is needed, since every theory receives a tone and character from the definition of inspiration which underlies it.

Inspiration can be reduced to two classes: i. Primary and personal; ii. Secondary or Biblical.

i. Personal inspiration is either intellectual or moral. The general definition, which I ventured to give, includes under it every form of personal inspiration. It was thus expressed: "The supernatural actuating energy of the Spirit of God on the mind and heart of an individual, preparing him for the reception, and the manifestation, of any of the gifts which He vouchsafes to bestow." For the apostle says, "All these worketh that one and selfsame spirit, dividing to every man severally as He will" (1 Cor. xii. 11).

1. That intellectual gifts, apart from the grace of sanctification, have been supernaturally conferred on men, is very evident from the instances recorded in

Holy Scripture of several persons so gifted, while their hearts were not right in the sight of God. Such was Balaam, the highly gifted prophet, whose gift was nevertheless perverted by ambition and avarice, "who loved the wages of unrighteousness" (2 Peter ii. 16).

Such, too, were many members of the Corinthian Church, who were endowed with extraordinary spiritual gifts; of these, however, St. Paul, testifying that though "enriched by Him (Christ) in all utterance and all knowledge, so that they came behind in no gift," yet if they wanted charity, says they were "nothing." Indeed we cannot abruptly confine inspiration merely to the enlightenment of the intellect, in all cases, so as not to touch the heart, since the latter conduces much to the knowledge of the truth.

It appears, also, that men filling certain divinely appointed offices, sometimes were endued from on high with the gift of inspiration, irrespectively of their moral character. Thus Caiaphas, a bad man, a prominent member of the Jewish Sanhedrim, thought it "expedient that one man should die for the people, and that the whole nation perish not." From a merely selfish principle, he was ready to perpetrate, under colour of patriotism, an unjust deed, and to shed innocent blood. There was, notwithstanding, in these words a deeper meaning than Caiaphas was aware of. The evangelist therefore adds,* " This spake

---

* John xi. 51, 52.

he not of himself: but being high priest that year, he prophesied that Jesus should die for that nation; and not for that nation only, but that also He should gather together in one the children of God that were scattered abroad."

According to the view taken in these pages of St. Paul's idea of prophetic utterance, revelation and inspiration must concur to the production of the knowledge of which such utterance is the expression. Now the measure of that knowledge is determined by the *degree* in which, as seems fit to Him, the Holy Spirit vouchsafes to impart one or both of those concurrent factors.

A suggestive revelation presented, at the moment, to Caiaphas, would be understood by him according to the degree of light and strength which inspiration might shed on his faculties, darkened as they must be by his evil heart.*

Well and truly Dr. Lee remarks, "The New Testament affords some striking illustrations of the fact that the full sense of a Divine revelation was frequently unperceived by the person who received it," and instances the case of Caiaphas. But on his idea of the nature of inspiration he gives no explanation of so singular a state of mind, merely observing the fact that "he spake under the influence of God. . . . The reference to the office of Caiaphas

---

* The unconsciousness of such men as Caiaphas is attributed by the Fathers to their personal unworthiness.

does not imply that St. John considered every high priest necessarily prophesied; but merely points out that he was the natural medium through whom God might at times reveal Himself."

The explanation above given by me also applies to St. Peter's partial knowledge at the time (until his mind was further enlightened) of his own utterance in his Pentecostal Sermon recorded in Acts ii. 39.

2. Moral inspiration, as taught in our Church, is a thoroughly scriptural doctrine, and is comprised in our definition of personal inspiration.

Very clearly is it set forth in the Collect for the Holy Communion: "Almighty God, unto whom all hearts be open, all desires known, and from whom no secrets are hid, *cleanse* the thoughts of our hearts by the *inspiration* of Thy Holy Spirit, that we may perfectly love Thee, and worthily magnify Thy holy name, through Jesus Christ our Lord."

Here is the essential characteristic of all inspiration—*preparation* by an imparted grace, "Cleanse the thoughts of our hearts," and acting inwardly: as in intellectual inspiration, the intromitted force of the Spirit prepares the mind and heart for the intelligent reception of the truths presented by revelation. The results following inspiration, in both cases, are perfectly analogous. The preparation in the one case begets knowledge resulting in its expression; and in the other, the preparation is succeeded by holy and loving* obedience to the commandments of God (1 Peter i. 2). In the one case the expression is words; in the other, acts. And as the inspiration in the latter case is antecedent to, and not to be confounded with, the result, or any guidance to it, so it is with the inspiration in the former case.

This is the doctrine of the Holy Scriptures. They teach that an inward and spiritual kingdom of God is set up in the hearts of all true believers, and that this kingdom is "righteousness and peace and joy in the Holy Ghost." And they teach that this gift is from the agency and operation of the Spirit of God. "Now (says St. Paul, Rom. xv. 13,) the God of hope fill you with all joy and peace in believing, that ye may abound in hope through the power of the Holy Ghost."

And still more fully is this stated by the same apostle in his Epistle to Titus: "But after that the kindness and love of God our Saviour toward man appeared: not by works of righteousness which we have done, but according to His mercy He saved us by the washing of regeneration, and renewing of the Holy Ghost, which He shed on us abundantly through Jesus Christ our Saviour."

And it is worthy of remark that St. Paul notices the *fruits* of the indwelling faith produced by the

---

* In Scripture phraseology, "to know God" is equivalent "to love God"—so intimately close is the analogy between intellectual and moral inspiration.

Holy Ghost in the heart, as *resulting from* the spiritual gifts shed on believers, and not as included in them; for he adds, "This is a faithful saying, and these things I will that thou affirm constantly, that they which have believed in God might be careful to maintain good works. These things are good and profitable unto men."*

The distinguishing marks which discriminate intellectual and moral inspiration, shall be presently more fully considered, particularly in reference to the apostolic and highest form of the gift. Meanwhile I observe, in the line of the fruits of moral inspiration, that the inspiration of Holy Scripture consists in the *capacity* for writing produced by the Holy Spirit, through personal inspiration and revelation, not in the *act* of writing. Thus the patriarchs were as much inspired when God revealed the truth to them, as they would have been had they anticipated Moses in recording it, being by inspiration qualified to place on record the things disclosed to them. In an early age of the world, the Father of Lights prepared by inspiration the patriarchs to receive and understand the revelations of His will; and, prompted by His Spirit, they officially transmitted these revelations to future generations, either *orally* or in *writing*,† being qualified for this work by the accurate

---

* Titus iii. 4—8.
† The contrary has been assumed without proof.

knowledge which revelation illumined by inspiration had supplied.

In the sacred writers, both kinds of inspiration—the intellectual and the moral—were combined in the same individuals. With them the fruits of the Spirit were exhibited, as well in holiness of life, as in the supernatural gifts of the understanding. By inspiration they were enabled to think the things that be good, and by His merciful guiding through Christ to perform the same: and by inspiration their mental powers were fitted and prepared to grasp, in their fulness and accuracy, the truths revealed ; and so qualified to communicate them to others. In fact, "*Holy* men of God spake as they were borne along by the Holy Ghost."*

Any definition of inspiration which in terms excludes the highest gift of the Holy Ghost,—and a gift of the Holy Ghost is the proper formal idea of inspiration, whether expressed by "being filled with the Holy Ghost," or "the Holy Ghost given unto us," or such like,—must be radically unsound.

To deny inspiration, in its primary sense, to such men as those "on whom the cloven tongues of fire rested, who were all filled with the Holy Ghost, and began to speak with other tongues as the Spirit gave them utterance," would, in every sense of the word, be unjustifiable.

---

* 2 Peter i. 21.

Now as in the popular definition, to which I have taken exception, the guidance to the outward act of speaking or writing, is not inspiration, so neither is it here. The gift of the Holy Ghost, here represented by their being "filled with the Holy Ghost," is a phrase unquestionably indicative of inspiration. This was an antecedent influence of the Spirit, and preparatory to the utterance in other tongues "of the wonderful works of God." The latter, in fact, was clearly a miraculous attestation and evidence of their inspiration, to the multitude of devout Jews then assembled for the festival at Jerusalem. Thus at the conclusion of St. Peter's address to Cornelius and his friends—the first-fruits of the Gentile Church—we read: "While Peter yet spake these words, the Holy Ghost fell on all them which heard the word. And they of the circumcision which believed were astonished, as many as came with Peter, because that on the Gentiles also was poured out the gift of the Holy Ghost. *For* they heard them speak with tongues, and magnify God."*

That there is a moral inspiration acting on the soul of man, to which the supreme faculty of conscience responds, St. Paul expressly states: "I say the truth in Christ, I lie not, my conscience also bearing me witness in the Holy Ghost."† In glowing terms the apostle appeals to his conscience, moved by the Spirit

---

* Acts x. 44—46. † Rom. ix. 1.

of God, how affectionately he yearned for the salvation of his brethren, his kinsmen in the flesh. For this inspiration we pray in the services of our Church; and it is the blessed heritage of all true believers, who "live by faith in the Son of God." Sanctification—the gift of the Holy Ghost—is appropriately designated, in the collect, inspiration, since in the language of Scripture the moral graces imparted are said to be the gift of the Holy Spirit. "The love of God is shed abroad in our hearts by the Holy Ghost, which is given unto us."* None can, on Scripture grounds, call in question the inspiration of the Gentile converts, spoken of by St. Peter: "God, who knoweth the hearts, bare them witness, giving them the Holy Ghost, even as He did unto us; and put no difference between us and them, purifying their hearts by faith."† And now, in the Christian Church, we only pray for the same blessing which the Spirit of God poured out on the multitudes of believing disciples in the days of the apostles. "And with great power gave the apostles witness of the resurrection of the Lord Jesus: and great grace was upon them all."‡

What the nature of this gracious influence of the Holy Spirit is, may be inferred from the antithesis to the character depicted by the proto-martyr Stephen in his Apology: "Ye stiff-necked and uncircumcised in heart and ears, ye do always resist the Holy Ghost.

---

* Rom. v. 5.   † Acts xv. 8, 9.   ‡ Acts iv. 33.

As your fathers did, so do ye." This is described by St. Paul as the character of the true Israelite: "He is a Jew who is one inwardly; and circumcision is that of the heart, in the spirit, and not in the letter; whose praise is not of men, but of God."* Being led by the Spirit, yielding to His motions, and having the love of God shed in his heart by the same Spirit, is, if there be any meaning in the word, a conception of inspiration, than which none is more genuinely true. And none is more orthodox. So our Church, in its Thirteenth Article, uses the words, "works done before the grace of Christ and inspiration of the Spirit are not pleasant to God."

Indeed, so true is this conception, and so likely therefore to recur uninvited to the mind of one who entertains a different idea of inspiration, that a late distinguished writer runs counter to Scripture itself, in asserting that the Tyrian prophets spoken of in the twenty-first chapter of the Acts, were not inspired, because, in fact, he thought that they wanted the elements of a genuine *moral* inspiration. Certain Tyrian prophets "said to Paul *through the Spirit* that he should not go up to Jerusalem." Dr. Lee thus comments on these words: "To them had been *revealed* what the Holy Ghost was witnessing in every city, namely, that bonds and afflictions awaited St. Paul in Jerusalem. These prophets, however, enjoyed

---

* Rom. ii. 29.

no inspiration: they adulterated the revelation they had received with human wishes and human feelings; and thus directly contradicted the will of God, which the guidance of the Spirit enabled St. Paul himself to understand. 'And now behold I go bound in the Spirit unto Jerusalem, not knowing the things that shall befall me there, save that the Holy Ghost witnesseth in every city, saying that bonds and afflictions abide me.'"

It is not easy to find a solution of the difficulty which this remarkable case of inspiration presents, on the commonly received notions concerning the nature of that influence. To concede inspiration to Balaam the prophet,—"who loved the wages of unrighteousness," and who advised the king of Moab to entice the Israelites to sin, by throwing a stumbling-block in their way,—and to refuse it to the Tyrian prophets, is unaccountable, on any other than an erroneous view of the nature of inspiration. For the precise scriptural formula descriptive of its manner and agency, is, "Thus saith the Holy Ghost,"* *i.e.,* *through* or *by* a human channel of communication. As " David himself said *by* the Holy Ghost,"† εἶπεν ἐν τῷ πνεύματι τῷ ἁγίῳ ; or, "certain Tyrian prophets "said to Paul, *through* the Spirit," ἔλεγον διὰ τοῦ πνεύματος.‡

Whatever explanation be advanced of the advice

---

* Acts xxi. 11. † Mark xii. 36. ‡ Acts xxi. 4.

given to the apostle—who felt himself "bound in the Spirit" to go to Jerusalem—by the Tyrian prophets, one thing is certain, that they were inspired. It is, in fact, a contradiction in terms, to say that a prophet, speaking through the Spirit, is not inspired. Nor is it conceivable that such an idea could be once entertained, were it not to support the foregone conclusion of the separability of inspiration from revelation.

Take what explanation you will (and three have been offered) of the manner in which this advice of the Tyrian prophets may be reconciled with St. Paul's felt obligation to visit Jerusalem, regardless of danger, all difficulties vanish and fade away in the light of the true scriptural distinction between inspiration and revelation, and in the light of the equally scriptural distinction of inspiration into intellectual and moral.

Here is a simple test by which can be judged the character of that view of inspiration which separates inspiration from revelation; making the latter the producing cause of the knowledge of Divine truth, and the former the director of its utterance. For although the Tyrian prophets are expressly—on the unquestionable authority of St. Luke—said to be inspired, yet because they directed St. Paul not to carry out the firm resolve of his own mind, they were not, it is alleged, inspired, since their directing utterance could not proceed from the Spirit of truth.

But if we accept the Pauline view of inspiration, and with the apostle distinguish also between moral and intellectual inspiration, we avoid this contradiction and inconsistency.

The Tyrian prophets were inspired that they might know the revelation presented to their minds, that bonds and afflictions awaited St. Paul at Jerusalem. The inspiration, illumining the revelation, gave them a certain knowledge of the future dangers which beset the path of their beloved friend, and truly "they spake that which they did know." And in like manner was Agabus inspired; and so understanding what was revealed to him, as a prophet both by symbolic act and word, predicted Paul's impending dangers.

The question now is, Did St. Paul visit Jerusalem on this occasion by revelation? and is this rightly inferred from Acts xx. 22—24, in his parting address to the elders at Miletus: "And now, behold, *I go bound in the spirit* to Jerusalem, not knowing the things that shall befall me there: save that the Holy Ghost witnesseth in every city, saying that bonds and affliction wait for me. But none of these things move me, neither count I my life dear unto myself, so that I might finish my course with joy, and the ministry which I have received of the Lord Jesus, to testify the gospel of the grace of God."

In matters of general interest to the Church, St. Paul had many revelations. By revelation he had visited Macedonia,* and for the furtherance of the Gospel he was by revelation directed to continue a considerable time at Corinth.† So by revelation had he at an earlier period come up to Jerusalem, when a question of vital importance to the propagation of Christianity among the Gentiles was by a solemn decree to be settled.‡ But here it is not said that he went to Jerusalem by revelation, though he felt constrained by a sense of duty to go. In things relating to his individual concerns, such as immunity from bodily danger, so far was he from being favoured with direct personal revelations, that, on the contrary, previous intimations were given of future hardships to be endured in the service of Christ. His ministerial career was in fact ushered in with the announcement, "I will show him how great things he must suffer for my name's sake."§ Such indeed was the destined lot of this soldier of the cross, and the lot of all the apostles of the suffering Saviour. Yet to them it was rather a matter of rejoicing; for they felt "that the trial of their faith being much more precious than of gold that perisheth, though it be tried with fire, might be found unto praise and honour and glory at the appearing of Jesus Christ."‖

Such feeling St. Peter very strongly impresses on the persecuted Christians whom he addresses in the

---

* Acts xvi. 9.   † Acts xviii. 9—11.
‡ Gal. ii. 2: ἀνέβην ἕκατὰ ἀποκάλυψιν.
§ Act ix. 16.   ‖ 1 Peter i. 6, 7.

consolatory words, "Beloved, think it not strange concerning the fiery trial, which is to try you, as though some strange thing had happened unto you: but rejoice inasmuch as ye are partakers of Christ's sufferings: that when His glory shall be revealed, ye may be glad also with exceeding joy."*

Animated by such hope, the apostle Paul could say, "Most gladly will I rather glory in my infirmities, that the power of Christ may rest upon me. Therefore I take pleasure in infirmities, in reproaches, in necessities, in persecutions, in distresses for Christ's sake: for when I am weak, then am I strong."†

While these servants of God, looking forward to the martyr's crown, patiently bore sufferings in their Master's service, the counsels of the Most High were being accomplished—and this too was to them a source of happiness—by the spread of Christianity; and the blood of the martyrs became the seed of the Church.

St. Paul does not say that, on this errand of mercy, he went to Jerusalem by revelation. On the contrary, the Holy Ghost, through many prophets, in particular Agabus, predicted and even specified what he should endure at Jerusalem; while to himself no such disclosure was made, for he avers that he knew not the things that should befall him there.

Archbishop Sumner's exposition is in point: "The

---

* 1 Peter iv. 12, 13. † Rom. xii. 10.

exact nature of his trials was not revealed to Paul. All that the *Holy Ghost witnessed* was what from the first he had been taught to expect. From the first he had been shown 'how great things he must suffer for Christ's sake.' It is mercy to man that a map of his wanderings is not laid before him. 'Sufficient unto the day is the evil thereof.' . . . This was Paul's support: he had a certain duty to fulfil, a certain course to follow; and he set out to meet the trials of every day in sure confidence of 'doing all things through Christ who strengthened him.' And this alone was his desire, that he might finish his course with joy."

What then does the apostle mean when he says, "And now, behold, I go *bound in the spirit* to Jerusalem, not knowing the things that shall befall me there—καὶ νῦν ἰδοὺ ἐγὼ δεδεμένος τῷ πνεύματι . . . ? "

Are we to suppose in this connexion that "the spirit" signifies the Holy Spirit, or the apostle's own spirit? Against the former several cogent reasons can be adduced, which are absolutely, in their combined force, decisive of the question.

1. The exegetical argument furnished by the context. This consists of two clauses. In the first occurs the phrase "bound in the spirit:" in the second the fuller form, "the Holy Ghost witnesseth." Now it is quite contrary to the genius of the language, and the established forms of construction in Greek, that if the τὸ πνεῦμα in the first clause, and the τὸ

πνεῦμα τὸ ἅγιον in the second, referred to the same Spirit, the shorter form should occur first.

2. On other missions of a similar kind, St. Paul expressly states that a revelation had divinely directed him. But here an inference is merely drawn from the words, "bound in the spirit," that such revelation had been vouchsafed to him. Not only the argument above is opposed to that interpretation, but the highest authorities—Rosenmüller and Middleton—explain the words differently, as expressing a fixed and decided resolve to accomplish a duty which, as a minister of Christ, he felt himself bound to fulfil.

3. The idea of a Divine revelation being given to the disciples of Tyre, and showing them that bonds and afflictions awaited Paul at Jerusalem, and still that "they enjoyed no inspiration," is both impossible and unscriptural. Impossible, since it is by inspiration that a revelation from God becomes intelligible: unscriptural, since St. Paul has declared, "We have received not the spirit of the world; but the Spirit which is of God (which latter influence on the human spirit is inspiration), that we might know the things that are freely given to us of God." It is indeed doubly unscriptural in this particular case, since St. Luke affirms positively that the warning voice of the Tyrian prophets was uttered "through the Spirit."

4. The consequences involved in the general principle, of which this is a particular instance, are

extremely perilous to the authority of the holy volume.

The principle that a direct personal revelation from God to an individual can be received and known to him without inspiration, and may therefore come to us as a message from heaven adulterated with the human wishes and feelings of the uninspired, is of portentous import. For, as in the case before us, it is alleged that the Tyrian prophets did not present the revelation which they had received from heaven; but that, so mixed up with their own wishes and feelings, as to render it quite another, namely, that Paul "should not go up to Jerusalem." And although Luke plainly and unreservedly asserts the accuracy and truth of the revelation communicated to these disciples, yet by inferences drawn from other passages in the Acts discredit is cast upon their representation.

Now it is scarcely possible to silence the obtrusive reflection that there may be other cases of a like kind —other revelations presented to persons without inspiration; and these mixed up with their own feelings and wishes, and yet presented as revelations from God. Suppose, then, that these were recorded by the sacred writers, as by Luke the case in question: What confidence can we have that the patriarchs and prophets have transmitted to us the pure unalloyed revelations of heaven? Or may they not be so mixed up with their own feelings and wishes, as to represent to us something very different from what God really revealed? Are we, then, to call in a verifying faculty in order that by collation with other parts of Scripture we may be enabled to select from the heterogeneous compound the Divine element which we can approve? Such is the doubt and alarming uncertainty which this principle would carry with it into every part of Scripture.

5. Cognate forms of expression occur in St. Paul's writings, having the sense here assigned to the phrase "bound in the spirit." The Greek verb συνέχω indicates the moral impelling power of duty, "The love of Christ constraineth us (συνέχει)"* So St. Luke speaking of St. Paul, in Acts xviii. 5, how, by a sense of duty, he was constrained to pursue a certain course of action, expresses it by συνείχετο τῷ πνεύματι.

It must, then, be admitted that these Tyrian prophets knew by the inspiration of the Holy Spirit the revelation presented to them. But whether we hold, with some, that the revelation was to them, as it was to others, simply a disclosure of the bonds and afflictions which awaited Paul; and that the words "he should not go up to Jerusalem" were added as their own advice; or that this too was really a part of the revelation, which therefore Paul should have obeyed as a command from heaven, especially when enforced by the additional prophecy of Agabus; the difficulty on either supposition is

---

* 2 Cor. v. 14. See also Philip. i. 23.

explicable, when the distinction between intellectual and moral inspiration is taken into account.

For a security against error in the knowledge of doctrine, and the knowledge of the future, had been promised by Christ to His apostles; and this implies that the teaching of the Holy Spirit is apprehended in the intellectual part of our nature. But this promise to the apostles, which guarantees an immunity from error to the word of God, as a faithful reflection of the teaching of the Divine Spirit, does not extend to the conduct of the morally inspired, even should they be apostles. True it is, the contingency of sinning under a watchful sense of duty, and a prayerful feeling of dependence on God, may be indefinitely diminished, at least so far as effectually to depose sin as a reigning power in the heart. Still there are sins of infirmity, and the purest among men are liable to be overtaken in a fault. Such was the case with David and Peter. Jesus Christ is the only sinless one.

Now the contrast between apostolic intellectual and apostolic moral inspiration exhibits itself strikingly in this respect.

The matters brought into correlation are error and sin. Of the latter you can say, "If any man sin, we have an advocate with the Father, Jesus Christ the righteous; and He is the propitiation for our sins." *

---

* 1 John ii. 1.

The former indignantly spurns any hypothesis of this kind: "If the apostles erred in writing the Scriptures,—in other words, if any Scripture err, we have the means of correcting it." This analogous form the Scriptures themselves sternly repel. For in reference to the revelation of God's will, the Divine command is, "Thou shalt not add to it nor take aught from it,"* and "the Scripture cannot be broken." †

Here, then, we arrive at a definite conclusion. On the undoubted authority of Scripture, which cannot be tampered with or altered, and on the testimony of St. Luke, we must say that the Tyrian prophets, under the inspiration of the Holy Spirit, delivered to St. Paul, either a warning "not to go up to Jerusalem," or a Divine communication, viz., that "bonds and afflictions awaited him at Jerusalem." In the latter case, the warning was from themselves, suggested no doubt by the revelation.

The warning was repeated by another prophet, Agabus, who came down from Judea to Tyre. Yet, under a strong sense of duty, Paul persistently refuses to yield to their urgent entreaties. Was St. Paul right or wrong in disobeying the warning voice of so many prophets? He may be right.

Doubtless, had he also received a direct revelation from heaven, as he had at other times, he would have

---

* Deut. xii. 32. † John x. 35.

considered himself obligated to yield to the friendly remonstrances of the Tyrian disciples, and of Agabus. But in the absence of this, his moral inspiration, and the sense of duty it imposed, would be likely to predominate over every menacing impediment which thwarted his fixed purpose, even to the loss of liberty and of life.

He might be wrong. For Agabus appears to have come down from Judea to Tyre, the bearer of a special message from heaven, to divert the apostle from this perilous journey.

What then? The grace of sanctification does not absolutely exempt God's free creatures from moral delinquency in the same manner, and to the same extent, as the gifts of personal inspiration and revelation—conformably to the Saviour's promise—hedged in and secured the apostles from error, in the knowledge of Divine truth, thereby conveyed to their minds.

If St. Peter was once deserving of St. Paul's rebuke for blameworthy conduct, is it not possible that St. Paul himself may be here in the fault?

Thus, on the principles laid down, taking either aspect of the question, whether St. Paul was right or wrong in continuing his journey to Jerusalem, we have an explanation of the difficulty.

So much, then, for the distinction between inspiration moral and intellectual, both of which, as being gifts of the Holy Spirit conferred on different parts of our mental constitution, are, on scriptural grounds, equally entitled to the designation of inspiration. No point is better established in theology than the relation of intellectual inspiration to revelation, which renders the knowledge communicated only possible; when the former, by enlightening and strengthening the cognitive powers of the mind, fits and prepares it for the intelligent reception of the Divine truths conveyed by revelation. Yet are the two kinds of inspiration, intellectual and moral, governed by different laws. For although you cannot separate intellectual inspiration from revelation, this form of inspiration, and the moral, are independent, have different spheres, and may not therefore coexist in the same person.

The most remarkable instance on record is that of Balaam. This highly gifted prophet, reprobated by St. Jude, St. Peter, and St. John as ambitious, avaricious, and in morals impure, was yet powerfully brought under the influence of a Divine afflatus. Although utterly devoid of the grace of sanctification, he possessed in an eminent degree intellectual inspiration, as a supernatural gift, opening his spiritual eyes, and enabling him to understand the special revelations with which the true God had favoured him. Such is by all admitted, and is evident from the narrative of Moses. Moreover, the sublime ode in which he portrays the future fortunes of Israel, is the utterance of the knowledge imparted to him by inspiration and revelation, and is strongly corroborative of the view here taken of the nature of inspiration: "And he took up his parable and said, Balaam the son of Beor hath said, and the man whose eyes are open hath said. He hath said who heard the words of God, and saw the vision of the Almighty, falling into a trance, but having his eyes open."

Submitting himself unreservedly to the Spirit's influence on the intellectual part of his nature, the more perfect knowledge thus acquired by him furnishes a proof of the potency of inspiration as an auxiliary to revelation.

The case of Caiaphas, who, lacking the grace of moral inspiration, was nevertheless intellectually inspired, and so enabled to utter a prophecy the full drift of which he did not clearly understand, has been already noticed.

In both kinds of inspiration the characteristic mark of all inspiration can be traced—*preparation.*

This has been considered at great length already in intellectual inspiration. The preparation in the case of moral inspiration (as touched upon in page 165) is in scriptural phraseology,—1. The cleansing of the heart (Psalm li. 10): "Create in me a clean heart, O God, and renew a right spirit within me." 2. "The strengthening with might by His Spirit in the inner man" (Eph. iii. 16).

Members of our Church must confess that this view of inspiration is the orthodox one; for in the most solemn sevrice of the Church, the Holy Communion, we pray to Almighty God, "Cleanse the thoughts of our hearts by the inspiration of thy Holy Spirit."

ii. After this full discussion, a few words will suffice to explain the nature and extent of secondary or Biblical inspiration.

Its nature is described as a compound process, the result and final outcome of which is the word of God. The Holy Spirit presents to the mind of the apostle or prophet a revelation in some form, fitted to suggest the conception of a Divine truth, which can be only spiritually discerned.

For this purpose the mind and heart are prepared by inspiration to grasp and receive the truth so presented. The combined operations of personal inspiration and revelation give an accurate knowledge of such truth; and this knowledge finds a faithful and spontaneous expression of the matter revealed to a person now fully master of the subject.

A person, moreover, so qualified and disposed by these gifts of the Divine Spirit, and thus "taught of God," utters words "which the Holy Ghost teacheth." In fact, he is in the position of Elihu, and is similarly moved. "I am full of matter: the Spirit within me, constraineth me. . . . . I will speak that I may be refreshed : I will open my lips and answer."*

---

* Jeremiah (chap. xx. 9) describes how the word as a burning fire in his heart found vent in expression.

Biblical inspiration is coextensive with the word of God. Hence the position that the Bible is not, but contains, the word of God, is untenable—a position unsupported by evidence, and savouring of impiety.

No such limitation is compatible with the promise on which its plenary inspiration is based; for our Lord unreservedly assured His apostles, who are the sacred writers or their instructors, that when the Paraclete was come, He would guide them into *all* the truth. Now the Holy Scriptures are "the words which the Holy Ghost teacheth" as the expression of that truth. Besides, St. Paul's formal exposition of the steps through which Divine truth finds a place in the written word, repudiates the idea of the holy book being a heterogeneous mixture of the fallible and merely human with the infallible and Divine.

Lastly, once open a door to a verifying faculty by which the human in the written word is to be discriminated from the Divine, and a faculty so varying among men will introduce its own uncertainty into the holy volume, and destroy its authority.

If with Tholuck it be held that the Scripture contains both "a kernel and a shell," errors may consist with 'truth in essentials. On this view it has been pertinently asked, Who is to be the judge of what essentials are, to say nothing of scriptures ambiguous even upon essentials?

Again, when it is said that "the Bible conveys to

mankind a revelation," and that "revelations were the prophetical announcements of the future and the peculiar doctrines of Christianity," limitations and restrictions as to revelation are hinted at, which prepare the way for the *à priori* method of investigating the nature of the inspiration of Holy Scripture.

The safe method, however, of proceeding, is to make no assumption whatever, but to tread in the steps of St. Paul : first, to consider a revelation presented to the writer ; next, to see how the mind is prepared by the Holy Spirit for the intelligent reception of that revelation ; then, to note how the conjoint spiritual moments of revelation and inspiration result in knowledge ; and, lastly, to mark how the writer, thus taught of God, expresses the knowledge so acquired, in words at once Divine and human.

Such, it is to be presumed, is the legitimate use of that which Dean Alford considers the true key of the whole inquiry.

The former method, on the other hand, refers at the outset to the expression or record, without analyzing the nature of that record, as it was taught by the Spirit of God to the inspired writer. This is the method of the theorists.

It is only on a wrong and hastily formed view of the subject—approvingly quoted by some—that Köppen fancies a certain mode of reasoning to be fallaciously employed. "In order," says this author, "to prove that the books of the Bible have been written under Divine inspiration, appeal is sometimes made to the extraordinary revelations which are here and there announced in the Bible: but this is plainly a false conclusion, and a weakness not to be concealed. Although God has revealed Himself to certain persons by means of a supernatural influence, the question, notwithstanding all this, still remains, How has the Divine influence exerted itself in the composition of the Bible?"

Revelations here and there announced!—who thus attempts to prove the inspiration of Holy Scripture? It would certainly be a weak and false conclusion, if any should argue in this manner. But it is not a fallacious mode of reasoning to conclude, from the mutually co-operating influences of particular revelations and inspiration, that the sacred writers, so taught of God (θεοδίδακτοι), were enabled to express accurately and faithfully the will of God in the written word.*

Still the great problem to be solved is well put by this German author; and it is this: "How has the Divine influence exerted itself in the composition of the Bible?"

---

* Thus Theodore of Mopsuestia, commenting on Hosea i., describes the power of recording or speaking the Divine disclosure as the result of the revelations having been thoroughly apprehended by the prophet :— Θείαν ἐνέργειαν κανταῦθα λέγει, καθ᾽ ἣν ἀποκάλυψις τῶν ἐσομένων ἐγένετο τῷ προφήτῃ, ἀφ᾽ ἧς περ αὐτῷ καὶ λέγειν καὶ μηνύειν τα ἐσόμενα δύναμις ὑπάρχεν.

It has been my endeavour to give a solution to the important question here proposed.

The Divine influence, according to St. Paul, thus exerts itself. 1. The Spirit of God presents revelations to the mind of the prophet or apostle. 2. He prepares the mind and heart by inspiration for the reception, intelligent and cordial, of these revelations. 3. From these two factors (revelation and inspiration) a knowledge clear and accurate of the truth revealed is formed in the mind. 4. So taught of God, the inspired apostle or prophet is enabled to express in representative words, faithfully and accurately, the matter revealed. Thus it would appear that, as perfect and complete *heaven-taught* knowledge finds a suitable and appropriate expression in words, the aim and purpose of the Spirit for that end was to impart full and accurate knowledge of the truth which He intends to reveal. In fact, St. Paul says, "We have *received the Spirit which is of God, that we might know* the things that are freely given to us of God."

Ancient writers, however confusedly they represent inspiration as the infusion of revelations, still, regarding it as an infusion, they steadily keep in view, as its aim, the impartation of religious knowledge. Thus Josephus, in his treatise *Cont. Apion.*, i. 7, distinctly states that "it was the prophets alone who had *learned by inspiration* from God facts the most remote and the most ancient; but that they described the events of their own time as they really occurred with perfect accuracy."*

Here are indicated two sources of the knowledge to which the prophets had attained: 1st, Divine inspiration as the equivalent of inbreathed revelation; and, 2nd, their own observation and experience. The historian does not say that they committed to writing either of these facts and events by inspiration, but that the former were learned (*i.e.*, became known) by inspiration; and merely, that the latter, as things well known, were written with accuracy; and so would the deep things of God, when revealed and fully understood by minds which inspiration had enlightened.

So too, at an earlier period, in a fragment of the high-priest Eleazer, addressed to Ptolemy Philadelphus, in the latter half of the third century before Christ, and preserved by Eusebius, the writer states how Moses had been equipped for his work by God through divinely imparted knowledge: ὑπο θεοῦ κατεσκευασμενος εἰς ἐπιγνωσιν τῶν ἁπάντων.

---

* ἀλλὰ μόνων τῶν προφητῶν τὰ μὲν ἀνώτατω καὶ τὰ παλαιώτατα κατα την επιπνοιαν την ἀπο' τοῦ Θεοῦ μαθόντων· τα ὃε καθ' αὐτοὺς ὡς ἐγένετο σαφῶς συγγραφόντων.

CHAPTER VII.

DIFFERENT MODES AND EXTENT OF INSPIRATION FURTHER CONSIDERED.*

ARE men of genius, poets, and philosophers, as such, inspired? Inspiration may find a faint counterpart in the natural man. The ψυχικος ἄνθρωπος has doubtless within him some basis or groundwork on which the Divine Spirit acts; and this, as an elementary principle of human nature, may exhibit certain dim traces of something akin to, or resembling, supernatural inspiration.

The Archbishop of Dublin, in his 'Synonyms of the New Testament,' has truly observed that the Spirit of God, indwelling and making His habitation with men, calls out an answering spirit in them. The ψυχίκος of Scripture is one for whom the ψυχὴ is the highest motive power of life and action, in whom the Πνεῦμα, as the organ of the Divine Πνεῦμα, is suppressed, dormant,—for the time as good as extinct: whom the operation of this Divine Spirit has never lifted into the region of spiritual things.

---

* The consideration of Inspiration in general conduces much to give precision to our ideas of the nature of Biblical inspiration.

Now it is not a matter of surprise, but what might be expected, that, since "the spirit of man is the candle of the Lord, searching all that is within him," or, as St. Paul asks, "What man knoweth the things of a man, save the spirit of man which is in him?" and since this Spirit, transformed by the energizing power of the Divine Spirit, can attain to the knowledge of things Divine, there is a point of contact between the two states of mind in which knowledge of things human and Divine, is acquired. In both the candle of the Lord is the enlightened instrument of knowledge; but in the natural man it burns dimly, and its light is unsteady and flickering in the atmosphere of the spiritual. Yet though faint, it exhibits some traces of latent light; and only needs to be resuscitated by the Spirit of Him "who is the true light, that enlighteneth every man that cometh into the world," in order to shine forth with undimmed lustre, as the fit organ of the Divine Spirit.

This influence of the Holy Spirit on the mind and heart of certain chosen servants of God, preparing them for the intelligent and cordial reception of Divine Truth, is the true scriptural idea of supernatural inspiration in its highest form.

But it is in the former sense only that inspiration can be predicated of men of genius, poets, and philosophers. Confining, however, the term to the supernatural operation of the Holy Spirit, as in this essay I have done, neither poets nor philosophers nor men of genius, as such, are inspired. It is another question, whether this limitation be in accordance with Holy Scripture. This is the point on which the propriety of such an application of the term turns. Now while it is affirmed in holy writ that "every good gift and every perfect gift cometh down from the Father of lights," it is not in these words implied that such gifts are supernaturally, and by a direct interposition of God, conferred on certain individuals who hitherto did not enjoy them. This only is intended, that, under the benign providence of the Most High, all natural endowments bestowed on man, which may be improved by culture, are, in their *origin* and in their capability of natural development, to be ascribed to the Author of his being. Men of genius, poets, and philosophers, move *as such* in the lower sphere of things human and mundane, or what the apostle calls "the things of a man." The "deep things of God"—of which even the Psalmist could say "such knowledge is too wonderful for me: it is high; I cannot attain unto it"—can be only spiritually discerned. Thus, what comes under the cognizance of prophets and apostles, is beyond the range of *their* vision who cannot know the things of the Spirit of God. And St. Jude states of natural men that they have not the Spirit ($\psi v \chi \iota \kappa o \grave{\iota}\ \pi v \epsilon \hat{v} \mu a\ \mu \grave{\eta}\ \check{\epsilon} \chi o v \tau \epsilon \varsigma$). Now, not to have the Spirit, is the negation of inspiration. Still if it be replied that in things human and mundane, especially in their relations to and in their bearings on the Divine, a more perfect knowledge may be supernaturally imparted by the Spirit's teaching: this is true, but it applies only to such persons as are competent to know things Divine. So in neither respect are poets and philosophers under the supernatural influence of the Spirit; or, in the language of St. Jude, they have not the Spirit. Nevertheless this faint semblance of inspiration—at most, a *quasi* inspiration, not obscurely throws light on the ever-recurring question, What is inspiration? For it indicates very clearly that inspiration is a power imparted by the Spirit of God to the human heart. For when the apostle says, "Neither have entered into the heart of man the things which God hath prepared for them that love Him," he distinctly states how the heart may be prepared to know these things—namely, by the impartation of a spiritual power: "Now we have received, not the spirit of the world, but the Spirit which is of God: that we might know the things that are freely given to us of God." The corresponding natural power is thus described by a great writer, whose bent of mind is to extend as far as possible the gift of inspiration. And yet, only in a very qualified sense does he venture to apply inspiration to men of genius, poets, and philosophers; and in doing so, fails to mark the line of demarcation which divides revelation from inspiration, making the latter the compound result of both, as preceding authors had generally set him the example.

Speaking of the creations of imagination, Mr. Robertson says, "Imagination is distinct from the mere dry faculty of reasoning. Imagination is creative—it is an immediate intuition: we call it popularly a *kind* of inspiration. Now imagination is a power of the heart,—great thoughts originate from a large heart. A man must have a heart, or he could never create."

It is a grand thing when in the stillness of the soul thought bursts into flame, and the intuitive vision comes like an inspiration; when breathing thoughts clothe themselves in burning words, winged as it were with lightning; or when a great law of the universe reveals itself to the mind of genius, and where all was darkness, his single word bids light be, and all is order where chaos and confusion were. Or when the truths of human nature shape themselves forth in the creative fancies of one like the million-minded poet, and you recognize the rare *power of heart* which sympathizes with, and can reproduce, all that is found in man."

It is this power of heart which fits the man of genius, the poet, and the philosopher to combine the materials presented to their imaginations into the wondrous creations which they are prepared to clothe in befitting forms of expression. It is this power of heart that is the analogue of Divine inspiration: while the materials on which it acts represent the revelations which, as supernatural presentations to the mind, the Spirit of God brings before the purged vision of prophet or apostle. Once more: the prayerful study, under the Spirit's teaching, of the lively oracles of God, that from its characteristic property of appealing to the hidden springs of feeling in the heart—finds a man in all the depths of his inner life, is dimly shadowed by the power which the lofty strains of poetry exercise on the mind of a reader. Thus Dryden, speaking of the creations of the poet's fancy, remarks, " Imaging is in itself the very height and life of poetry, which by a kind of enthusiasm, or extraordinary emotion of soul, makes it seem to us that we behold those things which the poet paints."

Let us try to classify the erroneous forms of inspiration, which, viewed in the light of Scripture, are false, or err in excess or defect. These may be reduced to three kinds:—

1. That which holds inspiration to be a guidance of the Holy Spirit to the unerring expression, oral or written, of Divine Truth.

2. That which still further limits inspiration solely to the field of Biblical composition.

3. That which, running into the opposite extreme, extends inspiration to all the higher endowments of the human mind, on the ground that every good gift and every perfect gift cometh down from the Father of Lights. In this point of view philosophers, poets, and skilled craftsmen, as such, are inspired, as well as prophets and apostles.

1. I have already examined, by the scriptural test, that form of inspiration, supposed to be a guidance to the external act of enunciating in words the *knowledge* which, according to St. Paul, the Holy Spirit had imparted to the inspired prophet or apostle through personal inspiration and revelation. And we have seen that if inspiration has had, previously to his enunciation, its effect as one of the factors in the production of that knowledge, any further guidance—if such be necessary—moving outwards, is not inspiration.

But as I have dwelt at great length on this vital element of the question, What is the nature of inspiration? suffice it now to add that the early Christian Fathers, who also claimed to be inspired, did not arrogate to themselves an infallibility on the score of what they had written on Christian doctrine, as being absolutely certain. And yet they freely conceded this prerogative to the inspired apostles of our Lord. While, on the other hand, without doubt or hesitation asserting their own inspiration in language that cannot be mistaken, they disclaim such an accurate and unfailing knowledge of the truth as St. Paul possessed. Thus Barnabas speaks merely as one of the members of the Church, and not as an infallible teacher, " non tanquam doctor, sed unus ex vobis."

Polycarp assures the Philippians. that he writes to them, not of his own choice, but as invited to do so ; " for neither I, nor any other like me, can fully attain to the wisdom of the blessed and glorious Paul, who at the time he was among you, in presence of the men then living, taught the word of God accurately and firmly." Hermes too, notwithstanding his claim to inspiration, has been refused by the writer of the Muratorian fragment a place among the certain and unerring teachers of the truth.

The Christian Fathers, therefore, could not have understood inspiration to mean an infallible guidance of the Holy Ghost to the utterance of Divine truth, as inspiration is now defined.

The only adequate, or even possible, explanation of this contradiction is to be traced to the untenable view of inspiration presented in the definition now employed, and to which we have taken exception as involving an idea entirely foreign to the nature of that influence. Admitting, indeed, that the apostles were so guided conformably to the promise of Christ, still this guidance is not inspiration, but the result of several Divine adminicles of which inspiration is one. The guidance, however, was really to *knowledge*, and inspiration was only one of the factors which produced it.

The question already discussed by me, opens once more on our view—What was the nature of those higher spiritual aids which constitute the special prerogative of the apostles of our Lord? Their minds and hearts were strengthened and illuminated by the Divine Spirit, and so prepared to receive and understand the truths disclosed to them by revelation.

This spiritual preparation is the true idea of this form of inspiration—the intellectual. Again, revelations were presented to their minds in any of the ways which Divine wisdom deemed best—either by visions or other representations, so as vividly to bring before and deeply impress on their intuitive consciousness the great truths of Christ's religion. Above all, the Spirit, by silent and yet to them unmistakable suggestions of the ideas of spiritual truths, revealed to them the mysteries of the kingdom of heaven. And doubtless, in this respect, no small part of the peculiarity of the abundant and Divine disclosures with which they were favoured, generally may have consisted; for it is to be noted that some of the Christian Fathers not only claim inspiration, but also profess to be the recipients of *express* revelations. The Pastor of Hermes abounds in such.

In the third place, accurate knowledge of the truths communicated resulted from the instruction imparted by this combined energetic action of preparation and presentation.

Lastly, the suitable expression of a knowledge, clear and accurate, divinely conveyed to their minds, spontaneously follows—*verba non invita sequuntur*—a matter fully mastered and fully comprehended, words which, as representing the ideas suggested by these spiritual appliances, are those "which the Holy Ghost teacheth."

But since this is a turning-point in a true answer to

the question, 'What is the nature of inspiration?' I must refer the reader to the fuller discussion of the matter in my first chapter.

2. The unauthorized limitation of inspiration, here confined to the oral or written expression of Divine truth, errs still further in defect when inspiration is contracted within the narrower bounds of the written form, or solely to the field of Biblical composition.

The application of the epithet 'God-inspired' to all Scripture, of itself suggests no theory as to the nature of inspiration. St. Paul, however, who uses the compound term 'God-inspired' in connection with Scripture, should be allowed to explain his own meaning. This he does most fully—and thus decides the point at issue—in the second chapter of 1st Corinthians.

The apostle by a regular synthesis ascends step by step from the revelations vouchsafed, and the preparation of the mind and heart of the sacred writers by inspiration, to the knowledge of the things freely given to them of God, and thence from the knowledge to its accurate expression " in words which the Holy Ghost teacheth." In fact, the Holy Ghost teaches them, by revelation and inspiration, the perfect knowledge of certain Divine truths; and the words being the representative signs of the ideas so formed in their minds by this Divine instructor, are truly the words which the Holy Ghost teacheth equally as if He uttered them Himself.* The words, although marked with the peculiarities of style and turn of thought of the several writers, yet bear on them the Divine image and superscription. For the Holy Spirit prepares such (as best suited to His purpose of communicating the truth in its different aspects to men of various temperaments and characters) by inspiration.

Now the Scripture coming to us by inspiration in this manner, and in words whose origin and generation are Divine, is 'God-inspired.' For this reason, the words are truly the utterances of the Divine Spirit; and as such the psalm of an inspired writer is quoted (Heb. iii. 7): "Wherefore, as saith the Holy Ghost." Now this, compared with the seventh verse of the fourth chapter, proves the inspiration of David, where it is stated that God speaketh in David, ἐν Δαβὶδ λέγων; or, as the formula is otherwise expressed in Matt. xxii. 43, Δαβὶδ ἐν πνεύματι . . . . καλεῖ. (See the foot-note, from Maimonides.) These general statements, however, positively affirming the utterances of the sacred writers to be spoken "in words which the Holy Ghost teacheth"—both sanctioned and appropriated by Him—say nothing about *the nature* of the inspiration of Holy Scripture

---

* The sense in which "the Holy Ghost speaketh the words" can be inferred also from Maimonides: "Daniel, the Psalms, etc., are all *written* by the Holy Spirit." Such idea of the most learned Jewish Doctors is very instructive on this point.—*More Nevochim*, ii. 45.

in the transition from the personal inspiration and revelation of the writers to the inspiration of the written word.

To obtain a clear view of this great question, we must study St. Paul's exhaustive exposition in the second chapter of 1st Corinthians. There the apostle, following a true constructive plan, ascends from revelation, presenting conceptions to the mind and heart, to inspiration, preparing them for the intelligent reception of that revelation, to accurate knowledge thence resulting, and finally to a faithful expression of the knowledge so imparted, in words "which the Holy Ghost teacheth" as the natural and spontaneous outcome of this preparatory instruction of the Divine Spirit.

Thus, again, we arrive at the correct view of Biblical inspiration held by our most eminent commentator of Scripture, namely, that "the men were inspired; the books are the result of that inspiration." For 'the Spirit in David,' or 'David in Spirit,' is the scriptural form for expressing David's inspiration; and the resulting words of David constitute that portion of the book of the Psalms.

It is only in this secondary or derivative sense that a book can be said to be 'God-inspired'—as coming to us through men directly inspired, and favoured with Divine revelations. For thus were they guided by the Spirit into an accurate knowledge of the truth, and fitted to express that knowledge in appropriate words.

Inspiration and revelation are gifts of the Divine Spirit by which the prophet or apostle is prepared to know and fully comprehend the truth presented. And as every charism of the Holy Ghost has its manifestation, that of the γνῶσις, communicated by these spiritual operations, has its manifestation to profit withal (1 Cor. xii. 7).

Neander correctly defines the nature of spiritual charisms "the predominant endowment of an individual, in which the power and energy of the Holy Spirit who animates them manifest themselves—the φανέρωσις τοῦ Πνεύματος peculiar to each." This manifestation of the γνῶσις—the joint effect of revelation and inspiration—is not inspiration, nor revelation, nor knowledge, but the verbal expression of that knowledge, which, as a permanent record, can profit the Church of God. Inspiration is, in fact, that supernatural aid by which the mind and heart are prepared to grasp and receive the revelation presented; and therefore powerfully contributes to the attainment of the knowledge imparted. The Holy Spirit guides the inspired into the knowledge of the truth. Here, in the inner sphere of consciousness, inspiration ends. If a further guidance to the external act of expressing this knowledge be needed, such is not inspiration,—at least according to the view of our Church clearly set forth in the collect for the Fifth Sunday after Easter.

I know no authority in the early Fathers for such

a limited use of the term 'inspiration' as is employed in the popularly received definition of Perrone, whom our divines generally follow.

When the name of Tertullian is offered as a proof of the position that 'Inspiratio'* "seems to have been used from the earliest times as expressive of the Holy Ghost's agency in the composition of Scripture," it may be replied that this Father, having quite another object in view, namely, to establish the authority of the apocryphal book of Enoch, is so far from throwing light on the nature of inspiration, that he advances a most dangerous and objectionable idea of inspiration. He holds that what relates to ourselves is not to be rejected, and what conduces to edify is divinely inspired.†

Tertullian merely quotes a passage of Scripture (2 Tim. iii. 16), which as the rendering of θεόπνευστος, implies only that the inspiration qualified men for certain outward acts, one being the writing of Divine truth,—but says nothing about the nature of that qualification. Tertullian is therefore no authority in support of the commonly received definition of inspiration.

We admit a 'superhuman guidance;' but in a defi-

---

* See 'Inspiration,' page 242, note ³. See page 86 for the view of Hagenbach.

† Quoting 2 Tim. iii. 16, Tertullian says, "Sed cum Enoch eadem Scriptura etiam de Domino prædicaret, a nobis quidem nihil omnino rejiciendum est quod pertineat ad nos. Et legimus omnem Scripturam ædificationi habilem, divinitus inspirari."—*De Cult. Fem.*, i. 3.

nition given to explain—as every definition must—the nature of the thing defined, to hide the actuating energy of the Holy Spirit under the veil of the negative phrase "in whatever degree or manner it may have been exercised," excludes this from the *rôle* of a definition. It is moreover as unscriptural as it is illogical. For St. Paul distinctly affords the information here suppressed, and plainly states that the guidance was to knowledge, and through revelation and inspiration; and adds that the utterance of that knowledge was the result of this teaching of the Divine Spirit.

3. If, on scriptural grounds, the idea of supernatural inspiration cannot apply to, or be limited by, the contracted bounds of a spiritual guidance to the unerring expression—oral or written—of Divine truth, or by the still narrower bounds of its written expression, on the same grounds, an undue extension of inspiration is liable to objection. This system errs in excess, as the two former erred in defect. Running into the opposite extreme, it extends inspiration to all the higher endowments of the human mind. In this point of view, philosophers, poets, and skilled craftsmen, *as such*, are inspired.

Two men of rare ability, Mr. Robertson and Mr. Swainson, take the side of those who are for extending the term 'inspiration' over a field much larger than in our purview had been contemplated.

"The Bible," says Mr. Robertson, "refers the inspiration of the poet, of the prophet, of the worker in cunning workmanship, to God. It makes no mention of our modern distinction between that inspiration enjoyed by the sacred writers, and that enjoyed by ordinary men, except so far as the use is concerned. God's prophets glorified Him. The wicked prophets glorified themselves; but their inspiration was real, and these Divine powers were perverted."

Now if Mr. Robertson hold the common idea of such extenders of the proper import of inspiration, his words imply that every true-born poet is inspired of God. This, we have seen, is scarcely consistent with what he says elsewhere where he designates it 'a *kind* of inspiration,' 'something like inspiration.' But if his meaning be, that the ordinary men for whom he claims the same inspiration as that enjoyed by the sacred writers, as such, must be spiritually minded—for he rightly holds that revelations of Divine truth would be unintelligible to the natural man—he breaks down the barrier that separates ordinary inspiration from apostolic inspiration, commingling too in one total effect revelation and inspiration.

These are the remarkable utterances of Robertson: "According to fixed laws of the spiritual world, obedient love has certain determined results." "Love God, and He will dwell with you: obey God, and He will reveal the truths of His deepest teaching to your soul. Not *perhaps*,—as surely as the laws of the spiritual world are irreversible, are these things prepared for obedient love: an inspiration as true, as real, and as certain as that which ever prophet reached, is yours, if you will."

The Scriptures, notwithstanding, undoubtedly make a broad distinction between the knowledge imparted to apostles and ordinary believers, which necessarily implies a corresponding distinction between the gifts of inspiration and revelation vouchsafed respectively to each.

In St. John xvi. 13, compared with xiv. 26, our Lord promised to His apostles *peculiar* gifts, in these words: "Howbeit when He, the Spirit of truth, is come, He will guide you into all the truth: for He shall not speak of Himself; but whatsoever He shall hear, that shall He speak: and He will show you things to come." "But the Comforter, which is the Holy Ghost, whom the Father will send in my name, He shall teach you all things, and bring all things to your remembrance, whatsoever I have said unto you."

From these decisive passages, very evident is it that *this particular* promise of the Holy Spirit can apply only to the apostles, since it is only to their remembrance that the Lord Jesus could bring those things which He had said to them. Moreover, the words "He will show you things to come," cannot apply to ordinary believers; since they do not claim or expect the gift of prophecy, however richly endued they may be with sanctifying grace.

Lastly, if it be affirmed that there is no real distinction of different kinds of *intellectual* inspiration, (for Robertson is dealing with such,) but only one kind belonging to the different persons inspired, it is enough to reply that prophet, poet, skilled artificer, cannot be considered in juxtaposition as distinct subjects of one inspiration. For the prophet, as such, is *supernaturally* inspired; whereas poets, and skilled workmen in cunning workmanship, are not of necessity supernaturally inspired. Judging from his great natural endowments, Saul of Tarsus may have been an accomplished and first-rate tent-maker; yet who, on that account, would say that he was inspired? On the other hand, Bezaleel and Aholiab, exercising a handicraft of the same kind, were subjects of Divine inspiration. Bezaleel and Aholiab were specially taught by the Holy Spirit to meet the urgent requirements of a particular emergency; otherwise, however great their skill, it would not have been said of them that they were inspired, or "filled with the Spirit of God."

The creative genius of the poet is also a natural endowment, and in Scripture this is not denominated a supernatural gift of God.

Mr. Robertson, indeed, in extending inspiration to its utmost limits, yet restricts the highest efforts of the poet and philosopher to the lower faculties, or those of the natural man. "All this is nothing more than the material man can achieve. The most ethereal fancies were shaped by a mind that could read the life of Christ and then blaspheme the Adorable. The highest astronomer of this age, before whose clear eye creation lay revealed in all its perfect order, was one whose spirit refused to recognize the Cause of causes. The mighty heart of genius had failed to reach the things which God imparts to a humble spirit."

Mr. Robertson's extension of prophetic inspiration and revelation to true believers in general, is however the most singularly remarkable part of his system. This is his view. The humble and spiritually minded Christian, besides enjoying the blessing of sanctifying grace, is open to receive from God, on the condition of sincere love and filial obedience, "a *revelation* of the *truths of His deepest teaching*—an inspiration as true, as real, and as certain as that which ever prophet or apostle reached." That this, however, is not the legitimate inference deducible from the premises supplied by the promised aids of the Spirit, as expressed by the Redeemer Himself, has, I submit, been proved.

The view of Robertson, which savours of the principles of the mystic theology, ignores the peculiarly pre-eminent knowledge of Divine truth, imparted by the Holy Spirit, through revelation and inspiration, to the apostles of Christ, according to the promise of unfailing certainty vouchsafed to them. A prerogative this, affirmed in the strongest terms in the Scriptures themselves. Thus St. Jude (ver. 17) exhorts Christian believers to beware of false teachers, and "remember the words which were spoken before by the apostles of our Lord Jesus Christ." In like manner, St. Peter stirs up the mind of the disciples of Christ, "that ye may be mindful of the words spoken before by the holy prophets, and of the commandment of us the apostles of the Lord and Saviour" (2 Peter iii. 2), in order to guard them against the Gnostic corruptions of the truth. For to protect their "pure minds," not yet contaminated by the heresies even then beginning to appear, the apostle Peter advises them not to depend on their own subjective ideas, as if these were necessarily revelations from God; but rather to trust to the words in which the true revelations presented to the inspired prophets and apostles are combined.

Mr. Swainson, who has very clearly shown the untenable position of those who limit inspiration to the power by which the writers of the Old Testament and the New were directed by the Holy Spirit in the composition of the books which bear their names, also extends the use of the term to an extreme length—much beyond the bounds to which, on scriptural grounds, in my humble opinion, it should be confined.

Although I object to this extension, I am bound to do this excellent writer the justice to say that, according to my judgment, no author of our day has so distinctly drawn the true line of demarcation which separates the inspiration of the apostles from that of every other class of persons to which this term has been applied.

His view rests on these words of the apostle Paul: "The manifestation of the Spirit is given to every man to profit withal. For to one is given by the Spirit the word of wisdom; to another the word of knowledge by the same Spirit; to another faith by the same Spirit; to another the gifts of healing by the same Spirit; to another the working of miracles; to another prophecy; to another discerning of spirits; to another divers kinds of tongues; to another the interpretation of tongues: but all these worketh that one and the selfsame Spirit, dividing to every man severally as He wills."

By a wonderful regularity, exhibited in the criminal statistics of every nation, man appears to be held in bondage by sin. And this might be expected from the explicit statements of Holy Scripture concerning the fallen condition of our race. Now over against this uniformity in the statistics of crime from year to year in every large community, there is set an equal regularity in the number of those who, by God's grace, are fitted to fill worthily offices of usefulness and trust for the preservation and well-being of the social fabric of that community.

The law which governs this general uniformity is not an iron necessity, but an unchanging ordinance of the unchangeable God. This law finds an echo in the principles which the Sovereign Creator has infixed deeply in the human heart. The social affections and rational self-love combine to prompt men who study their own interests to promote the well-being of the community to which they belong. But foreseeing danger to the state from the freedom of man's will, which may, by reason of its nature, verge to licentiousness, and often does, they impose on all the members of their society restraints, in order to control and keep within bounds the evil passions of such as blindly seek their own advantage in the detriment of the state.

Thus the ordinance by which rulers are placed over all, originate in, and spring out of, the very principles planted by God in the hearts of men. And so it is that "there is no power but of God," and that the apostle enjoins, "Let every soul be subject unto the higher powers" (Rom. xiii. 1); for "the powers that be are ordained of God."

Such a Divine institution, having for its end the safety of life and property, and the repression and correction of crime, and acting on this uniform principle, is truly an unchangeable ordinance of God. But administered by men, and on men, it encounters some disorder and disturbance from the occasional abuse of human liberty. On the other hand, the Divine ordinance which impressed on the heavenly bodies the laws that govern their motions, is entirely free from human interference. Accordingly, while the latter motions are susceptible of an exact mathematical determination at any given time, the natural perturbations correcting themselves in cycles of vast duration, (and this too is exhibited in the solution of the problem,) the former embracing in their sphere the actions, good and bad, of God's free creatures, cannot be subjected to the rules of any accurate calculation; nor can the disturbances introduced by the exercise of human liberty find a place in it. So, however remarkable the regularity of results in the statistics referred to, perfect exactness never arises, and is not to be expected.

Without interfering with man's responsibility, by a Divine ordinance such as this, and through the ordinary dispensations of an overruling Providence, individuals are fitted for situations in life to benefit society withal.

In every age of the world, under this benign economy, congruous means were provided to prepare and discipline men for the duties which they owe to their country, and to society at large. Thus a supply of suitable agents for this necessary work has been commensurate with the demand.

Nevertheless I cannot, with the learned author, extend the term 'inspiration' to the influences of that benevolent economy under which men generally were educated and trained to fill the parts assigned to them by Providence, in every well-constituted society even of the heathen world. Nor in Christian communities can the term be applied with propriety to men of genius such as Bacon and Laplace, of whom one first opened to the view of mankind the true method of discovering the secrets of nature; the other traced the laws which govern the movements of the great bodies circulating in the infinitude of space. Their range of thought was immense, and their powers of intellect almost superhuman; yet what says the Scripture of such wisdom? From it are we to affirm that men of genius are inspired by God? "We speak not in words which man's wisdom teacheth." "By wisdom the world knew not God." "God had made foolish the wisdom of this world." "We speak wisdom among them that are perfect: yet not the wisdom of this world."

This earthly wisdom cometh not from above: it is not, when alone, even compatible with the state of mind and heart which the Holy Spirit directs and rules. St. Paul's judgment is expressed on this subject in 2 Cor. i. 12: "Our rejoicing is this, the testimony of our conscience, that in simplicity and godly sincerity, not with *fleshly wisdom*, but by the grace of God, we have had our conversation in the world, and more abundantly to you-ward."

God, whose benign providence educes good out of evil, wills that men, whose free agency often leads them astray, should be under authority. All cannot govern, nor, ungoverned, be left to follow their own ways, according to the bent of their inclinations: for this would produce the total disruption of society. Hence, by a Divine institution, "The powers that be are ordained of God." "For there is no power but of God," and to resist them "is to resist the ordinance of God."

It is, however, to be observed that, in another sense, these powers are the ordinance of man. So St. Peter exhorts, "Submit yourselves to every ordinance of man, for the Lord's sake: whether it be to the king as supreme, or unto governors as unto them that are sent by Him for the punishment of evil-doers, and for the praise of them that do well. For so it is the will of God, that with well-doing ye may put to silence the ignorance of foolish men; as free, and not using your liberty as a cloke of maliciousness, but as the servants of God."

Individually, governors are appointed by men, and are a human creation, $\dot{\alpha}\nu\theta\rho\omega\pi\dot{\iota}\nu\eta$ $\kappa\tau\dot{\iota}\sigma\iota\varsigma$; yet as it is God's arrangement that men for their own welfare should be under authority, such is rightly denominated an ordinance of God not to be abused by Christian liberty, as if it were said, 'We will shake off all human rule, and obey God alone.' Thus although by mutual contract two persons become husband and wife, still matrimony is God's ordinance. In like manner, in social contracts where one governs and others obey, the general contract and covenant which bind the parties comes from God, the fountain of power.

Now this all-embracing Providence appearing in

the uniformity of results among the multiform diversities of human character, is no proof—as has been inferred from 1 Cor. xii. 11, by some eminent authors —of the direct influence of the Divine Spirit on the hearts of individuals, few or many, which constitute the communities into which mankind is divided. For the apostle opens this chapter by excluding from this special blessing the peoples of heathendom, however wisely governed, who did not acknowledge Jesus to be the Lord. Such, too, is St. John's test for trying spirits whether they be of God (1 John iv. 1).

The truth is, St. Paul in 1 Cor. xii. is only referring to the varieties of spiritual gifts required for the edification and progress of the infant Church. Hence it was that the Holy Spirit endowed the ministers of the early Church with many qualifications "given to every man to profit withal." And what has been advanced above about government and its implied authority being God's ordinance, is an answer to the assertion—at least too vague—that "the operations of the Spirit are not confined to the members of the living body of His Son." For still it may be asked, what operations?

With regard to the extension of inspiration to other things than matters of religion, the only question worth considering is this: 'Ought this term to be applied to every case in which the operations of the Holy Spirit are in any way concerned?'

The Scripture certainly justifies—nay, expressly

authorizes—its application to all cases in which the Spirit of God *supernaturally* acts on the mind and heart, for the purpose of imparting some gift which the individual had not by nature, nor acquired by the exercise of his natural talents, however aided they may have been by human instruction.

Such talents and such instruction, with their happy results, are the gift conferred by a Divine ordinance of Him "from whom every good gift and every perfect gift cometh down." These, in their origin, descend from the Father of Lights on the children of men, whom He had created in His own image. But in their growth and progress they exhibit no traces of that direct and immediate operation properly called inspiration.

To what, then, in Scripture terminology, are we authorized to apply inspiration?

1. To the direct influence of the Spirit supernaturally exerted for the purpose of communicating the knowledge of religious truth to chosen servants of God, such as the prophets and apostles of our Lord.

2. To the supernatural illumination and strengthening of the intellectual and moral powers of believers, so as to enable them to form a right judgment concerning the truths of religion, and, overcoming their prejudices, to dispose their minds and hearts to accept the truths of the Gospel. Such was the case with the disciples on the way to Emmaus, when Christ opened their hearts.

3. To the sanctification of the hearts and lives of Christians by the supernatural operation of the Holy Ghost, which is the practical aspect of inspiration.

4. To any supernatural influence of the Divine Spirit, by which men previously unfit for any particular office are directly qualified for the work and duties of the same. Thus Bezaleel and Aholiab were suddenly transformed into skilled artisans for executing the works of the tabernacle (Exod. xxxi.)

As to the inspiration claimed for poets and men of genius,—Newton, Bacon, Milton, Shakspeare, and the rest,—two considerations seem to be decisive of the point at issue.

1. The materials from which their ideas were formed were the very objects of sense, and of conception, and of imagination, which were *not* "the things of the Spirit of God," but on which, however, their natural faculties being exercised, produced the extraordinary works of science, or of art, or of imagination which illustrate the native powers conferred in some cases by the great Creator on the human mind.

Now these results, both because they are truly marvellous and beyond the reach of ordinary mortals, have excited, to the highest pitch, the admiration of mankind. They have, therefore, by a natural apotheosis of the mental gift of such favoured persons, put down rare endowments of this kind to the account of inspiration. But as their thoughts are not engaged about "the things of the Spirit of God," which "the natural man receiveth not," these thoughts are not suggested by the Holy Spirit, nor is their mind prepared by His sacred influence for the reception of the material or natural truths in which man's wisdom consists.

If then the view which I have taken of inspiration as a preparation for the reception of Divine truths be correct, neither philosophers, nor poets, nor men of genius, as such, are inspired.

2. Different powers were called into requisition.

By the eye, the ear, and the heart—the seat of conception and imagination—the naturally gifted derive from the phenomena of the material world all the knowledge they possess. But the prophets and the apostles, endued with spiritual senses, could perceive and comprehend "the things of the Spirit of God." They could grasp the spiritual truths by the inner senses of a mind and heart prepared by inspiration. "Eye hath not seen nor ear heard, neither have entered into the heart of man the things which God hath prepared for them that love Him."

This preparation is only needed for the distinct perception of "the deep things of God;" while the inlets of knowledge, through the senses, conception, and imagination, are absolutely required, where inspiration is not vouchsafed. If any one wish to call the power of genius, of philosophy, and of poetry, as such, inspiration, he may do so. It is, however, something entirely diverse from supernatural inspiration, of which we have been considering the nature in this essay. A natural inspiration of this kind—and it is even questionable whether such is a proper use of the term—has nothing in common with that which, as a supernatural actuating energy of the Holy Spirit, is in Scripture phraseology designated inspiration.

Mr. Swainson has shown that the inference from the fact of it being one and the same Spirit who administers the diversities of gifts is not legitimate, when it is asserted that "it is one and the same Divine inspiration which imparteth goodness to any and to all objects, however various those objects may be." For if there be any meaning in 'inspiration,' it is the infusion of some gift of the Spirit of God into the human spirit. Now if the gifts be different, as stated (1 Cor. xii.) in Scripture, the inspiration is not the same. The Spirit is one. But the different results produced in different beings—the word of wisdom and of knowledge, faith, prophecy—are produced by a different *action* of that one Spirit; and if the action is different, the inspiring, the *inspiratio*, the breathing into the minds of the persons inspired, is different too.

The Bible—the recorded result of Divine inspiration, illumining God's revelation to mankind—is Divine in its origin and in its subject-matter. The results of the natural gifts of Shakspeare, Milton, Bacon, and Newton, were human in both. Moreover, the point here is not the goodness imparted, but the power given, whether reference be made to the apostles or men of genius. It was, as Mr. Swainson remarks, " power that the apostles received, power that was given to Milton and Shakspeare." And yet, strange to say, he accepts the very vague and, from its vagueness, intangible definition of Mr. Macnaught: " Inspiration is that action of the Divine Spirit by which all that is good within us is originated and sustained." I close this chapter with the pertinent remarks of an acute writer, already quoted, in answer to this extension of inspiration, also advanced by Mr. Maurice,—remarks, be it observed, in unison with some of the utterances of Mr. Swainson himself: " I should reply that man is not so fallen that he has not in him 'some rays of his original brightness,' many mental powers, and also some moral affections, some love of virtue, some detestation of some vices; and that these may operate provided there be no strong counter-influence of temptation and pressure of opposing circumstances, and sometimes even when there are. There is therefore no need whatever to have recourse to the groundless hypothesis that all intellect and all kinds of noble actions spring from the Spirit of God."

CHAPTER VIII.

PROGRESS TOWARDS A SOUNDER AND MORE SCRIPTURAL VIEW OF INSPIRATION.

THE limitation of the term 'inspiration' (as it is now popularly used) to the special aid and direction of the Holy Spirit, for enabling the sacred writers accurately to express, orally or in writing, the truths communicated to them by personal inspiration and revelation, finds no support in Scripture. Neither is it sanctioned by the early Fathers, nor by the records of our own Church. "Such a limitation of the Spirit's influence, such a limitation of the use of inspiration," it has been truly remarked by a very distinguished author, "was unheard of in the times of the apostles; it was unheard of in the periods which succeeded them; it was unheard of until the end of the seventeenth century." At that time, A.D. 1689, in consequence of the sentiments of the Society of Friends, a proposal was made by the Royal Commissioners, who had been appointed to revise the Liturgy, to exclude the term 'inspiration' in the two places where it occurs in our Prayer Book. It was proposed in the collect for the Communion to change inspiration into operation; and in the collect for the Fifth Sunday after Easter, to substitute a new collect, from which the word inspiration should be omitted.

Not only does our Liturgy discountenance, but our Thirteenth Article lends no support to the limitation then proposed, and now acted upon, in the commonly received definition of inspiration. But so long as the book of Job shall be esteemed Holy Scripture, the text " There is a Spirit in man, and the inspiration of the Almighty giveth them understanding,"—in which not only the Vulgate, but the much older *versio Itala*, renders the Hebrew word *nishmath*, 'inspiratio,'—remains a standing protest that such limitation is warranted neither by Scripture nor by antiquity.

What, it may be asked, has produced the confusions and inconsistencies which have so often been pointed out in learned treatises on the subject of inspiration, but the wrong idea of its nature, presented in the definition now popularly received and borrowed from an old division in the dogmatic theology of Rome? For this idea formally, and by the very meaning of the terms employed, excludes its extension to other manifestations of the Spirit's operations on the mind of man. And such exclusion, as we have seen, has the sanction neither of Scripture nor of antiquity. But I have objected on the further ground that, even in this limited sense, the popular definition does not give a true idea of the nature of the inspiration of

Holy Scripture, such as is presented to us by St. Paul in the second chapter of 1st Corinthians. It suppresses, or rather ignores, the Pauline synthesis, viz.,

1. Revelation by the Holy Spirit of the deep things of God.
2. Personal inspiration as a necessary preparatory qualification, for
3. Understanding the revelations vouchsafed.
4. Knowledge clear and accurate of the revelation now fully understood.
5. Expression of that knowledge in words which through these means "the Holy Ghost teacheth."

There has been no lack of dogmatic teaching among the early Christian Fathers on the inspiration of Holy Scripture, considered as *a fact*. But on the deeper question touching the nature of this sacred influence, in consequence of the total neglect of noting the respective places assigned by St. Paul to personal inspiration and revelation, for the guidance of the apostles to a certain and definite *knowledge* of Divine truth, there is almost a complete blank in their voluminous writings, if we except a single reference given (without any steady persistence in this true and scriptural view) by Origen,* and which I bring forward in Chapter IX. of this essay. For it is to be carefully observed that the question concerning the

---

* Orig., 'Cont. Cels.,' lib. vii., c. iv.

nature of inspiration of the sacred Scriptures is not to be identified with that other question of fact—whether these Scriptures are inspired?

As to the latter—the question of fact—a painful reflection sometimes, at first blush, disturbs the mind, that in making a selection of the writings of which the holy volume is composed, many must have been omitted of equal authority with those chosen. This volume, consisting of several books written by many authors, and at times widely separated, has been considered as one organized whole. The conception, on the ground of the self-consistency of truth, has indeed much to recommend it; yet sometimes it has been put forward in an objectionable form.

A selection of certain books was made to the exclusion of others; and it has been assumed that those not taken into the canon "were regarded as fallible and human."*

Let us then revert for a moment to the appropriate idea by which the Bible, as an organized whole, has been illustrated. It has been compared to a grand edifice, constructed by the Divine Architect, of the choicest and most beautiful materials, joined together and fitted in perfect order. Now in rearing such a structure, suitable materials are to the God of all the earth at hand in richest profusion. We have no grounds for saying that the only good stones are

---

* Dr. Lee's 'Inspiration of Holy Scripture,' page 43.

those which shall be used by the wise Master-builder. As little reason have we for dogmatizing on the subject, by the assertion that the primitive Church, in forming the canon, had not omitted a single genuine composition of the inspired servants of God bearing the stamp of Divine authority, as that the only good acts of the Lord Jesus were selected out of all that the Redeemer had done, during His brief sojourn in the flesh among men. In reference to these, St. John's words imply that all Christ's marvellous acts (and all were good) need not be committed to writing, but that a few, selected by the evangelist, suffice for the Christian's faith. "These are written that ye might believe that Jesus is the Christ, the Son of God; and that, believing, ye might have life."

All we are justified in saying is that the most suitable for the purpose, under the providential care of the Spirit, were chosen, and these had their proper places assigned to them; and in the language of an ancient Father of the Church, "nihil otiosum," nothing was inserted that did not conduce to the main design, and nothing further than was necessary.

The best critics generally agree in the opinion that several books of the New Testament, written by the apostles of our Lord, have been lost, as there undoubtedly have been more than one of the Old, composed by the inspired prophets of God, and quoted in the canonical Scriptures, as of equal authority, which have not escaped the wreck of time.

It is indeed a gratuitous assertion to maintain that such were not inspired, though written by inspired prophets and apostles, in order to prop up a particular hypothesis. If, for example, it be accepted, with some commentators, as matter of fact, that the gentle and loving apostle John "wrote unto the Church" (3 John ix.) an epistle which has not been admitted into the canon, and St. Paul several which shared the same fate, on what principle has the primitive Church excluded them? Is it because these epistles were uninspired? or is it—if no doubt existed as to their being genuine—because, though inspired, the canon was deemed to be complete without them?

In the present state of this vexed question, few will hesitate to reject the guess of Augustine that such epistles might have been the fruits of "historic diligence," not of inspiration: a guess which, extended to the letters of the apostles of our Lord, whether addressed to churches or individuals, sounds somewhat incongruous.

The longer I have studied how the meshes of the net, by which this intricate subject is surrounded, have ensnared and entangled men, both in times past and in our own day, the more I am convinced that the greater part of the perplexities which all complain of have arisen from one or more of the following causes:—

1. A mistaken idea of the nature of inspiration as something *objectively* infused into the mind. In truth,

an objective presentation is the discriminating characteristic of revelation; whereas inspiration is a purely subjective influence.

2. The technical limitation of inspiration to the enunciation, oral or written, of the word of God.

3. A confusion of inspiration with revelation, by ascribing to the former suggestions of the Holy Spirit, which really appertain to the latter.

4. A mistaken notion that revelation *per se* gives knowledge, involving a wrong view of the true and proper function of inspiration.

5. The assumption of the written word as the starting-point of inquiry, and *prejudging* what is necessary in order to establish its unerring truth. Instead of such hypothetical reasoning, we should make no assumption whatsoever, but follow out to its conclusion the luminous synthesis of St. Paul which I have already fully submitted to the reader.

By steadily keeping these principles in view, the inconsistencies and contradictions, which are blemishes in the elaborate treatises that have appeared in recent times on the important question of the inspiration of Holy Scripture, would have been avoided.

Surely in ancient times there must have been some reason why the Fathers, who indulged in speculation, and who really in this respect did not overlook inspiration, considered as a fact, should have said little or nothing concerning its nature. One may naturally ask oneself, how it happens that modern authors, who follow Perrone's definition, are not able, in confirmation of this view, to adduce any of the great names which shed a lustre on the Church during long centuries whether of light, or gloom, or darkness? Or it may be asked, what was the use of collecting an enormous mass of Patristic extracts, if they cannot cull out of them some passages in support of this view of inspiration?

The only tangible passages really bearing on the question of the nature of inspiration are, 1, a reference by Melchior Cano to one in Basil, of which this Roman theologian gives his own interpretation, but which on examination will be found to support rather than oppose the Pauline view. This view I have taken pains to explain fully. The reference by Cano I give in the subjoined note.* 2, one in Origen.

In the former, it will be seen how Cano admits, 1. That the sacred writers had a clear knowledge imparted to them (*cognosebant*) by the Holy Spirit. Now St. Paul holds that it is by inspiration this knowledge was acquired. 2. He admits that it is

---

* Quæ sacri auctores scripsere, hæc in duplici sunt differentiâ. Quædam, quæ supernaturali solum revelatione cognoscebant : et ea Basilius tradit a Spiritû Sancto esse. Alia vero naturali cognitione tenebant, quæ scilicet aut oculis viderant, aut manibus attrectaverant. Atque hæc quidem supernaturali lumine et *expressâ* revelatione, ut scriberentur, non egebant. Sed egebant tamen Spiritus Sancti præsentiâ et auxilio peculiari, ut licet humana essent, et naturæ ratione cognita, divinitus tamen sine ullo errore scriberentur. Hæc vero illa sunt, quæ juxta Basilium, Paulus et Prophetæ de suo loquebantur.—*De locis Theolog.*, lib. ii., c. xviii.

only *express* revelations, which are not required in things naturally cognizable. Yet in that peculiar presence and direction of the spirit *suggestive* revelations are needed. So that inspiration is called into exercise in order to prepare the minds and hearts of the sacred writers for the clear and full knowledge of things presented, whether by express or suggestive revelations. In other words, conformably to the Pauline idea, inspiration is the gift of the Holy Ghost, which enabled the writers to receive, and thoroughly understand, the things brought before their mental vision in their proper connection and order. The passage in Origen, which holds the view I have given of inspiration, I reserve for Chapter IX. of this essay.

So here, again, is seen how impossible it is to prevent the true scriptural idea of inspiration from making itself felt, however theologians may try to exclude it as an unwelcome intruder. You may expel nature by force, yet she ever returns to assert her rights.

It affords me great pleasure to quote from Dr. Lee's treatise an admirable passage, in which he clearly sets forth the true nature and province of inspiration, the only regret being that he did not begin with, and steadily adhere to, this view:—

"The prophets tell us the energy of the Spirit of God mastered their natural strength; but they also tell us how their souls were supported and enabled to endure the sublime visions upon which they gazed. This is a fact which, while it proves that the object of their intuitions was no mere creation of their own imagination—no mere subjective phantasm—exhibits at the same time how their understanding was qualified to apprehend the Divine communication, and enabled to reproduce it for the benefit of others. . . . . So far are the facts of the case from suggesting a suppression of the prophet's intelligent consciousness, as being essential or even congruous, that we can at once discern how an elevation rather of all the powers whereby ideas are apprehended was of necessity required for the purpose of enabling him to receive, or to transmit to others, the mysterious truths which were disclosed to him. None felt more sensibly than the men of God themselves *how incompetent, without such spiritual support, are the ordinary faculties of man to grasp conceptions so widely transcending the natural limits of the human soul.*"

This is a happy illustration of the curative power which errors, founded on the ambiguities of language, possess of correcting themselves. The true and genuine significations of words cannot fail to assert their outraged rights, rising up often unconsciously and making themselves felt.

Although the early Fathers of the Christian Church dwelt much on the inspiration of God's word, while they overlooked the profound question of its nature so fully discussed by St. Paul, the subtle intellects of the schoolmen in the middle age, and not less the philosophic divines of Germany, might be expected to take up this phasis of the question; yet, strange to say, our authors do not produce any of the great writers of the scholastic and post-reformation periods who hold opinions confirmatory of their definitions of inspiration, and the ideas which they involve. The question at issue is this: What is the province and function of inspiration? Is its function an enlightenment and quickening of the mental faculties to enable the prophet or apostle to understand the revelations vouchsafed; or is it a guidance to the utterance of the truths revealed? In other words, what is the correct scriptural analysis of the communication of Divine knowledge? Are there no gleams of the true nature of inspiration bursting forth from the thoughts of those great men, and illumining the well-considered words of their writings?

One man, as a thinker, an acute reasoner, and of unrivalled ability, stands out among the rest of the scholastic divines, a burning and a shining light in a dark age—Thomas Aquinas. The simple statement of the analysis of the communication of Divine knowledge, according to Aquinas, will show very clearly his view of the nature and function of inspiration. Thomas Aquinas holds that inspiration, as well as revelation, is required to produce prophetic knowledge:—

"If to any one there be made, by Divine intervention, a representation of certain things by similitudes of the imagination (as to Pharaoh and Nebuchadnezzar), or by corporeal similitudes (as to Belshassar), such is not to be considered a prophet, unless his mind be illuminated for judging such presentations."

Aquinas, moreover, indicates the conditions on which revelations can be intelligible and communicable :—

"By the gift of prophecy, something else is conferred on the human mind, over and above what appertains to the natural faculty in two respects. First, in reference to the judgment through the influx of intellectual light ; and, secondly, as to the reception and representation of things which is effected by means of certain conceptions. As regards this second point, human doctrine can be assimilated to prophetic revelation, but not as regards the former. For man represents to his disciple some things by verbal signs ; but he cannot illuminate him within. This God only can do."

Under the following heads Aquinas presents his analysis of the communication of Divine knowledge to the prophet :—

"1. There are represented by God to the mind of the prophet, and sometimes even through the medium of the external senses, certain *sensible forms*, as to Daniel (chap. v.) when he saw the writing on the wall.

"2. Sometimes by means of *imaginary forms*, either

such as are entirely impressed by God, not being received through the senses, (as if there were in one born blind similitudes of colours in the imagination,) or even divinely produced out of those which are received from the senses, as Jeremiah (chap. i.) saw a seething pot facing the north.

"3. Also by imprinting intelligible ideas on the mind itself, as is evident from those who receive infused wisdom or knowledge, as Solomon and the apostles.

"4. But intellectual light is sometimes divinely impressed on the human mind for judging of those things which were seen by others; as is told of Joseph (who explained the dream of Pharaoh), and as was the case with the apostles, for whom 'the Lord opened their understandings that they might understand the Scriptures' (Luke xxiv. 45).

"To this head belongs the interpretation of religious discourses, either for determining the meaning according to Divine truth of those things which in the natural course man apprehends, or for deciding truly and effectually those things which duty enjoins to be done."

Thus this profound scholastic divine concludes that prophetic revelation is sometimes performed by the sole influence of light, sometimes by conceptions impressed, either entirely new or otherwise arranged. Hence Aquinas gives no authority to those who narrow the limits of revelation to supernatural presentations of sensible forms and forms of the imagination, since he includes in the wide sphere of revelation the supernatural suggestion of ideas (*intelligible species*), and also those revelations which come into spiritual view under the light of inspiration, brightening and quickening intuitional consciousness, and opening the understanding. Such are the matters contained in Holy Scripture, apprehended and discerned through supernatural illumination; and these are classed—as well as points of doctrine and practice, on which this light sheds its beams—under the general head of prophetic revelation. From these observations, derived from the writings of Thomas Aquinas, the master spirit of mediæval philosophy, and of a thinking age the greatest thinker, it can be seen how deeply his mind had been penetrated by the Pauline view of the respective functions of inspiration and revelation, and how entirely he had disowned the popular definition, which indeed conveys no precise and distinct notions of the nature and function of inspiration. When it is said that "the Bible conveys to mankind a Divine revelation," and, again, revelations were the prophetic announcements of the future, and the peculiar doctrines of Christianity," no more than the truth is said; yet to make this the starting-point of inquiry, is to open a door to the '*à priori* method' of investigating the nature of the inspiration of Holy Scripture.

The safe method, however, of proceeding, is to make no assumption whatever at the outset, but humbly to tread in the steps of St. Paul: first, to consider a revelation presented to the writer; next, to see how the mind is prepared by the Holy Spirit for the intelligent reception of that revelation; then to note how the combined spiritual moments of revelation and inspiration result in knowledge; and, lastly, to mark how the writer, thus taught of God, expresses the knowledge so acquired in words at once Divine and human.

The former method, on the other hand, begins by referring to the expression on record, without analyzing the nature of that record, as it was taught to the inspired writer by the Holy Spirit. This is the method followed by the theorists.

We are told that "Köppen draws attention to a fallacious mode of reasoning often employed." His words are, "In order to prove that the books of the Bible have been written under the Divine inspiration, appeal is sometimes made to the extraordinary revelations which are *here and there* announced in the Bible; but this is plainly a false conclusion, and a weakness not to be concealed. Although God has revealed Himself to certain persons by means of a supernatural influence, the question, notwithstanding all this, still remains—How has the Divine influence exerted itself in the composition of the Bible?" Revelations here and there announced!—who thus proves the inspiration of Holy Scripture? It would certainly be a weak and false conclusion if any one should reason in this way. But it is not a fallacious mode of reasoning to conclude, from the mutually co-operating influences of particular revelations and inspiration, that the sacred writers so taught of God ($\Theta\epsilon o\delta i\delta a\kappa\tau o\iota$) were enabled accurately to express the will of God in the written word.

Origen and Basil are the only examples adduced among the early Fathers as holding *the principle* from which has been derived the view of that distinction between revelation and inspiration, which, I submit, is not the true one. Nevertheless, neither Origen nor Basil held the view of inspiration embodied in the definition based on that supposed distinction, namely, "the actuating energy guided by which," etc. This, in fact, is not inspiration, but something resulting from an influence already exerted on the mind and heart. Nor is inspiration the only influence exerted in the composition of the Bible. Revelation and inspiration by their joint action gave knowledge; and knowledge, projected into the outer sphere of human language, found a suitable expression.

It is indeed inconceivable how—if a correct view is given here of inspiration as distinguished from revelation, and if the latter is and must be clearly understood by the early Fathers of the Christian Church— they failed to define the true nature and character of the former. For some of them, as Origen and Basil, are supposed to have marked the principle whence the distinction here laid down naturally flowed: viz., that some portions of the Scripture were *express* revelations, others not. And yet, until Cardinal Cajetan and Melchior Cano, late in the sixteenth century, took up the subject, was the distinction—based on this principle—between revelation and inspiration, unknown. There is one way, and only one, to account for this strange but undoubted fact. It is this. None of the Fathers of the primitive Church, or the great scholastic divines of the middle age, considered or acknowledged that to be inspiration which now goes by that name.

We have seen what a large step Thomas Aquinas made in advance of the theologians of former times, on the true nature of inspiration. I shall next show how some of the German divines had also moved forward to sounder views of inspiration than that presented by the popular definition, which describes it as a guidance to the outward act of speaking or writing. In this good progress, the love of the truth and the prayerful study of God's word will bring down God's blessing on His servants, who are struggling to free their minds from any doubts and difficulties, still clinging to this vitally important question. They may be grieved at heart that, up to this day, a matter of such transcendent interest in its bearings on theology, remains in a state so unsettled. Yet moving in this, which to Biblical scholars is the path of duty, let them not slack, but press forward, in the hope that their labours will be crowned with success, remembering the history of the ten lepers, how "as they went they were healed."

A vast amount of the embarrassing confusions in which this subject is involved arose from not keeping distinct, and considering in consecutive order, revelation (as presented to the prophet or apostle) and prophecy.

Now prophecy is the expression, in act or word, of a revelation received and apprehended by a mind prepared by inspiration. Knowledge, I repeat, is the result of the combined spiritual forces of revelation and inspiration; and the expression of that knowledge is teaching or prophecy. So in St. John's Epistle to the Seven Churches, the record of his revelation is the book of his prophecy.

Knowledge is also equally concerned in the right understanding of truths already expressed in the sacred Scriptures—such as were written in the Old Testament—in the days of the apostles; and for this intelligent apperception of Divine truths inspiration was equally needed. These Old Testament truths were very generally misunderstood even to a degree bordering on total ignorance, so that a supernatural inspiration was required to bring them out and teach them anew. This was the more necessary as natural acquirements proved to be inadequate for that end. Even some *inspired* persons did not fully understand the predictions of others, but "searched diligently into their meaning."

Equally to both, *teaching* applies.

The name of Hengstenberg, who clearly marked these distinctions,—however erroneous his idea concerning the ecstatic state of the prophets,—may be added to the list of those who rose to a truer view of inspiration than the one now commonly received: " What viewed in respect to the manner of receiving it is revelation; the same, when viewed in respect of the manner of its delivery, is prophecy." This writer refers to 1 Cor. xiv. 6: " Now, brethren, if I come unto you speaking with tongues, what shall I profit you, except I shall speak to you either by revelation, or by knowledge, or by prophesying, or by doctrine?" Here we have a double pair of corresponding parts: revelation and prophecy constitute the one, knowledge and doctrine the other.

The men of God, indeed, sometimes did not fully comprehend the sense of the revelations presented to their minds, yet by inspiration they were enabled to obtain a clear view of what came within the field of their spiritual vision. Then follows the expression of what they saw. This they could give accurately even without knowing the extent and remote bearing of the panoramic view exhibited to their mind's eye.

But without inspiration, again, after these mysterious truths had been put on record, they might remain hidden. And this, not obscurely, accounts for the apparently unaccountable ignorance of the Jewish people, who neither understood their own prophets, nor perceived the application of Christ's words to themselves. In fact, revelations original or recorded may be presented to the mind, and yet for ever remain unknown, or disregarded, unless inspiration open the eyes to see them. Inspiration is necessary both to him who is favoured with revelations, and to him who would rightly understand and appropriate them afterwards. I fully agree with those who, on Scripture grounds, claim a higher gift of inspiration for the apostles than that employed by ordinary believers. I further agree with those who hold that the promise of leading into *all* the truth applies to the apostles to whom it was addressed; and that truth, here means evangelical truth.

But I cannot agree with the inference drawn from these premises by Dr. Lee, when he asserts, "The plain inference from such expressions as 'all the truth' and 'shall teach you all things' is simply this, that when the apostles acted in any way as the official teachers of Christianity, not only was every species of error to be excluded, but new truths also were to be unfolded as need required." And again: "It is manifest that our Lord assured His disciples that they should be divinely guided in every particular which related to the *preaching* of the gospel."

There is here unquestionably a break or gap in the argument between being taught (which was the promise) and teaching. For what the promise of Christ guaranteed to these disciples was the sure and certain knowledge of all the truth, "to teach them all things," etc.

Now, though it be admitted that the holy apostles of our Lord, 'taught of God' in a manner so pre-eminently peculiar and powerful as to have a clear and accurate knowledge of Divine truths revealed to them, were above all others qualified to clothe the same in words the most suitable and expressive, and thus fitted to steer clear of all error in *their teaching*, still the argument above does not necessarily extend so far. For some hold—this qualification notwithstanding—the possibility of free agents not acting up to their qualification, at least in some minor respects which may not imperil the faith. This was the opinion of Erasmus, supported by the consideration that, even after the descent of the Holy Spirit, Christ in some things suffered the apostles to err.*

However faulty I deem the aforesaid arguments of Dr. Lee, I cannot once think that men under such mighty controlling influences of the Spirit, at the set moments in which they should place on record the things divinely revealed to their minds, illumi-

---

* "Non est necesse ut quicquid fuit in apostolis protinus ad miraculum vocemus. Passus est Christus errare suos, etiam post acceptum Paracletum, sed non usque ad fidei periculum."—*Erasm. Epist.*, lib. ii., tom. iv.

nated and strengthened as they were by inspiration, could fail to express them precisely and accurately.

For knowledge clear and perfectly communicated to minds fitted to understand it thoroughly finds naturally spontaneous and suitable expression, just in proportion to its own intrinsic accuracy. So in this extreme case of a divinely imparted knowledge, the chance of error in its expression is reduced to a minimum.

But the peculiar spiritual pre-eminence of the apostles over believers in general, in a great measure consists in the abundance and the extraordinary character of the revelations vouchsafed to them.

Now if it be the function of inspiration to prepare the mind for the intelligent reception of these revelations, it necessarily follows that apostolic inspiration was, at least, of a degree higher than ordinary inspiration.

It is, however, noteworthy that the revelations vouchsafed, it may be simultaneously, by suggestion, are sometimes not taken into account. Such may be the case at those thrilling moments in the public ministry of the apostles, recounted in Acts iv. 8, and xiii. 9, to which Dr. Lee refers as "clearly implying a special illapse of spiritual influence, distinct from any sense in which *inspiration*, as bestowed upon Christians in general, can be understood." Be it so. Yet this illapse, whether it be inspiration, or the total effect of inspiration and revelation, is an *intrinsic* power imparted to the mind; and something very different from the guidance to the accurate expression of Divine truth.

Hävernick, another eminent German, who cannot be cited as a supporter of the view of inspiration set forth in the commonly received definition, holds a correct idea of the true nature of that influence:—

"The prophets feel themselves elevated to a new and higher sphere, a world lying beyond common reality, in the midst of which they *hear* the truth, the voice of God. God is Himself the author of such a *state*. He *qualifies* the soul of the prophet for those intuitions; causes him to *see* visions; *opens his ears*, and also endows the inward organs of his spirit, so that they are capable of attaining to those intuitions.* By means of this Divine starting-point, as the principle operating in the prophets, the prophetic intuitions do not fall into the category of *mere* subjectivity, but lay just claim to be entitled actual *states*, which have objective reality."

Thus it is that prophetic knowledge is the joint result of inspiration and revelation.

Again: "God reveals Himself, externally, in the history of the people: internally, in the spirit of man by His Spirit: while neither the world nor humanity is brought into false identity with the Divine Being.

---

* Thus Augustine: "Hic insinuatur nobis, ea loqui prophetas Dei quæ audiunt ab Eo." Such is the explanation of St. Paul, " which we also speak in words which the Holy Ghost teacheth."

Thus Hebrew prophecy, according to its subjective starting-point, stands in contrast to all heathen notions: according to which the Divine life comes forth in the multiplicity of the powers of nature. Prophecy is not, like the heathen *Mantik*, tied to the concealed mysterious gloomy energies and powers of nature. Hence there is found in genuine Hebraism no divination of many different kinds; no uncertain fluctuating struggle and effort to place oneself in community with the Deity. . . . The essence and subjective peculiarity of prophetic inspiration lies in this, that it finds its origin, not in the natural consciousness of man, nor yet in any eminent natural parts and abilities, but proves itself to be the higher supernatural operation of the Spirit of God." See page 27 of this essay.

In confirmation of these lucid remarks on the true nature of inspiration, and its connection with revelation,* it may be added from the Holy Scriptures, "The word of the Lord that came to Micah, . . . which he saw." This inner word is perceived by the spiritual sense of the prophet. "The burden which Habakkuk the prophet did see."

These were seen, not mediately by the outer sense, but immediately and directly by the inner spiritual sense, by immediate intuition.

---

* Justin Martyr referring to the spiritual intuitions of the prophets, says, "They speak only what they have heard and seen, filled with the Holy Ghost."—*Dial. cum Tryph.*, c. vii., page 109.

It is scarcely accurate to say, with Dr. Lee, "their *knowledge* proceeded from an immediate intuition." The revelations were presented to their intuitive faculty, but this was illumined and quickened by inspiration, and the knowledge arose from the combined operation of both.

Their gift of prophecy was therefore not permanent, but depended on the Divine pleasure. For their prophecy was the utterance or expression of the prophetic cognition resulting from the revelations granted, and inspiration, which was their qualification for the intelligent perception and reception of those revelations. And this too affords a proof that such revelations did not owe their parentage to their own powers of reflection or imagination.

Thus in the prophetic vision with which Daniel was favoured at the river Ulai (chap. viii.), every part is described in order. The revelation in an ecstatic vision, the inspiration quickening his intuition, and the knowledge arising when he was hereby fitted to receive its explanation from the angel, "Make this man understand." The vision, or the first thing related, was the revelation. Here, as in many other instances, Dr. Lee considers, contrary to the tenor of the words, that the revelation is that which gives the knowledge to the prophet: "The revelation is now communicated; and he said, Behold, I will make thee know what shall be in the last end," whereas both it and the inspiration, fitting the prophet to receive the import of this revelation by vision as explained by the angel, were necessary pre-requisites for that cognition.

I cannot close the list of distinguished German authors, none of whom can be produced as supporters of that which is now improperly called inspiration, without adding the name of Twesten. This able writer, even while he levels the barrier separating apostles from ordinary believers, which is chiefly composed of the special and extraordinary revelations granted to the former, still presents a faithful portraiture of inspiration as represented by St. Paul in the passage from which my idea of the true nature and function of inspiration had been derived.

"If," says this writer, "all Christians have the Holy Ghost (as Scripture teaches), can every religious statement of a Christian be called inspired? But we make a distinction between apostolic writings and others—between inspiration and Christian illumination, although this too must be looked upon rather as gradual than specific. For of a specific contrast between apostles and other Christians, Scripture says nothing, but only of the distinction between them and the world (John xiv. 17); so that we shall not go astray if we suppose inspiration to be something analogous to *illumination.*

"Although the disciples of the apostles stand a degree lower than the apostles, still we must place them higher than other enlightened Christians (*e.g.*,

Clemens, Ignatius, Polycarp, who had seen, no doubt, some of the apostles, but had scarcely associated long with them). . . . The nearer or more remote connexion with Christ, as the centre of our faith, presents a measure according to which we can distinguish what is to be deemed more or less essential for Christian consciousness, and therefore more mediately or immediately under the influence of the Holy Ghost."

The presence or absence of revelation, even to the apostles, is generally overlooked or slurred over by writers who treat of their inspiration. This is a fatal defect which hides from view the true nature of inspiration.

Olshausen has truly observed that "the agency of the Holy Ghost in the apostles is not to be considered a permanently operating power, but as a power called forth at different times, in different degrees and forms of activity."

Now the apostles might sometimes have believed, at the first moment, that the thoughts that first rose up in their minds were the suggestions of the Spirit; and yielding to the impulses of their own souls might have prescribed to themselves a certain line of ministerial duty. But at such times, if wrong, an inward controlling power arrested them, or the higher influence of the Spirit by revelation would correct their mistake, and teach them what to do. Thus Paul's impulses would lead him to preach in Galatia, but he was forbidden by the Holy Ghost. He assayed to go into Bithynia, but the Spirit suffered him not. The apostle could distinguish the impulses of his own soul from the suggestions of the Spirit. Still this was, or might seem in some cases, only negative guidance. Continuing to doubt where God would lead him, he seemed to be embarrassed and perplexed, when lo! an express revelation is vouchsafed to give him positive directions. "A vision appeared to Paul in the night. There stood a man of Macedonia, and prayed him saying, Come over into Macedonia and help us. And after he had seen the vision, immediately we endeavoured to go into Macedonia, assuredly gathering that the Lord had called us to preach the Gospel unto them."

Not to mark carefully the part occupied by revelation, in the diverse results of spiritual agency, on the minds of the apostles, as recorded by the historian of their acts, has been, I have no doubt, the offspring of the popular erroneous view of inspiration which, in its turn, has helped to confirm and perpetuate that error. Thus no notice is taken of revelation in the following stirring incidents of St. Paul's life. "St. Paul could strike Elymas blind because he was so directed by the Spirit, (spiritual direction being taken for inspiration,) but he could not miraculously restore to health Ephaphroditus, his brother and companion in labour. He had the spirit of prophecy as to Antichrist, and he was enabled to predict the safety of his fellow-travellers, but he could not foresee what was to befall himself at Jerusalem."

Indeed, revelation is regarded more in its scriptural record than in its presentations to the mind of the inspired; and yet it is only when viewed in relation to the comprehending mind that it affords an adequate explanation of results so diverse as those above referred to.

The cause of the fallacy which lurks in this omission is the wrong view taken of inspiration as a particular guidance of the Spirit. In this way, being enabled to predict by "the spirit of prophecy" is (using the phrase in a restricted sense) taking it for a guidance of the Spirit to foreknowledge of future events; and this satisfies without analyzing the nature of that guidance.

The Revelation, however, as a written record is—I have already explained—the final result of the Spirit's operations; and we are to consider how authority attaches as well to the teaching of the apostles, as to the knowledge they possessed of the truths themselves. This knowledge may consist of three parts: 1. Knowledge derived from revelation, presented by the Spirit to minds enlightened by inspiration, of things not cognizable by the unaided human faculties. 2. Knowledge of truths recalled to their remembrance, only partially understood, or forgotten. 3. Knowledge bearing on the subject, of which they were in possession by natural means of information.

The two former were the new things; the last, the old mentioned by our Lord in Matt. xiii. 52 : "Therefore every scribe, which is instructed unto the kingdom of heaven, is like unto a man that is an householder, which bringeth forth out of his treasure things new and old."

When, therefore, Grotius said, " There is no need that historical facts should be dictated by the Holy Spirit,—it was enough that the writer have a good memory,"* he seems to have doubly erred : first, in supposing that simple dictation of the Holy Ghost were needed in things not cognizable by the unaided powers of man ; secondly, that human memory needed not to be refreshed and quickened by the suggestive aid of the Divine Spirit.

In fact, every constituent part of the knowledge so imparted, which passed through a mind enlightened and elevated by inspiration,—and possessing thereby, in one complete whole, the Divine and human elements combined,—received the full sanction of Divine authority. For everything imperfect, or only partially known, was made perfect by the suggestive revelations of the Spirit, and what had been already fully known was accepted. Thus the entire subject-matter was composed of one or more or all of those parts, adjusted in due proportions, while the part known by natural reason, clustered round and fitted

---

* " A Spiritu Sancto dictari historias non fuit opus. Satis fuit Scriptorem memoriâ valere."—*Grotius, propace Eccles.*, tom. iii., p. 672.

into the central revelation. So the whole, expressed in words, would be the record of one indivisible revelation constituting a certain portion of the Bible.

You cannot, therefore, (as I have remarked,) detach the part known naturally by the writer—as it has been sanctioned equally with the rest by the Spirit of truth, and has been incorporated with the parts supernaturally revealed—from this one revelation now recorded at full in appropriate words; for this separation would destroy the sense and intention of that Divine revelation forming an integral portion of the Holy Bible.

Such detached sentence is part and parcel of a revelation, though by itself it may not be more than expletive matter; still was it needed to give form and consistency, according to the intention of the Spirit, to that revelation. Such of themselves may be thought lightly of, as no real parts of a Divine revelation; yet are they bands and ligatures, binding the whole into one compact body, in the same manner as, in the earth, sterile rocks are bands and pillars that keep together the entire mass, whose surface is here and there diversified by beautiful scenery, and teeming vegetation. Such seem to be the dry genealogies in the gospels written by Matthew and Luke, yet these furnish proofs that the testimony of Jesus is the spirit of prophecy.

It is therefore scarcely legitimate to illustrate the distinction between inspiration and revelation by what is itself a part of a revelation. Moreover, it is not a fair representation of the matter, to assert—as a proof of a distinction between revelation and inspiration—that such detached sentences are not revelations, while they and every other part of Scripture are inspired. For, separated from the context, there are many sayings which, as utterances of erring mortals—sometimes wicked and unholy persons—are not inspired. These, in their isolation, are neither inspired nor revealed; but as recorded by the sacred writers, they are both. As the words of inspired authors, whose minds were enlightened by the Spirit of God for the intelligent reception of the matters presented, they are inspired; and they are revealed, since, by the suggestions of the same Spirit, the authors were, in the selection of such matters for record, guided, and so preserved from error. For guiding this selection, refreshing their memory, and correcting their judgment, even in things already humanly known to the writer, so as to impart a thoroughly accurate knowledge of the subject under consideration, the Holy Spirit unfolds—*i.e.*, reveals—the truth to its inspired recipient.

In that most ancient of Biblical compositions, the book of Job, the greater part of the reasonings of the patriarch's three friends are untrue, as are also those of Job himself. These are refuted by Elihu. A man so much their junior, to whom the truth of the deep sayings then discussed was revealed, and who was inspired that he might know it, excused himself for criticising their arguments, by an appeal to his spiritual gifts.* "But there is a spirit in man: and the inspiration of the Almighty giveth them understanding." And thereby knowing the truth, he feels an impulse to speak that he does know: "I said, I will answer also my part: I also will show mine opinion. For I am full of matter; the Spirit within me constraineth me."

By a visible miracle, the Lord, approving the inspired judgment of Elihu, answered Job out of the whirlwind, and said, "Who is this that darkeneth counsel by words without knowledge?"† The view, therefore, which holds every isolated passage in the Bible to be inspired, and many such to be no revelations, though, as integral parts of the context, and put on record by an inspired writer, they are both inspired and revealed, is not correct, and furnishes not a true basis for the distinction between inspiration and revelation.

No objection lies against this view from the consideration that it seems to involve the idea that there may be revelations of facts and truths already known. For if an apostle had forgotten such, or if such had nearly faded away from his memory, the suggestions of the Holy Spirit to the sacred writer, which would recall the former or refresh the latter, is a revelation.

Again, I must repeat that conscience approves the

---

* Job xxxii. 7, 8, 17, 18.   † Job xxxviii. 1, 2.

moral commandments of God before they are revealed by word; yet conscience in fallen and sinful creatures is not a safe guide on which to depend; therefore to make them authoritative, God revealed them from heaven.

From these remarks, I submit that we are not justified in limiting revelation to those portions (isolated) of the Bible, the contents of which were unknown to, or undiscoverable by, the sacred writers.* The confusion, which in this view is so embarrassing, disappears entirely when the true nature of inspiration—indicated by its etymon—is strictly adhered to, namely, that it is a subjective influence of the Holy Spirit, wrought within the spirit of man to qualify his mind and heart for the intelligent and cordial reception of Divine revelations.

The work of the blessed apostles in advancing the gospel of the kingdom to perfection from the incipient stage of its existence, is well described by Professor Blunt, in language which shows how fully he coincided with the view of inspiration and revelation here set forth and deduced by me from the writings of St. Paul:—

"How, then, are we to account for this phenomenon, this rapid transition of the Gospel from a state of solution, so to speak, to a state of consistency and consolidation? Doubtless, the gift of

---

* See page 121.

the Holy Ghost had been meanwhile sent down from on high, and had wrought a great change in the character and sentiments of the apostles, opening their minds to understand the Scriptures of the Old Testament, unveiling to them the real nature of Christ's kingdom, stimulating their consciences, increasing their faith, and bringing vividly to their recollection all that Jesus had imparted to them, and with a deeper penetration into its meaning than had been vouchsafed to them at the time He gave utterance to it. But if it be questioned, as perhaps it may, whether it would fall within the precise province of the Comforter directly to prompt or prescribe the details of the constitution of the Church, and to quicken it thus rapidly into life, it may be open to us perhaps to trace the initiation of it to our Lord Himself, and to the instructions He was pleased to give, during the period which more immediately preceded the day of Pentecost; whilst He committed it to the third Person of the blessed Trinity here, as in other departments of revelation, to perfect the work, by reproducing in the memory of the "apostles all the suggestions of Jesus Himself, and enduing these His ministers with the temper and wisdom necessary for carrying them successfully into operation."

CHAPTER IX.

THEORIES OF THE INSPIRATION OF HOLY SCRIPTURE.

FIRST our attention must be recalled to the Pauline or true theory. This I have discussed at full length in the first chapter. From what is there brought out, it appears that every theory is, and must be, based, in the last resort, on the fundamental idea of the nature of *personal* inspiration, or on its accurate definition,—so much depends on a correct and scriptural answer to the question, What is personal inspiration?

Next, in the transition from personal to Biblical inspiration, it has been shown that the idea of the inspiration of Holy Scripture is a complex conception, embracing personal inspiration, personal revelation, knowledge imparted by their united action, and the expression of that knowledge, in words the immediate result of such teaching of the Holy Spirit.

In the luminous synthesis of St. Paul, and the logical concatenation of its several parts, in a true constructive form, we have unquestionably the desired scriptural theory. This theory implies that the Pauline idea of personal inspiration is radically different from the commonly received conception of that Divine influence. Besides, at the point where a theory is needed, the view of St. Paul rationally unites the Divine with the human element in the spoken or written word. For while the connecting link in the popular definition of the inspiration of Holy Scriptures is, we know not what, impulse, "in whatever degree or manner exercised;" in the Pauline it is *knowledge* having, as *taught* by the Divine Spirit, a peculiarly *brightening* effect on the words which represent it.

The popular idea of inspiration rests too upon a distinction which is, I submit, untenable; and even if it were, the idea is not the correct one. The distinction is this: the Bible, as an organized whole, is an inspired record, but all its parts are not revelations.

1. Here revelation is unwarrantably reduced to limits too narrow; for the largest class of revelations—the suggested—are excluded. And it seems to be forgotten that Melchior Cano, an early supporter of this view of inspiration, in set phraseology, while discussing the matter, does not absolutely refuse the name of revelation to the latter kind; only he thinks that the word is not properly applied to any Divine communication unless *express* revelations. Thoughts nevertheless suggested by the Holy Spirit to a mind enlightened by His influence, in the sacred Scriptures

take perhaps the most prominent place among revelations.*

This, in my judgment, is a sufficient answer to the error of a Roman Catholic theologian, wedded by indissoluble ties to the doctrines of his own Church, of which the peculiar teaching necessitated a belief of the distinction in question.

Whether in fact a writer draws from his treasure things new or old, I have shown that there is need of revelation to bring up *on demand* the materials required to give order and consistency to his composition. Materials of such a nature, which the natural man cannot receive, are not to be summoned up at will into their fitting places, without both a revelation to present them, and an inspiration to qualify the mind for their reception.

2. Even admitting to the full this distinction, the notion of inspiration derived from such a distinction is not a correct one. For this is the true distinction between inspiration and revelation. Revelation is a Divine presentation to the mind of an object distinct from any product of the human faculties, whether the object be a thought directly suggested by the Holy Spirit, or something else, bringing up such thought before the intuitive vision. Inspiration is not direction or guidance, but preparation of the mind by the Spirit

---

* Thus Dr. Henderson, in his able treatise on 'Divine Inspiration,' places suggestion first in his classification of the different modes of revelation.

for the intelligent reception of the revelation which, in its natural state, the mind cannot receive.

The direction or guidance follows the inspiration, which was indeed a transaction already completed before a word was uttered or written. On no account whatever could this outward movement to speak or write (to which the sacred writers were otherwise morally impelled) be denominated inspiration.

That the formal and precise scriptural idea of inspiration is '*preparation*'—and this the turning-point in the whole controversy—is now quite evident. It may therefore be desirable to enter a little more fully on the proof of this position.

Manifest it is, in the first place, that no knowledge of Divine truths ("which the natural man receiveth not," 1 Cor. ii. 14.) can be attained unless on two conditions expressly stated by St. Paul: 1. That a revelation be presented to the mind ("God hath revealed them unto us by His Spirit," 1 Cor. ii. 10). 2. That the mind be fitted and prepared to understand and receive the revelation, ("We have not received the spirit of the world, but the Spirit which is of God," $\tau\grave{o}$ $\pi\nu\epsilon\hat{v}\mu a$ $\tau\grave{o}$ $\dot{\epsilon}\kappa$ $\tau o\hat{v}$ $\theta\epsilon o\hat{v}$, 1 Cor. ii. 12, that *we might know*, etc.) Both conditions are necessary; for without a revelation, man would mistake his own thoughts for suggestions of the Divine Spirit; and without a suitable preparation, he could not grasp and receive these realities of the spiritual world. In the former case, the possibility of such an event is thus strikingly represented by the prophet Ezekiel: "Son of man, prophesy against the prophets of Israel that prophesy, and say thou unto them that prophesy out of their own hearts, Hear ye the word of the Lord: Thus saith the Lord God, Woe unto the foolish prophets that follow their own spirit, and have seen nothing." (Ezek. xiii. 2, 3.) In the latter case, the revelation is unintelligible. So far is it from being true, that revelation of itself gives knowledge. For antecedently to inspiration, man is in the natural state—$\psi\nu\chi\iota\kappa\grave{o}\varsigma$—and "the natural man receiveth not the things of the Spirit of God, for they are foolishness to him, neither can he know them, because they are spiritually discerned."

What then is the nature of that preparation which is the act of the Divine Spirit, and which, in its effect on the mind and heart of the apostle or prophet, is denominated inspiration?

It appears to consist of three constituent elements.

1. Illumination. So St. Paul prays for his converts at Ephesus, "that the God of our Lord Jesus Christ, the Father of glory, may give you the spirit of wisdom and revelation in the knowledge of Him: the eyes of your understanding being *enlightened*—$\pi\epsilon\phi\omega\tau\iota\sigma\mu\acute{\epsilon}\nu o\upsilon\varsigma$ —that ye may *know*," etc. (Eph. i. 17, 18.) Such too is the purport of the phrase "opened their understanding," in Luke xxiv. 45, and of a similar phrase in Job xxxiii. 16: "Then openeth He the ears of men," etc. The latter is very remarkable as confirming

our position that inspiration is necessary to render a revelation intelligible, and so an indispensable factor in the production of the knowledge of Divine truth.

2. Divinely imparted strength to man's spiritual faculties. For writing to the same Church, St. Paul earnestly supplicates God, in behalf of its members, "that He would grant you, according to the riches of His glory, to be strengthened with might by His Spirit in the inner man; that Christ may dwell in your hearts by faith; that ye, being rooted and grounded in love, may be able to *comprehend* with all saints what is the breadth, and length, and depth, and height; and to know the love of Christ, which passeth knowledge, that ye may be filled with all the fulness of God." (Eph. iii. 16—19.)

3. A disposition for receiving Divine truth implanted in the heart by the Spirit of God. Thus in the tenth Psalm, David prays, "Lord, Thou hast heard the desire of the humble: Thou wilt *prepare* their heart," etc.

Illuminating, strengthening, disposing,—such is the triple efficacious instrumentality of the Holy Spirit, by which, in its combined operation, the mind and heart are duly prepared to understand and receive "the things freely given of God" by revelation.

Now the Hebrew verb which expresses the act of preparing for any intended purpose is כון, as in 1 Chron. xxix. 2. "I have," says David, "prepared with all my might for the house of my God the gold for things to be made of gold," etc. A similar use of the same word occurs in Exod. xxiii. 20.

According to the appropriate import in the different conjugations of this verb, it has different significations, such as aptavit, præparavit, disposuit, stabilivit,—so nearly related, that sometimes our translators seem to have been in doubt which to use. Thus in the tenth Psalm, "Lord, Thou hast heard the desire of the humble; Thou wilt *prepare* their heart," they give in the margin 'establish;' while in Genesis xli. 32, "And for that the dream was doubled unto Pharaoh twice; it is because the thing is *established* by God, and God will shortly bring it to pass," the marginal rendering is 'prepared of God.' This free interchange of the meaning is natural enough, since, in reference to the matter in hand, a preparation from the Lord of man's mental powers must necessarily improve and strengthen them.

Preparation, therefore, in every aspect, and in reference to each of its constituent elements, is the exact and essential characteristic of inspiration. Illumination imparts, in its effect, clearness to the spiritual vision of the prophet. David prayed, "Open Thou mine eyes, that I may behold wondrous things out of Thy law." Spiritual strength, divinely bestowed, gives power and full mastery over the thoughts, suggested by the Holy Spirit, to the servants of God.

A disposition of the will to receive "the mysteries of the kingdom," by inclining man's heart towards them, powerfully contributes to this end. Lydia of Thyatira, "whose heart the Lord opened, that she attended unto the things which were spoken of Paul," is an instance of one prepared for the knowledge of the truth in this way.

Thus inspiration, the gift of God's Spirit, acting on the minds and hearts of His chosen servants, prepared them for the due reception of the truths which the Most High vouchsafed to reveal. And thus were they fitted both to receive and to know the deep things of God, which, in their natural unprepared state, they could not understand, and would not receive.

In reference to preparation—as the fundamental characteristic of inspiration—the passage quoted already from the Epistle of Eleazar to Ptolemy Philadelphus, is in point. In it he relates how Moses was *instructed* by God in the *knowledge* of things Divine—ὑπὸ Θεοῦ κατεσκευασμένος εἰς ἐπίγνωσιν τῶν ἁπαντων.

In like manner, the apostles of Christ were instructed by inspiration, receiving thereby "the Spirit which is of God," "that they might *know* the things that were freely given to them of God." And in the same manner as Moses were they thus "taught of God,"—qualified and able to express the will of God, in words which, though exhibiting an unmistakable human element, were truly Divine in their origin and production.

A legitimate theory of the inspiration of Holy Scripture can be arrived at only by investigating the true nature of personal inspiration and revelation, as expressly stated and given to us in the written word,—antecedently proved to have come from God,—and by ascending in a constructive scheme from these Divine factors to the knowledge thus imparted of revealed truth ; and thence to its expression in representative signs or words which are therefore also Divine.

The investigation moves in a wrong line, either when—assuming the perfect and infallible certainty of the word of God—it lays down *à priori* conditions, on which that certainty may be realized, or when, without this assumption, judging beforehand, by the light of reason, what are the characteristic properties of the written word, it determines the conditions on which this written word has been so composed.

The organic theory of the inspiration of Scripture, and also the dynamic, come under the former head of non-legitimate theories; while the latitudinarian systems broached in the 'Essays and Reviews,' are non-legitimate theories of the latter kind.

The fabrication of particular theories of inspiration must, in no small measure, depend on the very meaning attached to the term itself. And how this was likely to be encouraged will appear from the formidable list of its significations enumerated by Professor Jowett :—

"The word inspiration has received more numerous gradations and distinctions of meaning than perhaps any other in the whole of theology. There is an inspiration of superintendence, and an inspiration of suggestion,—an inspiration which would have been consistent with the apostle or evangelist falling into error, and an inspiration which would have prevented him erring,—verbal organic inspiration by which the inspired person is the passive utterer of a Divine word, and an inspiration which acts through the character of the sacred writer. There is an inspiration which absolutely communicates the fact to be revealed or statement to be made, and an inspiration which does not supersede the ordinary knowledge of human events. There is an inspiration which demands infallibility in matters of doctrine, but allows for mistakes in fact. Lastly, there is a view of inspiration which recognizes only its supernatural and prophetic character, and a view which regards the apostles and evangelists as equally inspired in their writings and in their lives, and in both receiving the guidance of the Spirit of truth in a manner not different in kind, but only in degree, from ordinary Christians." The Professor, on this variety, remarks: "Many of these explanations lose sight of the original meaning and derivation of the word: some of them are framed with the view of meeting difficulties; all perhaps err in attempting to define what, though real, is incapable of being defined in an exact manner."

All appeal to Scripture; yet all error lies in the principle on which this appeal is made. Thus Professor Jowett, it might at first sight appear truly, says, "The nature of inspiration can only be known from the examination of Scripture. There is no other source to which we can turn for information; and we have no right to assume some imaginary doctrine of inspiration, like the infallibility of the Roman Catholic Church."

When, however, an appeal is made to Scripture, in order that by the examination of its contents we may obtain the desired information respecting the nature of inspiration, without at the same time specifying and acting on the principle upon which the inquiry is to be conducted, what is this but an attempt "spargere voces ambiguas," and thus to add one more perplexity of the same kind to the many which the Professor complains to have embarrassed the subject?

For the examination of Scripture, touching its inspiration, may and does strictly mean, an inquiry into those passages of Holy Writ which expressly treat of the sacred influences of the Divine Spirit on the minds and hearts of the writers, enabling them to express accurately the truths which God deigns to reveal.* Such an examination I have fully entered into of several passages of the Bible, all bearing on

---

* See page 52, where Bishop Ellicott is quoted: "The Bible itself shall explain the nature of that influence."

the subject *directly*, in particular that decisive one in the second chapter of 1st Corinthians.

But with Mr. Jowett 'the examination of Scripture' is viewed in a different light, for the quotation above given is continued by Mr. Jowett in these words: "To the question, 'What is inspiration?' the first answer therefore is, 'That idea of Scripture which we gather from the knowledge of it.' It is no mere *à priori* notion, but one to which the book is itself a witness. It is a fact which we infer from the study of Scripture,—not of one portion, but of the whole."

This vague view of the inspiration of Holy Scripture, however redeemed it may seem to be from the common error of proceeding on *à priori* notions, rests notwithstanding on a weak and insecure foundation. For if the examination of Scripture as a whole, according to the judgment of each inquirer, has, in matter of fact, impressed different minds very differently respecting the nature and character of the written word, how wavering and unsteady must be the idea of Scripture which is gathered from the knowledge of it? Mr. Jowett in himself has supplied an example; for this eminent scholar has derived from his own study of Scripture, in reference to inspiration, that "for any of the higher or supernatural views of inspiration there is no foundation in the gospels or epistles." A singularly unaccountable assertion this! which one Biblical student out of a thousand would not endorse. The danger here evidently is, that a favourite idea, already formed from a general impression concerning the Bible at large, or, in reference to this particular question, from an insufficient induction, may prove to be unscriptural. Such in the present instance is undoubtedly the case; for St. Peter expressly states the contrary in his second epistle: "Holy men of God spake, as they were borne along by the Holy Ghost," which is perhaps the strongest language in the Bible, or that can be conceived, to represent the supernatural actuating energy of the Spirit of God in the act of inspiration. And even should the canonicity of 2nd Peter be called in question, other passages are at hand to supply the place of that cited. Above all, the second chapter of the 1st Corinthians settles the point at issue, beyond controversy, that the higher and supernatural view of inspiration is the true and scriptural one. Here the apostle points out how the knowledge of the mystery of Christ is reached by supernatural spiritual agency. Moreover, so deeply was St. Paul impressed with this view of inspiration, that he returns to the subject in the third chapter of the Epistle to the Ephesians, referring again to this source of Divine knowledge: "If ye have heard of the dispensation of the grace of God which is given me to you-ward; how that by revelation He made known unto me the mystery, (as I wrote to you before in few words, whereby, when ye read, ye may understand my knowledge in the mystery of Christ,) which in other ages was not made known unto the sons of men, as it is now revealed unto His holy apostles and prophets by the Spirit."

Now this talented writer, who breaks down the barrier which, as others think, definitively separates the apostles and prophets of the New Testament from ordinary believers, should, I humbly submit, consider whether in holding different degrees of inspiration,* and in attributing errors and mistakes to these chosen servants of God, he has not prejudged the question at issue, by proceeding on '*à priori* notions,' just as much as those who, recognizing "the supernatural and prophetic character of inspiration," deem those apostles and prophets to have been divinely guarded against error.

The truth is, each one who studies the Bible brings to this study a particular bent of mind, the result of many forces, acting often unconsciously to the individual himself, but arising from the various positions into which he may have been thrown in the earlier stages of his life. It may be, too, that at this time a slight cursory reading of the Scriptures presents to his view either the all-perfect certainty of the written word, sanctioned and certified by Him who is "the true Witness;" or certain apparent discrepancies in the gospels, and fanciful mistakes in

---

* The phrase 'degrees of inspiration' is used ambiguously. It sometimes refers to portions of Scripture as more or less inspired; sometimes to the greater or less inspiration vouchsafed to certain men or classes of men; sometimes, again, to different modes of this influence.

the epistles, as well as supposed errors in the Old Testament, may, in magnified proportions, rise up before his imagination, according to the bias of each. Nothing is more natural than that new principles may now occur to minds so predisposed, confirmatory of their particular views, or perhaps leading to those views. Such are the following: one regards conscience, in imperfect and fallen creatures, as an unsafe guide in the determination of scriptural difficulties; the other accords to it a supremacy over the Bible. Reason at length matured, and so fortified, each enters on the deeper study of the Bible. One sees in it nothing but the unerring truth of God; and setting out from this principle, seeks a theory of inspiration to explain how the Scriptures, coming to us through a human channel, can yet be the pure word of God. The other, proceeding on the principle that there may be, and are, errors and mistakes in the written word, fails to recognize its supernatural character, and therefore with him the inspiration of apostles and prophets does not differ from that of ordinary believers—"an inspiration which would be consistent with the apostles falling into error." And because he truly considers that "we have no right to assume some imaginary doctrine of inspiration," cuts the matter short by merely defining inspiration to be "that idea of Scripture which we gather from the knowledge of it." What is this? Or is it a theory of inspiration which, holding only some parts of the

Bible to be inspired, by divinely ordered assistance and guidance enables the inquirer to select those portions of the holy volume which bear the stamp of Divine truth?

The subject-matter of inquiry, however, is not the idea of Scripture *we* gather from our knowledge of it; but the spiritual aids and gifts bestowed on the sacred writers, for the attainment of their knowledge, of which the Holy Scripture is the record.

If, then, in order to abate as much as possible the dangers of prepossession, we take the untutored minds of the young, and try what idea of Scripture they may gather from their knowledge of it,—before the current of popular opinions, above all the opinions of the religious party to which they attach themselves, may turn their pure thoughts into a particular channel, and warp their judgments,—what is likely to be the result?

An experiment made many years ago, on this very subject, sufficiently indicates what ideas the young, without proper and suitable instruction, would form of the nature and character of that blessed Book, and of the influence by which it is pervaded and quickened. At an institution in Daventry a trial was made by the celebrated Dr. Doddridge, and under his superintendence, of the effects of a religious education conducted upon purely abstract principles. Confining himself solely to the study of the Bible, no boy was to be taught any particular tenet or doctrine of religion. Every boy was to have the Bible, and read it for himself. Now what was the upshot? Many young men went from the institution Deists, and not a few Atheists.

The minds of children must be trained by catechetical instruction in order that the reading of the Holy Scriptures may to them be attended with profit. A distinguished prelate of our Church says, "The single ordinance of such instruction has, under Providence, been the great stay throughout Christendom of orthodox unwavering Christianity. . . . . The principal elementary truths of religion become fixed in the memory; and with these the Scriptures, as they are read, harmonize; and these they elucidate and confirm. The truths of religion, to be beneficial to the soul, must be comprehended by the understanding. This was clearly intimated by Philip's question to the eunuch, 'Understandest thou what thou readest?' and the eunuch's candid reply contained a truth of general application: 'How can I, except some man guide me?'"

On the other hand, leave the minds of children untrained, and therefore unfitted for such profitable study of the Bible, and the deplorable consequences that must follow are patent to all. Wrong views of Christianity as the revealed religion of God, and of the Spirit's influence which animates and sustains it, must inevitably succeed. Wrong too must be the idea, under these circumstances, of inspiration arising from their knowledge of Scripture.

Bolder, however, in assertion, but, as proceeding on the same *à priori* notion of the supremacy of conscience over the Bible, equally to be ranked with non-legitimate theories, is that of Dr. Rowland Williams. With him, the Church is an inspired society, and the Bible the written voice of the congregation. If such a Spirit did not dwell in the Church, the Bible would not be inspired. "Bold as such a theory of inspiration may sound," Dr. Williams remarks, "it was the earliest creed of the Church, and it is the only one to which the facts of Scripture answer. The sacred writers acknowledge themselves men of like passions with ourselves, and we are promised illumination from the Spirit which dwelt in them. Hence, when we find our Prayer Book constructed on the idea of the Church being an inspired society, instead of objecting that every one of us is fallible, we should define inspiration consistently with the facts of Scripture and human nature."

Here the same observation applies as in the former case. The inquiry touching the inspiration of Holy Scripture does not relate to the illumination of the Spirit in our study of its contents, which the pious and faithful Christian prays for, and hopes to obtain; but to the gifts and aids of the Divine Spirit vouchsafed to the sacred writers, for the purpose of conveying *to them* the knowledge of the truth, which they may commit to writing for the benefit of the Church in future ages.

Now we do not "define inspiration consistently with the facts of Scripture and human nature," if we view the Church as an inspired society in which the Spirit of God dwelling, directs and rules the whole body in the aggregate, without taking into consideration the special acts of this Divine agent on the minds and hearts of certain chosen servants of God, by which they are prepared and fitted to benefit that religious society called the Church in its collective capacity. These are the facts of Scripture. The apostles of our Lord, though men of like passions as other members of the Church, were nevertheless a chosen few at that time, who, receiving a higher illumination and more abundant revelations, were taught *the knowledge* of the deep mysteries of Christianity, and thus were enabled to preach Christ, and to place on record, for the benefit of future generations, the saving doctrines of the Gospel.

It was one of "the facts of Scripture" noticeable in the apostolic age, that, conformably with a special promise of the Saviour, certain chosen men were enabled through a peculiar illumination of the Holy Spirit, and the gift of abundant revelations, *to know* clearly and fully the great truths of the redemptive scheme, and so enabled to express them "in words which the Holy Ghost teacheth." This is a fact which has no counterpart in the Church of the present day; for although illumination in the study of God's word, and the grace of sanctification—in other words, intellectual and moral inspiration—find a place in our Prayer Book, there are none gifted by the Spirit to add that to the Bible which could be deemed the word of God. What must be the nature of the examination of Scripture, and how to be conducted, in order to ascertain the true idea of its inspiration, has already been shown in page 237. The *à priori* sceptical principles with which the last-named authors have begun the investigation, exclude their theories from the rank of legitimate.

The existence of *à priori* notions may be traced as well in the dogmatic assertions of writers of an opposite school of thought, who proceed from assuming what they take to be the characteristic properties of the written word of God. We are not to commence the investigation in this way, but to explore in the sacred writings the several statements of the procedure by which the Holy Spirit imparted to the writers the knowledge of Divine truth, thereby fitting them to communicate it to mankind. We are not to begin with results, but with the steps, *indicated in Scripture*, by which these results were arrived at. We cannot subscribe to the view of Dr. Lee that "the real question with which our inquiry is concerned is the result of this Divine influence, as presented to us in the pages of Scripture, *not* the manner according to which it has pleased God that this result should be attained."

Theories constructed on this plan, are, as I have shown, unsafe, and to be classed also with the non-legitimate. Such are the theories called the Organic and Dynamic, invented for the explanation of the inspiration of Holy Scripture. Pertinent and in point are the well-considered words of Dean Goodwin: "I believe it will be found to be true that the chief difficulties concerning the question of inspiration have arisen, not from anything in the Bible itself, so much as from theories respecting it which have been built upon insecure foundations by pious men zealous for the integrity of the truth."

Mr. Swainson, too, whose thoughts on the subject run in the same groove, but who yet, deeming it unnecessary, did not supply any scriptural theory in the stead of those which he discarded as unscriptural, profoundly remarks, " Our theory of inspiration of the writers of the books of the Old and New Testaments must be drawn from the language of the writers themselves, and not from the statements of early Christian divines, or from assumed opinions as to the necessities of the case."

Such are the sage and well-directed observations of two eminent divines, who, by way of caution, point the finger to the devious paths of investigation into which theorists are naturally tempted to enter. In order to avoid these dangers, it should be our object and aim to settle and fix the true idea of personal inspiration in precise terms, on scriptural authority; and, ascending from this, to point out how the inspiration of Holy Scripture is connected with the personal inspiration of the sacred writers. For it is the inspiration of the writers which makes the Bible the word of God.

Nevertheless, a course directly opposite is that which hitherto has unfortunately been adopted. The simpler conception of inspiration in the individual is slurred over; and inspiration is, in the first instance, defined relatively to the written word. St. Paul says, "We have received the Spirit which is of God, that we might know:" modern theorists, "that we might write." The problem then proposed for solution is this: 'Given a form of words free from all error, yet coming to us through a human channel, on what conditions has it been secured against, and preserved from, every taint of human infirmity?'

1. The first solution of the problem is the Organic or Mechanical Theory.

From a view of God's word which assigns such a predominant and engrossing prominence to the Divine element as to eclipse and practically ignore the human element, is raised the organic theory of the inspiration of Holy Scripture.

This theory proceeds on *à priori* conceptions of what the true nature and character of the Divine word should be, and the necessary conditions to be satisfied in order that they may be such. This word, as God's word, is true, and exempt from all admixture of error. In every portion of it—even the smallest particle—there is no verbal inaccuracy whatsoever, for the words are those "which the Holy Ghost teacheth." Now, regarding this latter, and kindred forms of expression, in the light of dictation, the necessity is imposed of viewing the person inspired as a passive instrument in the hands of the Divine Spirit, wielded by Him at will, with an absolute controlling power which extends to the body as well as the mind.

Although the internal origin and the true nature of inspiration, as explained in the writings of St. Paul, were quite independent of the influence of any philosophic system of the age, and above all of the Oriental-Platonic philosophy which had its chief seat at Alexandria, yet a reference to Philo may be useful. For representing this philosophy, in its bearing upon Judaism, and being a contemporary of the apostles of Christ, however little his influence *directly* extended to them, he seems, at least as to the external form and didactic development of the Gospel, to have impressed his views on some of the early Christian fathers. For a speculative tendency now began to spring up and grow among them, and it became customary to adapt the logical definitions of the schools to Christian theology. Thus Platonism makes its appearance among the fathers of the Alexandrian school, notably in the writings of Justin Martyr. And it is remarkable what a close resemblance exists between the mechanical theory of Philo and that of Justin. The idea seems to be taken up also by Clemens Alexandrinus and some others of the early fathers. Philo was more of a philosopher than a religionist, and was the first who transferred the ancient heathen idea of the Mantik to the prophets of the Old Testament.

Now this idea, which supposes the prophet at the moment of inspiration to be seized with a divine furor, to be unconscious, and for the time bereft of reason, naturally, and indeed necessarily, demands an organic theory to account for the utterance of words not his own. This state of mind, in the language of Philo ('De Vitâ Mosis,' lib. iii.) is called τὸ ἐνθουσιῶδες, furor fanaticus seu divinus—a divine frenzy. It however derives no support from the rational and sober statement of St. Paul, according to whom "the spirits of the prophets are subject to the prophets" in their moments of intensest rapture. Nor is it sustained by the instances on record of ecstatic visions. In these exciting moments, entranced prophets and apostles enjoyed a conscious exercise of their rational faculties. Peter and Paul are notable examples of this kind.* Even Balaam, who saw the vision of the Almighty, falling into a trance, had his eyes open.†

If, therefore, the view be correct, that a revelation cannot be intelligently apprehended without the

---

* Acts ix. 5 ; x. 14. † Numbers xxiv. 16.

mind being first prepared for its reception,—that no knowledge can be had of it until "the Spirit which is of God"* be previously imparted,—a theory which overlooks or omits this indispensable pre-requisite, this necessary element of Divine Inspiration, is no theory at all of inspiration, at least no legitimate theory, unless it be said that the absence of reason, implied in the Μαντίκη, be that preparation. Taking the utterance as the starting-point, it may perhaps be called a theory of prophecy, based on *à priori* assumptions, and invented for the purpose of accounting for the unerring truth of this Divine result of inspiration, but, properly speaking, it is no theory of inspiration, of which it slurs over—in fact, omits—the essential factors. Viewed in this light, the *locus classicus* of Philo, in which his theory is said to be conveyed, as presented to us in his life of Moses, is rather a classification of the different *species of prophecy*, according to the divers nature of its utterances—the sacred oracles (λόγια)— than a theory of inspiration.

In this celebrated passage the mental state supernaturally induced, which is properly inspiration, and of which prophecy is merely the result, is referred to very slightly by Philo; yet, in several remarkable words and phrases—partly applied to Moses, "inspired and under the Divine afflatus"† partly to prophets in

---

* The Pauline idea is expressed in singularly coincident terms by Josephus: κατὰ τὴν ἐπίπνοιαν τὴν ἀπὸ τοῦ Θεοῦ.

† ἐκ προσώπου Μωϋσέως ἐπιθειάσαντος καὶ ἐξ αὐτοῦ κατασχεθέντος.

general, "actuated by a Divine frenzy,"* and receiving a special "gift or power of prognostication by which they are enabled to foretell future events."†

This state of mind and heart is cursorily slurred by the writer, without analyzing it, after the manner of St. Paul, into its constituent elements. Yet all the while Philo was well aware of the distinction—and that there was such—between inspiration, the source, and prophecy, the result. Thus in a passage which he gives elsewhere, in all the extravagance of his system, the distinction is clearly indicated, though not analyzed; for speaking of the prophet Jeremiah, he says, ὃς καταπνευσθεὶς ἐνθουσιῶν ἀνεφθέγξατο, where Philo appears to satisfy himself that he fully understands the true nature of inspiration, when he identifies it with the heathen *Mantik*, and fixes his attention solely on the utterance of the prophet, as if this was necessary and sufficient to convey the true idea of inspiration.

According to this system, he regards the words (his sole concern) as purely dictated by God Himself to a person who for the time is not master of his own thoughts—*non compos mentis*. "The prophet is an interpreter, God suggesting to his mind within, the words τὰ λέκτεα."

---

* τὸ τοῦ λέγοντος ἐνθουσιῶδες. Thus Cicero, speaking of Epimenides, says, "futura præsentiens et vaticinans per furorem.—*De Divin.*, lib. i.

† μεταδόντος αὐτῷ τοῦ θεοῦ τῆς προγνωστικῆς δυνάμεως ᾗ θεσπιεῖ τὰ μέλλοντα.

Philo, however, does not in this passage divide inspiration into the two species of 'interpretation' and 'prophecy,' as Dr. Henderson, whom Archdeacon Lee follows, seems to think. But in a perturbed and illogical order, divides prophecy or the sacred oracles (λόγια)—"for everything that is written in the sacred books" Philo holds to be oracles—into three classes:

1. When a Divine prophet acts as an interpreter of oracles spoken directly as from the person of God. This is the highest form of prophecy, called by Philo ἑρμηνεία.

2. When the prophet inquires, and receives an answer from God. In this case, there is a mutual intercourse between the Divine and human, the prophet consulting God, and God answering and teaching him.

3. The third species of prophetic utterances are such as are attributed to the lawgiver: God imparting to him the prognostic gift by which he can foretell the future.

Such are the species of *prophecy* (not of inspiration) according to Philo. And it is to be observed, as noteworthy, that he gives the well-known philosophic name of species (ἔιδος) to this third class, calling it τὸ τρίτον ἐέιδος. Philo says that ἑρμηνεία and προφήτεια differ. Of course they differ, as the species differs from its genus: for he distinctly states that the former is prophecy. Hence the necessary consequence is, that if there be a division of inspiration here really intended, inspiration is prophecy—the fountain is the issuing stream, the cause its effect.

The author then adds, "Of the second I shall presently try to give the explanation, having interwoven with it the *third species* also, that in which the Divine mental alienation or religious frenzy of the speaker exhibits itself; on which account it is that he chiefly and legitimately is "considered a prophet." So Cicero, "concitatione quadam animi, aut soluto liberoquo motû futura præsentiunt, ut Baris Bœotius, ut Epimenides Cres."—*De Divin.*, i. 18.

Such is some of the disorder in thought and language which this wrong method of taking the initiative from results has produced. These results are the forms of expression embodied in the written word-oracles concerning which, as touching their nature and true import, assumptions are made necessitating a theory, more or less plausible, to explain. Moreover, as, bearing on the popular views now current, this is a most instructive example: I thought it right to dwell on it at great length; for the same wrong method still prevails, alas! in our day, and is the fertile source of many errors and inconsistencies which yet abound in the hidden and fugitive intricacies of this confessedly difficult subject.

To suppose that we are only concerned with the results as presented in the written word, is a superficial view of the question, "What is meant by the inspiration of Holy Scripture?" For as the nature of prophecy cannot be understood by simply considering it in the utterances of the prophet, without regard to the source of these utterances, in the Divine communications made to him; so the inspiration of the sacred Scriptures is not fully intelligible in the written word without special reference to the subjective conditions according to which they were written. Philo's theory of prophecy, which he (as others who follow him) confounds with inspiration—whether προφητεία be that species of it which he calls ἑρμηνεία, or either of the two other species—is a purely mechanical theory thus expressed by the author: "Our own intellect departs on the arrival of the Divine Spirit; and on His departure it again re-enters. For it is not right that the mortal and the immortal should dwell together. Hence the setting of reason, and the darkness about it, has generated an ecstacy and a divine frenzy."* In another place he says, "A prophet manifests nothing at all of his own, but is an interpreter, another suggesting all that he utters, and himself during the time he is inspired (ἐνθουσιᾷ) being unconscious (γεγονὼς ἐν ἀγνοίᾳ), reason having withdrawn, and surrendered the citadel of the soul; and the Divine Spirit having entered and occupied it, and moving the entire organism of the voice, uttering sounds for the plain manifestation of what he predicts."

We come next to the Apostolical Fathers. Of

---

* Philo, 'Quis rerum,' tom. i., p. 404. Colon, 1613.

these Justin Martyr is said to be the first who presents a more definite explanation, on *à priori* grounds, of the process which is supposed to take place in inspiration.

This is a supernatural endowment: "For it is not possible for mankind, either naturally or by the force of human intellect, to know things so great and Divine but by a gift which then descended from above upon those holy men, who needed not the art of elocution, nor the power of disputation and controversy; but to submit themselves *unreservedly* (καθάρους) to the energy of the Divine Spirit, in order that this Divine plectron, descending from heaven, using these just men as an organ (ὀργάνῳ) of a harp or lyre, should *reveal to us* the knowledge of things divine and heavenly."* Hence Justin infers that "these men, at different times and places, have taught us the great doctrines of Christianity with perfect agreement among themselves."

Justin here supposes the inspired to be merely passive organs, who must submit themselves entirely to the Spirit's influence, herein regarding inspiration rather as the immediate necessary result of the Divine act, than as the outcome of the effect produced by that act on the conscious subject (which is the view of modern writers). Now neither is the exact formal idea of inspiration set forth by St. Paul. Not the former, since to emit musical sounds, the instrument

---

* 'Cohort. ad Græc.' § 8.

must be tuned; and this tuning is the true analogue of that preparation of the mind and heart which is really inspiration; while the strokes of the plectron symbolize revelation: nor the latter, since it is the effect itself on the mind and heart, and not its outcome, which, speaking properly, is inspiration.

By this sad deviation, after so short an interval, from St. Paul's clear and full statement of the real transaction that took place in fitting the sacred writers for the task assigned to them, we may learn how it had arisen.

Considering that they had no concern with anything but the written word, as presented to them in the pages of Holy Scripture, and this being the word of God, and therefore infallibly true, Justin Martyr, Clemens Alexandrinus, and a few others of the apostolic fathers, precipitated the inquiry, without patiently following the steps of the Pauline investigation. Instead of proceeding from the inspiration of the writers—which fitted them to understand and receive the revelations vouchsafed—to the knowledge thus communicated, and from this knowledge to its expression, they, at once assuming the absolute truth of the verbal form of that expression, invented a shorter *à priori* theory to account for it.

Justin seems to be tinged in some degree with the philosophy of the Alexandrian school. He informs us how he came to be a Christian: "I also was once an admirer of the doctrines of Plato; and

I heard the Christians abused. But when I saw them meet death, and all that is accounted terrible among men, without dismay, I knew it to be impossible that they should be living in sin and lust. I despised the opinion of the multitude; I glory in being a Christian."* And it is very natural that the apologist, being imbued with the principles of the same philosophy as the Alexandrian Philo, should exhibit a kindred view to that held by his predecessor on the great question of prophetic inspiration. More especially might this be so, since Justin's idea of *the spermatic word*, as related to the absolute Divine Logos, with him constituted the transition between Christianity and all that was true and good in the times anterior to Christianity. Be this as it may, they both regard the subject of inspiration as a passive instrument in the hands of the Divine Spirit, for the time unconsciously moved by an extraneous force, as κάθαρους in his statement seems to imply. Our own Hooker convincingly shows the scriptural unsoundness of this view, which its author illustrated by sounds given out by a musical instrument.

"The difference," says Hooker, "is only this: an instrument, whether it be a pipe or harp, makes a distinction in the times and sounds, which distinction is well perceived by the hearer; the instrument it self understands not what is piped or harped. The

---

* Apolog. I., pp. 50, 51.

prophets and holy men of God not so. 'I opened my mouth,' saith Ezekiel, 'and God reached me a scroll, saying, Son of man, cause thy belly to eat, and fill thy bowels with this I give thee: I ate it, and it was sweet in my mouth as honey.' Herein were they not like harps or lutes, but they felt the power and strength of their own words. When they spake of our peace, every corner of their heart was filled with joy: when they prophesied of mourning, they wept in the bitterness and indignation of spirit, the arm of the Lord being mighty and strong upon them."*

When Justin's own statement is carefully considered, "I also was once an admirer of Plato," and that this philosopher (Tim. 72, *b*) derives μάντις from μαίνομαι, and distinguishes (as the Greek authors) μάντεις from προφῆται, the former being persons who uttered oracles in a state of divine frenzy, the latter the interpreters of these oracles, new light is cast on the subject. For when we add to this Justin's conception of the connexion of Christianity with all that was good and true in the times antecedent to this era, especially in the classic age of Plato, it is more than probable that there was a much nearer similarity of the view of Justin and others, who took their illustration of the nature of inspiration from the harp or pipe, to that of Philo, than Mr. Westcott seems to think.

This very distinguished scholar says, "As applied

---

* 'First Sermon on Jude 17—21.'

to men who are agents of the Holy Spirit, we should remember that the tone and quality of the note depends as much upon the instrument itself, as upon the hand "which sweeps over the strings." Now the question at issue is this, 'Did these teachers hold the view that the inspired agents at the time were unconscious as well as passive organs of the Divine Spirit?'

Mr. Westcott's observation is clearly decisive of the point that there is a human as well as a Divine element in the written word. But it leaves untouched another point of transcendent and vital importance, namely, that neither in the living nor dead organ do the tone and quality of the note, such as the performer desires, proceed, before the organ has been duly prepared and fitted for that purpose. To compare therefore the living organ to the dead one, *before it is properly tuned*, and from such comparison to explain the nature of inspiration, is a *petitio principii* which presupposes the human instrument to be already prepared by inspiration, in order to give out notes of the required tone and quality.

If, dazzled by the fanciful and engrossing illusion of the lyric illustration, these fathers forgot to allude to the suppression of the conscious exercise of reason at the moment of the Spirit's illapse which had been prominently set forth by Philo, their *silence*, on the other hand, of the scriptural proof of consciousness so forcefully advanced by Hooker, and which, if they had not contrary leanings, must have suggested itself to their minds, is a convincing argument that they held a wrong view of inspiration, too closely allied to that of the Jewish philosopher.

The real state of the case appears to be this: Montanism was the natural outgrowth of so general an opinion; but the extravagance of this extreme party, as naturally produced a reaction in the Church, and this brought their view into disrepute. Neander had indeed reason on his side when he arrived at the conclusion that "this mode of regarding inspiration, which had passed over from the Jews, had up to the time of Tertullian prevailed even among the teachers of the Church; but now, in consequence of the opposition to Montanism, this view was *gradually* suppressed."

This conclusion of the learned historian is greatly confirmed, when it is considered how deeply these sentiments would take root in the Alexandrian soil by the teaching of Clemens. Such too may be the case, although the illustration of the lyre had been handed down among the Christian Fathers for centuries, even to the time of Chrysostom and later; for it may be admitted that this similitude does not *necessarily* imply the unconscious state on the part of the inspired, though, as a matter of fact, such an opinion might have been entertained by many at the first, and long afterwards.*

---

* "The theory of inspiration which is founded upon the illustration of the lyre began with Justin about the year 140, previously to the rise

For shortly after Justin Martyr, there arose another teacher in the Church, Clemens of Alexandria. He also was a Platonic philosopher of the second century, converted to the Christian faith—the disciple of Pantænus, whom he succeeded in the Alexandrian school, where the celebrated Origen was one of his scholars.

Clemens, incidentally alluding to this matter, ('Pædag.,' lib. ii., cap. iv.,) while he quotes the 150th Psalm, uses the similitude of the musical instrument, and applies it even to the material structure of the human body. Referring, in the fourth verse, to the words "Praise Him with stringed instruments and organs," Clemens says, "He calls our body an organ; and its nerves, chords, by which it receives that tension which attunes it to harmony, and struck by the Spirit gives out human voices."

What a favourite illustration the harp or lute was at this time, appears from Origen's extension of it to the organism of the Bible itself! and shows how much wider in application, and how different in the minds of these teachers, had been the idea of inspiration from that of a guidance to the outcoming acts of writing or speaking which in modern times has usurped its place. For, according to Origen, the

of Montanism; and although the opinions of Montanus were still maintained in the sixth century, we can trace a series of writers by whom the same similitude was employed, down to Chrysostom, who on more than one occasion falls into the same train of thought."—*Lee on Inspiration*, Lecture ii., p. 83.

inspiration of the holy volume is that which sends its music right into the heart of man.

In Origen's view, "Scripture as a whole is God's one perfect and complete instrument, giving forth, to those who wish to learn, its one saving music from many notes combined, stilling and restraining all striving of the evil one, as David's music calmed the madness of Saul." ('Comment. on Matt. v. 9.') Besides, this great father has the credit of first presenting the true idea of personal inspiration as opposed to the fanaticism of the Montanists : "The Jewish prophets were illuminated by the Divine Spirit, their intellects becoming more perspicacious, and their souls more lucid, by the touch of the Holy Ghost." ('Cont. Cels.' lib. vii., cap. iv.) Now what is this but the preparation of the mind and heart, which, collecting my information (as Origen says he has done in the same matter) from the sacred Scriptures, I have proved to be the true scriptural view of inspiration. This, Origen in his own forcible language expresses as a Divine act, in these words : "Illumined by the Divine Spirit, so far as was useful to those who prophesied," and, as an effect, in the still more remarkable words, "by *which touch*, as it were, of the Holy Ghost, they were rendered more perspicacious in their understandings, and more lucid in their souls."*

---

* καὶ διὰ τῆς πρὸς τὴν ψυχὴν αὐτῶν, ἰν' οὕτως ὀνομάσω, ἀφῆς τοῦ καλουμένου Ἁγίου Πνεύματος, διορατικώτεροι τε τόν νοῦν ἐγίνοντο, καὶ τὴν ψυχὴν λαμπρότεροι.—*Orig.*, *Cont. Cels.*, lib. vii., cap. iv.

This ἀφή, *touch*, of the Divine Spirit on the mental powers of the prophet, *this tuning* of the human organ, imparting perspicacity and light to his mind, by which he "receives the Spirit which is of God," is the true scriptural idea of inspiration. And then only is he fitted to receive and understand the revelations communicated to him.

Such was the organic theory of the inspiration of Holy Scripture, whose attractive and imposing illustration held its votaries spell-bound for many centuries, even from the earliest dawn of Christianity, until, at the Reformation period, it appeared in its intensest form.

Yet how did it happen that a theory so illusive had led captive for so long a time minds of the highest order? Simply because it was based on plausible *à priori* assumptions respecting the written word, which it had made its starting-point. The assumptions that the words themselves are "inspired by God," and that "the Holy Ghost speaketh" them, were interpreted as literally necessitating their pure dictation by the Divine Spirit.

The test of a true theory of Biblical inspiration is that it explains all the phenomena of the written word. Now one of these, about which all are and must be agreed, is the union of the Divine and human elements in its composition. A theory, therefore, such as the Organic, which fails to account for this undoubted characteristic of God's word, cannot be true.

The proper method of proceeding, as I have already remarked, is to begin by tracing out diligently the notices which Scripture itself gives of the nature and properties of inspiration; and not to lay down, at the outset of the inquiry, certain conditions which are to be satisfied. This latter course is perilous in the extreme; for it is possible to exceed or omit some of the necessary conditions, or to misinterpret one or more of them; and we have seen that such really had been the case in the Organic or Mechanical theory.

The Dynamic theory seeks to assign its proper place to the human element, while it accords to the Divine its due influence on the faculties of the mind, not—as in the Mechanical theory—acting *on* man, but *through* man. This is well and forcibly expressed by Dr. Lee: "The human element, instead of being suppressed, becomes an integral part of the agency employed,—moulded, it is true, and guided, and brought into action, by the co-operation of the Spirit, but not less really on that account participating in the result produced. Nay, more, the peculiar type of each writer's nature was even essential to the due reception of that particular phase of truth presented by his statements: his share in the great work was apportioned to the order of his intellect, and the class of his emotions, while his characteristic form of expression was absolutely requisite for the adequate and complete conveyance of the Divine message." Hence, as Mr. Westcott finely remarks, "The Bible is authoritative, for it is the voice of God; it is intelligible, for it is in the language of men."

Such is the Dynamic theory,—invented more expressly with the view of combining in due proportions the Divine and human elements, and so intended to supply the failure, in this respect, of the Organic theory.

It must be admitted that it is a great advance on the former, and seems to exhibit more truly the *modus operandi* of the Divine Spirit, or the steps of the process by which He qualified certain chosen servants of God to give an accurate expression to the very clear and definite knowledge which He had communicated to them, by revelation and inspiration.

But whether this be the true Pauline view of the inspiration of Holy Scripture, or the Pauline bound too tightly by dogmatic fetters, so as not to include within its scope and sphere some of the phenomena which the Bible presents, it is to be classed among non-legitimate theories; for that only is legitimate which is deduced *directly*, as to its characteristic properties, from the *express statements* concerning the latter, by the sacred writers, as by St. Paul in the second chapter of 1st Corinthians. In this chapter the apostle states explicitly that the *knowledge* of Divine truth is the result of inspiration and revelation combined; and that, under the Spirit's instruction, this knowledge finds its natural and spontaneous expression in words at once human (which "*We* speak"), and Divine ("which the Holy Ghost teacheth").

Instead of deriving the theory from the express statements of the sacred writers about this influence, *à priori* conditions of the problem concerning the written word *in general* are laid down—conditions which a true theory must satisfy.

Dr. Lee limits to two, all the conditions which a true theory of the inspiration of Holy Scripture, must satisfy. These are the following :—

1. "The Bible consists of both a Divine and human element. This leading fact may be regarded as the first of two conditions of our problem—a condition which can only be satisfied by showing how the two elements may be combined."

2. "The second condition is the distinction between revelation and inspiration. This condition arises from that class of facts which indicate that a considerable portion of what the Bible contains, consists of matters already known to the sacred writers: other portions are such as they could not have become acquainted with except by an immediate communication from heaven."

Now here the objections to this method of investigation, urged above by me, reappear in their full force. It is unsafe to assume conditions *à priori* which a true and adequate theory must satisfy. For those conditions, conceived according to the judgment of each, may be too few or too many; or they may be—one or more—untrue.

If the Organic theory did not satisfy the first condition, and was therefore rejected; on the same grounds the Dynamic theory also must be rejected, since it does not satisfy the second. For the criterion of the adequacy of a theory of the inspiration of Holy Scripture must be its fitness to account for every characteristic feature of the written word.

Now Dr. Lee candidly admits the failure of the Dynamic theory to satisfy all the conditions of the problem, in these words: "It appears to me, however, that the dynamical theory, taken alone, is not sufficient to account for all the phenomena which the Bible presents to our view. By it the first condition *only* of our problem is satisfied. We must, therefore, seek for a further principle according to which the remaining condition may also be complied with." He says that the class of facts specified above in the second condition, on which he bases his idea of the nature of inspiration, is satisfied by the distinction between revelation and inspiration.

Thus is the matter brought to an intelligible issue; for while the first condition, as expressed above, has been accepted by all, the second has not. Now this latter is either true or false. If true, the Dynamic theory, which then is not sufficient, must be given up : if false, there remains only one condition to be fulfilled ; and on this supposition, the Dynamic, satisfying the only condition required, is true. Accordingly, on the assumption that no other condition, further than the two, were to be satisfied, and the Dynamic theory be true ; its truth, as an inevitable consequence, necessitates the renunciation of his view of the distinction between revelation and inspiration, and with it the renunciation of his idea of the nature of the inspiration of Holy Scripture, which rests on the difference he supposes to exist between the two classes of facts mentioned in his second condition.

Now it is not unknown to him, that while all admit the truth of the first condition, as perfectly harmonizing with the Pauline or Scriptural view of inspiration, regarded as a factor in the acquisition by the prophet or apostle of the knowledge of Divine truth, many have called in question the distinction between revelation and inspiration which Dr. Lee holds, and the difference between the two classes of facts on which he builds that distinction.

Indeed some eminent divines have been so disconcerted by the relation, *on this view* (which is the popular one) of inspiration to revelation, that they have been forced to give up altogether this distinction as unnecessarily confusing and embarrassing the whole question.

The acute and learned Dr. Henderson observes,

"The strict theological distinction between revelation and inspiration is of comparatively modern date. No traces of it are to be found in the Fathers; nor was it at all used by the Reformers, how strenuously soever they contended for the Divine authority of the Scriptures. It appears to have been first introduced in the seventeenth century by Calovius. It was improved upon by Quenstedt, and afterwards more scientifically by Baumgarten, Seiler, and others; but has since been abandoned as unnecessarily clogging the subject. Even Quenstedt himself was compelled to admit that it could not be absolutely maintained."

An anonymous writer presents to the public in 'The Journal of Sacred Literature,' the ablest article 'On Inspiration and Revelation' that has appeared in our day. This argumentative writer proves by an irresistible logic, that the common notion concerning the nature of inspiration, adopted and enforced by Dr. Lee, cannot on scriptural grounds be accepted. Yet failing to perceive, or not adopting himself, the simpler view of inspiration, as stated by St. Paul, by which the Holy Spirit prepares the mind and heart for the intelligent reception of the revelations vouchsafed, he halted midway before he had reached the goal to which his reasoning was pointing and guiding him. This is to be regretted; for although the distinction against which he protests, cannot be maintained, there is a real distinction between revelation and inspiration. But instead of reasoning out this, he rather counsels Dr. Lee to renounce the distinction completely, or to make inspiration more scriptural by introducing into its conception many ideas which really belong to revelation.

Thus while he maintains that Dr. Lee has not succeeded in establishing the distinction between revelation and inspiration, he relegates to the domain of inspiration many of those facts which are justly by him reckoned among revelations; and, breaking down this distinction, prefers the confusion thence resulting, to leaving inspiration, when divested of those revelations, something quite unmeaning.

But I must let this clever writer speak for himself: " Revelation has a wider scope than simply the communication from heaven of truth, absolutely unknown to the recipient of it. It may be very true that inspiration is given to men without making to them a revelation of what was wholly unknown to them; but unless we define inspiration to be a mere wild, unintelligible impulse to we know not what, we must suppose that it always exerts some influence in the direction of, and partaking truly of the character of, revelation, as correcting or reviving memory, correcting and guiding judgment, correcting and imparting a proper apprehension of the subject in hand. All this is of the nature of revelation, or the making known. And if we strip the inspiration which we attribute to a man of everything of this kind, we reduce it to we do not well know what. It is then either nothing—absolutely nothing but a name, or else a wild, headlong impulse, unintelligible, unreasonable, and ridiculous."

The writer of the article winds up his argument in these words: "We think revelation and inspiration, if different, yet inseparable and different only in so far as inspiration may be called the manner, and revelation the matter, of the Divine communications. . . . We can only express our judgment, that were Dr. Lee to modify his view in this respect, he would remove from his work that which mars its effect."

St. Paul's idea, I conceive, more precisely marks the true difference (for there is such) between revelation and inspiration. "We have received," says St. Paul, "the Spirit which is of God, that we might know"— *i.e.*, that our spirits might be prepared for understanding the Divine communications,—"the things freely given to us of God,"—the things presented to us by revelation.

And this idea of preparation is clearer by far, and much more in unison with the sentiments of the apostle, than anything which the *manner* of the Divine communications can signify. Still this writer, by exhibiting a true view of the extent of revelation, has made an immense step in advance towards the correct and scriptural view of the nature of inspiration. But it is, I repeat, unsafe to dogmatize, anywhere, on a subject so profoundly mysterious as that of the operations of the Holy Spirit on the spirit of man;

for may it not be asked, Are there not other phenomena, recorded in the pages of the Bible, which a true theory must satisfy, as well as those specified by Dr. Lee in his two conditions? And is there no objection that can be raised against the Dynamic theory, except its failure to account for the class of facts presented in the second condition of the problem?

The latest article published on inspiration pronounces the Dynamic theory unsatisfactory, "because it does not meet the cases where we are taught, on the authority of Scripture itself, that the inspired writers did not fully understand the scope and meaning of their own predictions." (1 Peter i. 10—12.) The writer concludes with the sage remark that "plenary inspiration is not to be identified with any special theory of any kind, but deals reverently with the Divine element of Scripture, as a fact, without presuming to explain its operations."

It is still, however, an open question whether all who volunteer this advice, "to deal reverently with the Divine element," have acted up to its spirit; for we do not treat the Divine element with becoming reverence, unless we, to the utmost of our ability, inquire and search diligently for every intimation of the nature of this characteristic of the written word, in all parts of the Bible, particularly in the utterances of that apostle who specially discusses this very subject.

Now, while it must be admitted that no theory

of the same kind as those used in the physical world can group together the results of the operations of God's Spirit upon the spirit of man, because in the latter we cannot appeal to the testimony of man's natural senses, nor higher unaided faculties, as we can in the former; still an appeal can be made to that testimony of inspired writers which is recorded in the Bible, antecedently proved—as having come from God—to be true; and a further appeal touching the reality of those Divine operations can be made to every spiritually minded believer.

I have pointed out how St. Paul has grouped together in a regular and methodical constructive argument, the effects of the several operations of the Divine Spirit, of which the combined forces result in the written word of God. And a devout and careful examination of these in the second chapter of 1st Corinthians will, I submit, bring to light the several steps of the process by which the Spirit had prepared the minds and hearts of God's chosen servants to *receive* and to *know* the deep things revealed, and so instructed them to express the knowledge imparted "in words which the Holy Ghost teacheth;" for when God fits men to speak, He speaks by them.

CHAPTER X.

GENERAL REMARKS, AND CONCLUSION.

AT the close of the last chapter, an important matter, already briefly brought under the reader's notice, turned up again, in the discussion of the theories of the inspiration of Holy Scripture. The matter to which I refer is whether St. Paul's full, formal, and authoritative exposition of the combined result of the several spiritual forces which divinely acted upon the minds and hearts of God's chosen servants,—constituting, in fact, the apostle's proof 'that their written word was the word of God,'—is to be regarded as a theory of the inspiration of Holy Scripture.

In answer to this inquiry, it may, in the first place, be remarked, that the real scriptural facts, which furnish the only reliable data on which a legitimate theory should be based, happen in this case to be simpler and more intelligible than those of either the Organic or Dynamic theory. The conjoint effect of a revelation presented to the mind, and an inspiration which prepared and improved its faculties, so as to enable it to receive and understand that revelation,

—that is, "to know the things freely given of God,"—is a process which clearly accounts for the knowledge imparted. Moreover, when the perspicacity and light—also certified in Scripture—which such a preparation involves are included, how perfect must that knowledge be?

Once again: on the principle that in proportion to its clearness and accuracy, men give expression to their knowledge in appropriate words, the best fitted to convey the precise meaning of their thoughts on such subjects as they have thoroughly mastered, accuracy of knowledge begets accuracy of expression, whatever may be the style and turn of thought of each speaker or writer.

Thus St. Paul, in a form of demonstration, as beautiful as simple, combines the Divine and human elements. The words are at once human—"*we speak*" them; and Divine—the words are such as "*the Holy Ghost teacheth.*"

This theory has a double advantage over the Organic and Dynamic; for the Organic is quite intelligible, but does not explain the union of the Divine and human elements: the Dynamic theory explains this union, but in a way not so easily understood; and fails to satisfy all the arbitrary and because arbitrary (in character and number) uncertain conditions of the problem. On the ground, therefore, of simplicity and comprehensiveness, the Pauline view is to be preferred. This is its first, but not its greatest advantage. It is the scriptural and therefore the true view of the inspiration of Holy Scripture. Resting, moreover, on the explicit statements of the Divine word itself, it is not bound rigorously within the limits of any assumed conditions whatsoever, other than what those statements impose (page 40). The Scriptures do not interpose any new supernatural link in the chain of causes between the acquisition of the knowledge divinely imparted to the apostle or prophet, and the communication of that knowledge by either to mankind, whether by writing or word of mouth. The Saviour promised to His apostles "the Spirit of Truth shall guide you into all the truth;" and this promise was fulfilled when the Spirit of God, presenting revelations, and preparing by inspiration their hearts and minds to receive and understand these revelations—the mysteries of the kingdom of heaven, thus imparted to them the *knowledge* of Divine truth.

"We have," says the apostle, "received the Spirit which is of God, that we might *know* the things that are freely given to us of God." Revelation had brought before their spiritual vision "the deep things of God;" and inspiration—in the language of Origen—imparting to their spiritual faculties increased light and perspicacity, enabled them to know thoroughly the mysteries of the kingdom.

In the absence of any other *supernatural* link, recorded in the Bible, of this chain of causes—namely, revelation, inspiration, knowledge, expression,—interposed between the knowledge and its utterance, we are not justified to introduce another. It would indeed be very unphilosophic to do so, more especially since the causes assigned, which are scriptural, are also sufficient to explain all the phenomena. The revelation, the knowledge of which was presented to the inspired recipient, was not (as some please to say) left to itself, but the brightening effects of such Divine knowledge, imparted by a previous inspiration to all the faculties and powers which subserve the use of language, naturally and spontaneously flow into the words. And thus the Pauline theory is amply capable of explaining all the facts of the case; whereas a theory more definite (made such by an assumption) cannot be safely attempted (page 57). Besides, this would not be inspiration at all, but its result.*

The Holy Spirit teaches the knowledge of Divine truths so clearly and fully, to minds prepared by His inspiration to understand them, that by the laws which govern the utterance of truths entirely within the grasp of knowledge, they are able to express, what they know so perfectly by Divine instruction,

---

* "It seems pretty generally agreed among thoughtful men at present that definite theories of inspiration are doubtful and dangerous. . . . . The exact relation of the human element to the Divine, it may be difficult to define. Yet some thoughts may aid to an approximation to the truth, perhaps sufficiently clear for practical purposes."—*Bishop Harold Browne, Aids to Faith,* page 302.

in the natural and spontaneous outflow of words which exactly represent the knowledge divinely taught. In fact, of truths so taught, and so precisely presented by the Spirit to the mind, the words, which are their exact representatives—especially as to a great extent men think in words—thoroughly exhibit the nature. Consequently the apostle adds, as a sequel to the knowledge imparted, " which we *also* speak in words which the Holy Ghost teacheth." For what is all this but fitting men to speak? and it has been observed that when God fits men to speak, He speaks by them.*

Now try to explain, in a different manner, if possible, the form here employed by the apostle, "which we also speak in words which the Holy Ghost teacheth," and you will be the better able to judge St. Paul's explanation, and that it is the only possible one.

Two other modes of explanation have been attempted: 1. That the words have been dictated directly by the Spirit of God. 2. That by some unknown impulsive force of the Divine Spirit, the servants of God have been guided to the very words, which guidance has been taken for inspiration. For such has been defined, "The actuating energy of

---

* Exodus xxiii. 22, compared with xxx. 2, 3. The latter shows that the Angel was distinguished from God; and yet while the Angel speaks, God speaks by him.—See Patrick *in loco*, and Kalisch's Historical and Critical Commentary, page 463.

'the Holy Spirit, in whatever degree or manner it may have been exercised, guided by which the human agents chosen by God have officially proclaimed His will by word of mouth, or have committed to writing the several portions of the Bible."

The former of these explanations, which is that adopted by the supporters of the Organic theory, is quite intelligible, but, ignoring the human element altogether, is at present by every one exploded as unsound. The second, overlooking or mistaking the steps of a process not noticed in the Dynamic theory, though minutely analysed by St. Paul, is for this reason, however plausible, unsatisfactory; and simply stating the ultimate fact, without telling how the transition is made from the actuating energy to its outcome in words, explains nothing. For the guiding process, ending with the words, consisting of several parts, is here taken in mass, and lumped into one operation, called inspiration. Now to regard this *total* guidance as inspiration, while it really partakes so much, and in so many respects, of the nature of revelation—as has been proved—is intelligible only by an intolerable confusion of revelation with inspiration. Such blending of things so diverse in their respective natures has indeed been the fruitful source of perplexing confusedness of thought and language.

We have seen that our Church holds this guidance, whether to words or acts, to be a result of inspiration, not inspiration itself; and that the same is the view set forth by the Holy Scriptures themselves.

Let us, for the sake of brevity, pass over the numerous instances that might be adduced, and again refer to one very remarkable case. The aged Simeon was inspired: "The Holy Ghost was upon him; and it was revealed unto him that he should not see death before he had seen the Lord's Christ. And he *came by the Spirit* into the temple." He was inspired both when the Spirit fitted his heart and mind to receive and understand the revelation imparted to him, and when "he came *by the Spirit*" into the temple to witness the realization of the hopes he had been cherishing.

The words which followed his faith, that the child whom he took up in his arms and blessed was in very deed the Lord's Christ, are to be considered the outcoming result of his inspiration, conformably to the Old-Scriptural maxim adopted by the apostle (compare Psalm cxvi. 10 with 2 Cor. iv. 13): "We having *the same Spirit* of faith, according as it is written, 'I believed, and therefore have I spoken;' *we also believe and therefore speak.*"

In the second place, the argument usually brought forward against St. Paul's exposition being regarded as a theory of the Divine character (or inspiration) of Holy Scripture, is answered by the analogy of physical theories.

It has been urged that in our ignorance of the laws

which govern the acts of our own spirits, much more those of the Divine Spirit,—and above all of the laws which govern the operations of God's Spirit on the human spirit,—we have not sufficient knowledge of the facts, as data on which to build a theory of the inspiration of Holy Scripture.

Now this objection applies as strongly to the Organic and Dynamic theories, which are moreover admitted to be, the one false, the other insufficient. But in answer to this common defect of all theories relating to spiritual acts, it may be replied, that physical theories are open to a similar objection, owing, in like manner, to our ignorance or scanty knowledge of the nature and properties of the elementary particles of matter,—whether, in relation to matter or mind, the facts to be observed and classified are the results of certain exciting causes. The powers inherent in matter are deduced from facts which are classified, and for convenience denoted by general terms.

Thus amber (or electron), in common with several other substances, by friction present phenomena so similar, that to the *source* of the power of attraction, exhibited by all, we give the general name of electricity. Its analogy to what may take place in the spiritual world, appeared so striking to Thales, six centuries before the Christian era, that he considered the amber had become, by the act of friction, animated. This fancy of the philosopher notwithstanding, it may be remarked that in the operations of the Spirit of God on the human spirit, whether regard be had to moral or intellectual inspiration, of which the end is either the communication of sanctifying grace or the knowledge of religious truth, and its suitable expression in words, there is a manifest analogy to the operations of the powers of nature in the world of matter. For the Holy Spirit prepares the mind and heart; and whether the enlightened understanding fits man to comprehend the truth revealed, and disposes the heart to receive it, or the love of Christ constrains the renewed Spirit of the pious Christian to do works pleasing to God, this implanted love and that enlightenment are real facts,—something more than mere figures of speech.

Such preparations are unquestionably true motive forces, true exciting causes,—as true and as real as friction is the exciting cause of, and the preparation for, electricity. And as, when a proper object is presented to, and brought within, the sphere of its influence, the prepared amber draws that object to itself, so the mind and heart, prepared by inspiration, take in and grasp the truth which revelation presents.

Now at this point of our inquiry we have before us clearly enough the phenomena whether of our material illustration, or of the spiritual problem of the inspiration of Holy Scripture. In the one case, friction brings out the facts of electricity; in the other, personal inspiration concurring with revelation, as an object presented to the mind, produces religious knowledge, and this knowledge emerges in the word of God.

Thus the preparation of personal inspiration, when a revelation is placed before the mental vision, brings in its train the resulting phenomena of religious knowledge and the Divine word. The whole compound process is aptly designated 'the inspiration of Holy Scripture.' But when we inquire further what is the nature of *this* inspiration, the question, in the last resort, is reduced to the simple issue, 'How is the knowledge expressed by man, the word of God?' Of this several solutions have been given, in which much of conjecture and assumption appear. Still there have been fully as much conjecture and hypothetical reasoning employed in the explanations advanced to account for the phenomena of electricity; and yet these have been dignified with the rank and title of theories.

If, in the one case, Franklin and Faraday have given hypotheses to explain the nature of electricity, and these have been called theories; in the other, the hypothetical explanations of the inspiration of Holy Scripture may be as justly denominated theories. So far, indeed, as these are not clear and well-defined utterances of God's word, uncertainty hangs over them; and at best they are only hypotheses. But even so, they can claim the rank of theories just as much as those of electricity—a great force veiled under the obvious phenomena of nature.

The case then stands thus. The utterances in the Bible, on the authority of Scripture, already proved to have come from God, are accepted as God's word: 'How then can that be the word of God, of which men were the utterers?'

First theory: Man, the agent employed, is a passive instrument, and merely an amanuensis of the Spirit who dictates the very words. This, merging the human element in the Divine, gives no explanation of the former.

Second theory: The Holy Spirit employs the human faculties in conformity with their natural laws. The actuating energy of the Divine Spirit, co-operating with the subordinate agency of man, leads the human agent to the accurate and certain utterance of the words. This may be very true, and doubtless is; but merely gives the agents, not the agency employed. And this latter, a legitimate theory must of necessity clearly set forth. The former theory is free from this fault.

The third theory is the Pauline. This, besides embracing the Dynamic view—that the result springs from the co-operation of the actuating energy of the Divine Spirit on the human faculties, employed in conformity with their natural laws—explains the agency used, namely inspiration, to prepare the heart and mind to receive and comprehend the objective truth presented by revelation; the knowledge arising from the combined spiritual forces of revelation and inspiration; and the expression in words by the agent divinely taught.

The principle, on which the accuracy of the words depends, is the *brightening effect* of such divinely taught knowledge. Even under human teachers, if the knowledge of any subject is improved, the persons so taught express that knowledge more correctly; and if the knowledge be further increased, the expression becomes more correct;—how much more when the teacher is that Spirit who was to guide the disciples of Christ into all the truth? At any rate, beyond this point we are not, on scriptural grounds, justified to go.

I cherish a hope that the all-important questions, What is the true nature of inspiration, personal and Biblical? and, What is the true relation of the latter to the former?—which Dean Alford considered the key to the solution of this deep problem—will engage the attention of some of our distinguished theologians having more ability to grapple with the difficulties of the subject than I can claim.

In my humble opinion, the many inconsistencies and contradictions which eminent scholars of our day have pointed out in modern treatises on inspiration, are to be attributed, almost entirely, to wrong ideas concerning inspiration, and the answer which each of the authors would give to the short question, 'What is inspiration?'

The true answer to this question is a desideratum,

bequeathed to us by our predecessors in this field of inquiry. And the hope that I entertain of its final and satisfactory solution rests upon the following considerations. With much praiseworthy diligence, many writers have accumulated an immense mass of patristic materials, adding to it the rich treasures of the scholastic age, and extending their investigations to the post-Reformation period. But, unfortunately, making their starting-point a definition arbitrarily assumed from the dogmatic theology of Rome, and not, as it should be, derived from the notices of inspiration in the Bible,—for, with little variation, their definitions are all resolvable into Perrone's,—the consequences are such as might be expected. One advantage, however, and that of great value, these consequences bring in their train: they prove unquestionably that this definition is radically unsound. Still, making such a definition our point of departure, how are we prepared to read and candidly examine the passages in the Fathers which bear on the subject?—nay, how are we prepared to read and examine those that relate to it in the Bible?

As Archbishop Whately has excellently well remarked, "Whoever sets out with a favourite theory of his own, and then searches the Scriptures for confirmations of it, will hardly ever fail to find them. He will be viewing objects through a coloured glass, which will impart its own tint to everything he looks at."

And yet how amazingly little, if any, proofs from Scripture have the supporters of this view been able to gather? The case with them is rather that of men who view objects through a glass so deeply stained that it renders them invisible. And so they do not perceive what others, whose minds are free from prejudice, see distinctly—an awfully real state of spiritual dulness, such as the Jewish Rabbis, who had made the word of God of none effect by their traditions, laboured under; and for which our Lord rebuked His hearers, in the prophetic language of Isaiah, " Seeing ye shall see, and shall not perceive."

How can minds preoccupied with something, such as Perrone's definition of inspiration,—which is really no definition of inspiration at all, and which gives no information, but is of such a negative character that a singularly powerful reasoner has pronounced it "*absolutely nothing,*"—deduce a more correct view from St. Paul's full, elaborate, and complete statement of the true nature of Biblical inspiration, set forth, on set purpose, in his First Epistle to the Corinthians?

Reading the Fathers, too, with the same prepossessions, we are not likely to benefit much by the hints occasionally thrown out by them, which might otherwise suggest more correct views. For though Hagenbach truly observes that "they speak of inspiration in very general terms; and in quoting passages from the Old Testament, they indeed use the phrase λέγει το πνεῦμα τὸ ἅγιον, or similar forms, but do not give any more definite explanation regarding the manner of inspiration;" yet are there some few remarkable intimations to be found in the Fathers which might point candid inquirers to a more accurate idea of the true nature of inspiration; such as when they speak of the co-operation of the Holy Spirit with the sacred writers, and still more when they indicate the effects of the Spirit's operations on their minds and hearts.

Modern authors have collected some singularly expressive passages of this kind, which to a marvel agree with the Pauline ideas of inspiration. But committed, one and all, to some form of Perrone's definition—which explains nothing, except stating the mere result—do not avail themselves of the helps these passages afford towards the formation of a *correct* definition.

Origen has done much in this way. He not only states that the Holy Spirit co-operates (συνεργοῦντος) with the writers, but he tells us how,—namely, by imparting to them enlightenment and perspicacity.

Dr. Lee's extensive reading of the Fathers brought before him many points which should have smoothed the way to a correct definition, exhibiting the proper and essential characteristic of inspiration. It brought before him " the condition of the sacred writers when under the influence of inspiration." " The Fathers," he adds, "reject the idea that this at all resembled that state of unconsciousness which the Montanists represented as the essence of true prophecy.* On the contrary, the notions of quickened intuition and enlightenment of the faculties of the prophet are strongly insisted upon. Thus Cyril Alexandrinus frequently argues, not merely that the future events, which they predicted, flashed upon the minds of the prophets by the illuminating influence of the Holy Spirit, but that they actually saw the events themselves."

Now what is this preparation of the Divine Spirit, which enlightens the mind, imparts strength and quickness to the power of intuition, and disposes the heart to receive the revelation presented—which the former enabled it to understand—but inspiration?

"We have received," says the apostle, "the Spirit which is of God, that we *might know* the things freely given to us of God." And what does Cyril, quoted above, really say? "The prophets were instructed on suitable occasions, not by mere [verbal] messages: the Holy Ghost flashing upon their minds the *knowledge* of each thing," etc.

The communication of the knowledge of Divine things is the point on which both St. Paul and Cyril fix their thoughts, as the immediate effect of the Spirit's operations. And this should not be omitted by Archdeacon Lee in his translation of Cyril's words,

---

* In this the Montanists followed Philo exactly. See the closing remark of the *locus classicus* quoted by me in the note, page 336-7.

(see p. 508). St. Paul analyses this knowledge into its constituent factors—revelation and inspiration; but this finds no place in the commonly received definitions of inspiration. Knowledge so imparted may, however, suggest a more accurate definition of inspiration, being, in the mind of St. Paul, its prominent idea.

In fact, it is through knowledge that the Spirit's teaching of the words comes ; and for this purpose it is that inspiration exercises its effect as an internal operation on the soul of the recipient. What follows is not inspiration, but its outcoming result: in the same manner as in the grace of sanctification (moral inspiration), for which we pray, the performance of the righteous acts is not inspiration, but something to succeed it, for which we *also* pray, in the collects for the Holy Communion and the Fifth Sunday after Easter.

The course of inquiry in these pages has been chosen on Scripture ground ; and it has been my object and aim to determine, in the first place from the word of God itself, the nature of that which all regard as its great characteristic—inspiration. It has been, moreover, my earnest endeavour to enter on that course without seeking to fortify my position by any *à priori* assumptions borrowed from the early Fathers of the Christian Church. The only question in reference to their very valuable literary remains is the place which they should occupy in an investigation relating to the nature of the inspiration of Holy Scripture.

'The judgment of the Fathers,' as affording confirmation of what has been proved already by the word of God, cannot be prized too highly. Kept in their proper place, how many precious corroborations of truths, established by Scripture, do these venerable defenders of the faith supply? But to those who began with them, adopting arbitrary definitions and divisions, and next studying the Holy Scriptures with the view of finding out proofs for their assumptions what has been the result? In particular, what confirmations of the old division of 'inspiration' into 'revelation and Divine direction,' or of the new arbitrary definition of inspiration—the offspring of the former—has the most laborious of compilers, been able to extract from the voluminous writings of the Fathers?

I am constrained to answer, absolutely none worth noticing. On the other side, I am bound to say that the great majority of those extracts,—and the same observation extends to the scholastic and German divines,—lends powerful support, in many beautiful and touching passages, to the scriptural view of inspiration given by St. Paul, on collateral points bearing on the subject. The direct discussion of the apostle they scarcely enter on. For the problem, What is the nature of inspiration? is of comparatively modern growth, and can only be solved with certainty by an appeal, on proper principles, to the Bible itself, as stated by me in page 268.

With Dr. Lee, 'the judgment of the Fathers' is indeed a careful and painstaking compilation; yet far too discursive and ambitious in its character is this collection of extracts to stoop to a formal discussion of the simple question, 'What is inspiration?' Though of great variety, and soaring high, it was too speculative to confine itself to the pure region of scriptural truth.

'The judgment of the Fathers'—although not supporting his view of inspiration—is, indeed, a very able, elaborate, and otherwise useful compilation. But the Fathers, indulging much in speculative conjecture, failed to notice the primary question, 'What is inspiration?' It is, I think, Lord Bacon who observes that men, aiming at high things beyond their grasp, often missed the discovery of truths quite within their reach, and before their eyes. The earth-born giants heaped Pelion on Ossa, and were still as far from heaven as ever.

But seeking in the holy volume itself, on a right principle, the nature of that Divine influence which actuated and quickened the writers, and fitted them for their work; next, proceeding to inquire, in the same blessed book, how and by what appliances the knowledge of religious truth was formed in their minds; and, lastly, how this knowledge emerged in words which "the Holy Ghost teacheth,"—a rational and well-grounded hope may spring up that the true scriptural idea will be reached in the light of God's word, when it is reverently studied in the direct notices which it supplies of the matter under consideration.

On the other hand, make, *in the first instance*, the idea you form of this influence, according to the terms of some arbitrary definition of inspiration, your starting-point, and then seek in the Bible proofs of that definition,—a definition borrowed, it may be, from some doubtful source, and scarcely supported by one of the early Christian Fathers,—and mark the consequences which are likely to follow. No doubt one *so predisposed* will find in the Bible some proofs, and some confirmations perhaps in the Fathers. Still, what are the consequences likely to be? and what, in fact, have they, under these circumstances, actually been? Doubt takes the place of certainty, self-contradiction of consistency, error of truth; for now, living in an atmosphere surcharged with impurities, the discords which it conveys to the mind jar upon the ear of the soul, not harmonizing with the hallowed utterances of the Divine word.

Here is a touchstone by which to try any proposed definition of inspiration. The distinguished theologians who, dissatisfied with the principles on which the popular treatises on this subject had been constructed, and had pointed out the inconsistencies of their authors, have thus subjected the prevailing idea of inspiration

—implied in every treatise which adopted Perrone's definition—to a decisive test.

It has been the anxious and careful endeavour of the writer of this essay, by a strict exegesis of the language of Scripture, to steer clear of these inconsistencies. Still, feeling how imperfectly he has accomplished his task,—although fully persuaded of the scriptural accuracy of the view he has taken of inspiration,—if any of the distinguished theologians referred to would point out a flaw of another kind in the argument by which it has been established, he will be found open to conviction, and ready to correct where correction is necessary. Meanwhile, until one of them finds a better way to answer the difficulties and to remove the inconsistencies of which he* complains, the writer of the essay offers to his serious and prayerful consideration this small contribution to so desirable an end; and, bidding him farewell, invites him to continue the work here begun, under the teaching of the blessed Spirit.

> Perge, vale : si quid novisti rectius istis
> Candidus imperti ; si non, his utere mecum.

---

* Mr. Swainson was one of the most distinguished of the theologians who complained of such inconsistencies. To these I have referred in pages 317 and 318.

APPENDIX.

NOTES AND ILLUSTRATIONS.

CHAPTER I.

Page 3.—Mr. Robertson, convinced of the danger of making the idea which men form of the written word the starting-point of an inquiry into the nature of inspiration, and persuaded that all reliable positive teaching on this subject must be taken from *express statements* of Holy Scripture, illustrates a character divinely impressed on the inspired word.

In fact, on this principle, the nature of inspiration may be legitimately investigated in either of two ways. We may either consult the holy volume for *direct statements* of the Spirit's agency in producing in the minds of prophets and apostles "the *knowledge* of the things freely given to them of God;" (and a knowledge clear and definite, passing through minds specially prepared by the Spirit to receive and thoroughly understand the truths conveyed, finds a suitable expression in words which, however marked by individual peculiarities, must bear the Divine impress;) or we may seek, on the same principle of *direct statement*, what the characteristics of the word, as an inspired document, are.

In this way, by a rigorous logic, Robertson deduces from Romans xv. 1—4 an undoubted characteristic of the inspired word—namely, that "Scripture is of *universal application*, all its lines converging towards Christ."—*Robertson's Sermons*, 4th Series, page 299.

I have adopted in my Essay the former method, as applying to all the characteristics impressed by the Holy Spirit on the word of God.

Page 10.—Jesus, the Son of Sirach, the translator of his grandfather's book, thus speaks of his composition :—

"Παρακέκλησθε οὖν μετ' εὐνοίας καὶ προσοχῆς τὴν ἀνάγνωσιν ποιεῖσθαι, καὶ συγγνώμην ἔχειν ἐφ' οἷς ἂν δοκῶμεν τῶν κατὰ τὴν ἑρμηνείαν πεφιλοπονημένων τισὶ τῶν λέξεων ἀδυναμεῖν· οὐ γὰρ ἰσοδυναμεῖ αὐτὰ ἐν ἑαυτοῖς Ἑβραϊστὶ λεγόμενα, καὶ ὅταν μεταχθῇ εἰς ἑτέραν γλῶσσαν."

Side by side with this, read Cano's guarded statement, " hæc supernaturali lumine et expressâ revelatione ut scriberentur non egebant."

Page 18.—In his 'University Sermons' Professor Salmon argues from several passages in St. John's Gospel that "the superhuman knowledge which our Lord, as man, possessed, did not exist in Him necessarily by virtue of the hypostatical union of the two natures, but was communicated to Him by that Spirit which dwelt in Him without measure. . . . All these passages (St. John vii. 16, xii. 49, xiv. 10, and v. 20) point to the conclusion that His human knowledge admitted of increase by *Divine revelation*, and that it was therefore naturally finite."

In pages 235, 236 of the present Essay, Thomas Aquinas enumerates suggestion as a class of revelations.

Page 31.—"Those which are called *real* definitions, viz., which unfold the nature of the thing, (which they may do in *various degrees*,) to these the epithet 'true' may be applied; and to make out such a definition will often be the very end (not as in mathematics the beginning) of our study."—*Whately's Logic*. I have therefore postponed defining inspiration and revelation until I had ascertained their essential properties.

Page 39.—The second paragraph should begin thus: "According to the commonly received view of inspiration, some are supposed to have thought;" and the notes in pages 41 and 43 should change places.

CHAPTER II.

Page 51.—On the ground that theories of inspiration have been called forth by emergencies, and drawn up to meet difficulties which may have arisen from assuming beforehand that such and such are the genuine properties of Holy Scripture, instead of appealing first and foremost to Scripture itself for information on these very points, the Bishop of Gloucester and Bristol justly (see page 73 of this Essay, and also page 110,) advises the rejection of all theories of inspiration. This advice, however, only extends to *extra-Biblical* theories; not to one (such as I hold the Pauline to be) truly scriptural, based on no assumptions whatever, but on the very words of the inspired apostle himself. And a lucid statement of this kind in a systematic order, ascending from personal inspiration and revelation to knowledge, and from this divinely imparted knowledge to its expression in words, on which the enabling and brightening effects of that Divine knowledge are stamped, is a theory in every sense of the word; nor would it have escaped notice, had not *this knowledge* been hitherto kept in the background most unaccountably.

Page 76.—The following is Dr. Lee's observation to which I have referred: "When the apostles acted as instruments of God for the edification of the universal Church, they were supplied with every needful qualification. Their understanding (νοῦς) was enlightened so as to be in perfect accordance with the spiritual influence (1 Cor. xiv. 18, 19). For the attainment of this end, the following gradation in the conferring of gifts had been (as he points out in ver. 6) observed: revelations or new communications of Divine truth (ἀποκαλύψεις) had been conveyed to their minds; *unclouded insight* and *clear perception* (γνῶσις) had next been granted; the power of expounding (προφητεία) had also been conferred; to all which had been added the gift of doctrinal application (διδαχη)."

Now what is the enlightening of their understanding, so as to prepare it for the Divine communications, but the unclouded insight and clearness of perception imparted by the Holy Spirit to enable them to *know* the things freely given to them of God? First were granted revelations; next, "the Spirit which is of God," or inspiration. Such is St. Paul's order, both here and in 1 Cor. ii. 10, 12. So the unclouded insight or perspicacity is not knowledge, but inspiration—a necessary factor of knowledge. This knowledge is succeeded by its prophetic announcement, and is well and truly expressed by Dr. Lee (p. 208 of his treatise) in these words: "The continued preservation of the human agent's intelligent consciousness, and the elevation of his natural faculties for the reception of the Divine suggestions, are the characteristics of true prophecy."

In fact, out of the two factors—a revelation presenting an object to the mind, and an inspiration fitting that mind to receive and understand the truth which it infolds—springs knowledge; and the outflow of this divinely imparted knowledge in representative words is the Pauline theory of the inspiration of Holy Scripture. Other theories (it has been shown in page 73) as being extra-Biblical, have not the same claim on our consideration.

CHAPTER III.

Page 100.—Defining in a logical form 'inspiration' regarded as a general influence of the Holy Spirit, we take the genus, under which every species of it is to be classed, 'a gift or energy of the Divine Spirit.' Thus too the peculiar properties of the two species under consideration—revelation and inspiration—are their essential differences, by which they are severally discriminated from other gifts of the same Spirit. See pages 106, 107.

CHAPTER IV.

Page 111.—Revelation, regarded as something disclosed by God (and in this sense it is used by Bishop Butler), refers to the matter divinely communicated to the world. But when reference is made to revelation and inspiration as the factors of the knowledge imparted by the Spirit of God to the minds which were to be the media of its transmission to mankind, revelation is understood as an act of the Spirit by which He presents objective truth to minds prepared by inspiration to receive and understand it. Such an idea did not escape the subtle intellect of Butler. "In like manner," he remarks, "we are wholly ignorant what degree of new knowledge it were to be expected God would give mankind by revelation, upon supposition of His affording one ; or how far, or in what way, He would interpose miraculously to *qualify* them to whom He should originally make the revelation for communicating the knowledge given by it."

CHAPTER V.

Page 137.—Inspiration of prophets and apostles is peculiar at least in the higher degree of light imparted to them.

Ewald in the introduction of his work on the prophets, while considering that their inspiration was special and different from that of other men, yet holds that the difference was in its object and in its form, and not in its essence.

CHAPTER VI.

Page 161.—Although a guidance to an external act is not inspiration, there is, notwithstanding, a real guidance, in a double sense, connected with a divinely inspired revelation—that is, with a revelation known and received through inspiration. The prophets and apostles were the teachers and guides of the people, and designed to be such, whether by oral or written communications of the truth disclosed to themselves. But to be such, they must themselves have been taught of God, and guided by His Spirit into the knowledge of that truth. The consideration of the latter is the key to the right understanding of the former, or the Divine guidance through the word writter by inspired men.

Page 163.—By the enlightenment of the intellect, when the heart also is reached and touched by the Spirit of God, the knowledge of Divine truth is much enhanced. This our Lord testifies in John vii. 17 ; and proves the close connexion the exists between intellectual and moral inspiration noticed by St. Paul in Eph. iv. 17, 18, and v. 8.

CHAPTER VII.

Page 193.—The consideration of inspiration *in general*, even in those forms of it which can be properly called only 'a quasi inspiration,' points clearly to the genuine nature of that which is truly supernatural. For it implies that the latter is a *power* impressed by the Holy Spirit on the mind and heart, qualifying God's chosen servants for the manifestation of spiritual gifts. This manifestation is not the inspiration, but the result of it (see page 204), which can profit the Church by oral teaching, and still more by a written permanent record.

The historic origin of spiritual gifts is traced in the following manner by Neander. The natural relation of the Church-members to each other points of itself to some organic form as indispensable in the constitution of the community; and as the Christian life shaped itself to the form of these natural peculiarities, which it ennobled, the natural talent was elevated to a charism. So may the rise of the charisms of γνῶσις and διδασκαλία and others be accounted for; and by these a chosen number of God's servants become qualified to render priceless service to the Church.

Page 219.—Whatever may be the effects on the mind and heart of inspiration—whether these effects be speculative or practical—whether they lead to words or to actions,—exhibiting, that is, either in set forms the truths of religion, or, in righteous conduct, holiness of life,—it is itself an influence wrought inwardly on the soul by the Divine Spirit. The words and actions are only the outcome of that influence. For the idea invariably assigned to inspiration is that of something infused or inbreathed, antecedent to and distinct from, and therefore not to be confounded with, any subsequent acts or results springing from them. This, in the Wisdom of Solomon (xv. 11), is expressed by the verbs ἐμπνέω and ἐμφυσάω.*

---

* ὅτι ἠγνόησε τὸν πλάσαντα αὐτὸν καὶ τὸν ἐμπνεύσαντα αὐτῷ ψυχὴν ἐνεργοῦσαν καὶ ἐμφυσήσαντα πνεῦμα ζωτικόν.

CHAPTER VIII.

Page 225.—While we have no reason to complain of diversity of opinion, among the early Fathers of the Christian Church, on the *nature* of inspiration, since they scarcely touched on the subject, we can console ourselves, as Bishop O'Brien has done, on a question very much akin to the present one. The question concerning "the nature and effects of faith," on which these Fathers differed very much, is discussed by this great thinker with singular power and clearness of expression. "For myself," says this eminent prelate of our Church, "in all such conflicts of ancient opinions, I feel ready heartily to adopt the spirit of Calvin's summary decision of one of them: 'Scio eos posse Origenem et Hieronymum citare, suæ expositionis suffragatores: possem et illis vicissim Augustinum opponere: sed quid illi opinati sint nostra nihil refert, *si constat quid voluerit Paulus.*' And I think, in the present case, that I have shown—I am sure I see—that we are able to make out Paul's meaning very clearly without their assistance."

With a similar object in view, I have stated in page 237 of this essay, the only safe and reliable method of investigating the nature of the inspiration of Holy Scripture. And if I have succeeded in tracing out, in clear outline and arrangement, the meaning of St. Paul, I feel the more confident as to the scriptural accuracy of my conclusion.

Page 232.—"We can at once discern how an elevation rather of all the powers whereby ideas are apprehended was of necessity required for the purpose of enabling him to receive or to transmit to others the mysterious truths which were disclosed to him," etc. Such a clear and precise view of the real nature of inspiration abundantly shows that this Divine influence consisted in the qualification imparted by the Holy Spirit to the mind and heart, which fitted the recipient for the subsequent efficient discharge of certain duties he was bound to perform. In fact, inspiration had been exerted, and produced this necessary qualification, before he spake or committed to writing the truths divinely communicated to himself."

"The misrepresentations of the true signification of *faith*, and of its true place in the work of our justification,"—as the subject has been ably and skilfully treated by Bishop O'Brien,—afford striking illustrations of similar misrepresentations of the genuine scriptural doctrine of inspiration.

In a profoundly interesting chapter this prelate discusses at great length 'The Corruptions of the Doctrine of Justification.' The confusion which arises from mixing up the principle and source of good works with the latter, which are results flowing from that source, finds its counterpart in the matter whose nature we have been discussing. As faith is misrepresented by those "who include obedience in the notion expressed by the term *faith*," for "this is to deviate manifestly from its meaning in common language; as I presume all who contend for this as its scriptural sense, would be ready to acknowledge;" so inspiration is misrepresented by a similar deviation from the popular signification attached to this word, viz., an influence of the Holy Spirit, producing a new character or state—intellectual or moral —of the mind and heart. As in the former case, faith is not a guidance to good works, which yet spring from it; so in the latter, inspiration is not a guidance to the expression, oral or written, of the knowledge imparted by the Spirit, which expression, however, even with more unerring certainty* flows from it, than good works from faith. If 'with the heart, man believeth unto righteousness' (Rom. x. 10),—if, that is, faith is an inward principle leading to good works,—still more is inspiration an influence wrought within man's soul, as one of the spiritual operations by which a knowledge of the truth is imparted, and thus leading to the external act of its expression. So much for an internal character, which is common to both faith and inspiration."

Again, I may remark, a similar confusion, arising from a similar extension of the idea of repentance to the outward form which it assumes in the Church of Rome. The idiomatic phrase by which this grace has been expressed in the Latin language, has

---

* We are here chiefly speaking of the results of the inspiration promised by Christ to His apostles, as stated in page 181.

fostered and strengthened the misconception. This phrase, 'agere pœnitentiam,' being literally translated to do penance or to act penance, has turned men's thoughts from the true notion, expressed by μετανόια, to the outward discipline which the Church imposes, or the self-inflicted austerities by which the flesh may be mortified.

CHAPTER IX.

Page 261.—As has been stated in page 26, the factors of divinely imparted knowledge are revelation and inspiration. For no knowledge of Divine truth can be attained unless on two conditions: 1, That there be a revelation, or an intelligible object, presented to the mind; 2, That the mind be prepared by the Holy Spirit to understand the revelation, or, in the language of St. Paul, that " we receive the Spirit which is of God." This latter is—in express terms—inspiration, as the former, or the presentation of the intelligible objective truth to the mind, (whether directly by suggestion or indirectly through sense or conception or imagination,) is revelation. See page 33.

Now since a *Divine* revelation is presented only that it may be understood, and since the apostle positively avers that inspiration is the only condition on which it can be known, there can be no revelation, which is *a making known*—implied in the very meaning of the word—without inspiration. It is therefore a great error to suppose that a Divine revelation can exist separately and apart from inspiration. Thus is explained the statements of St. Paul when he says certain things were made known to him by revelation, and their seeming inconsistency with his positive and explicit affirmation in 1 Cor. ii. 12. The truth is, there is a perfect agreement between them, since in the revelation, which makes known, is necessarily implied inspiration.

Page 266.—" The investigation moves in a wrong line," etc. The book of nature had for ages been read, as the book of revelation is, even yet, read by many. Men did not interrogate nature, but—as if they were its masters, not its interpreters—accounted for the phenomena which it presented by assigning final causes such as they might judge the most suitable to the ends designed by the great Creator. Thus, as the circle was conceived to be the most perfect figure, the planets must move round the sun in circles. Again, matter in one form or another filling all parts of the earth on which we live, and entirely surrounding it with the atmosphere, which we breathe, on all sides and above its surface, the idea prevailed that all space was replete with matter: so the rise of water in pumps, siphons, and other engines had been for a long time attributed to Nature's abhorrence of a vacuum.

In like manner *à priori* reasoning of this kind had gained a footing among Biblical students. Certain principles are assumed relating to the text of the Holy Scriptures, and conditions laid down which each may think necessary in order to secure its perfect accuracy. How an appeal to Scripture can be legitimately made on the question before us I have shown in page 268.

Page 282.—I here subjoin the *locus classicus* of Philo, as it has been misunderstood. I fail to find in it *his* theory, or any theory, of inspiration. This celebrated passage rather gives Philo's classification of prophecy, or the result of inspiration, under three heads embracing so many species of the Divine oracles (λογία). His theory of inspiration he gives elsewhere (*De Præm. e Pœn.*, t. ii., p. 417, and *Quis. Rer. Div. Hær.*, t. i., p. 511). This Divine influence, reducing the mind to absolute unconsciousness, using the subject as a passive instrument, extending to and moving the entire organism of the voice, presents a mechanical theory of inspiration the most thorough-paced on record.

"Οὐκ ἀγνοῶ μὲν οὖν, ὡς πάντα εἰσὶ χρησμοὶ ὅσα ἐν ταῖς ἱεραῖς βίβλοις ἀναγέγραπται χρησθέντες δι' αὐτοῦ. Λέξω δὲ τὰ ἰδιαίτερα, πρότερον εἰπὼν ἐκεῖνο· τῶν λογίων γὰρ, τὰ μὲν ἐκ προσώπου τοῦ Θεοῦ λέγεται δι' ἑρμηνέως τοῦ θείου προφήτου· τὰ δὲ ἐκ πεύσεως καὶ ἀποκρίσεως ἐθεσπίσθη· τὰ δ' ἐκ προσώπου Μωϋσέως ἐπιθειάσαντος, καὶ ἐξ αὑτοῦ κατασχεθέντος. Τὰ μὲν οὖν πρῶτα ὅλα δι' ὅλων ἀρετῶν θείων δείγματ' ἐστὶ, τῆς τε ἵλεω καὶ εὐεργέτιδος, δι' ὧν ἅπαντας μὲν ἀνθρώπους πρὸς καλοκαγαθίαν ἀλείφει· μάλιστα δὲ τὸ θεραπευτικὸν αὐτοῦ γένος, ᾧ τὴν πρὸς εὐδαιμονίαν ἄγουσαν ἀνατέμνει ὁδόν. Τὰ δὲ δεύτερα μίξιν ἔχει καὶ κοινωνίαν, πυνθανομένου μὲν τοῦ προφήτου περὶ ὧν ἐπεζήτει, ἀποκρινομένου δὲ τοῦ Θεοῦ καὶ διδάσκοντος. Τὰ δὲ τρίτα ἀνατίθεται τῷ νομοθέτῃ, μεταδόντος αὐτῷ τοῦ Θεοῦ τῆς προγνωστικῆς δυνάμεως ᾗ θεσπίζει τὰ μέλλοντα. Τὰ μὲν οὖν πρῶτα ὑπερθετέον· μείζονα γὰρ ἐστιν ἢ ὡς ὑπ' ἀνθρώπου τινὸς ἐπαινεθῆναι, μόλις ἂν ὑπ' οὐρανοῦ τε καὶ κόσμου, καὶ τῆς τῶν ὅλων φύσεως ἀξίως ἐγκωμιασθέντα, καὶ ἄλλως λέγεται ὡσανεὶ δι' ἑρμηνέως. Ἑρμηνεία δὲ καὶ προφητεία διαφέρουσι. Περὶ δὲ τῶν δευτέρων αὐτίκα πειράσομαι δηλοῦν, συνυφήνας αὐτοῖς καὶ τὸ τρίτον εἶδος, ἐν ᾧ τὸ τοῦ λέγοντος ἐνθουσιῶδες ἐμφαίνεται καθ' ὃ μάλιστα καὶ κυρίως νενόμισται προφήτης."—*De Vita Mosis*, lib. iii., t. ii., p. 163.

This classification of the prophetic utterances, though confused, has considerable merits. In it not only the Divine communications which transcend human reason to discover, but also everything written in the sacred books, are regarded as bearing the stamp of divinity. Whether God reveals *directly from Himself* deep truths which man taught of God can only interpret, that interpreter is a prophet; or man inquires and God answers and teaches, the man so instructed is a prophet; or, lastly, when God imparts the gift of foreknowledge, it is to a prophet.

Now the power (δύναμις) is *the inspiration* which enables him *to know* the truths communicated, and so qualifies him to exercise the function of a prophet. In all the three kinds of prophecy, the prophet is God's interpreter. But how is he enabled to interpret? This is the question which St. Paul has answered, but which Philo *in the present passage* has left unanswered. Philo gives a theory of inspiration in his treatises above referred to, but it is not St. Paul's.

The only allusions to the mental state of the inspired, in the passage under consideration, are two contained in the third head of his division; which Mangey translates, 'Ex Mosis personâ, instinctû divino afflati, et intus correpti;' and 'tertiam iis speciem attexans in quâ divinus furor loquentis apparet.'

Now, the true nature of inspiration is to be sought in the mental state from which, as its source, prophecy flows. This state is, according to Philo, very different from what it is as represented by St. Paul ; and such being the basis upon which the theory of each has been constructed, how different must the theories themselves be ! See pages 286, 290 of this Essay, and the reference to Plato (*Timæus* 72. *b*) for the historic origin of Philo's view.

The great cause of Philo's confusion in his division of the λογία or prophetic utterances arose from his general statement that every prophet is an interpreter ; and yet he held that prophecy applies only *legitimately* (κυρίως) to the cases in which the Divine frenzy is visibly exhibited (τὸ τοῦ λέγοντος ἐνθουσιῶδες ἐμφαίνεται), therefore he made a distinction between the two kinds of prophecy—interpretation, and prophecy properly so called.

Page 294.—It is not intimated here that other Christian Fathers had not insisted on the necessity of quickened intuition and illumination of the faculties of the sacred writers, when they were under the influence of inspiration. Thus, even with greater accuracy than modern authors exhibit, when they say that "inspiration is an imparted gift for guiding to the expression of Divine truth, orally or in writing, with unerring certainty," Cyril of Alexandria speaks of the enlightening influence of the Holy Spirit, and speaks of it too as ancillary to *knowledge*. He does not, however (while he also omits the factors of the imparted knowledge) impress with equal precision this essential idea of the direct end and aim of that inward influence—merely saying, "The Holy Spirit *flashes* on them the knowledge of each thing" —as Origen in the passages here referred to. For Origen clearly points to an influence that fitted the recipient not only to understand but also to receive the revelations vouchsafed to him, and defined the true character of inspiration as a preparation for that very purpose.